RA

BOOKS BY LETITIA BALDRIGE

1956
Roman Candle (Houghton Mifflin)

1958
Tiffany Table Settings (Bramhall House, Clarkson Potter)

1968
Of Diamonds and Diplomats (Houghton Mifflin)

1972
Home (Viking)

1977
Juggling (Viking)

1978
The 1978 Revision of *The Amy Vanderbilt Complete Book of Etiquette*
(Doubleday)

1980
Amy Vanderbilt's Everyday Etiquette (Bantam)

1981
The Entertainers (Bantam)

1985
Letitia Baldrige's Complete Guide to Executive Manners (Rawson)

1987
Letitia Baldrige's Complete Guide to a Great Social Life (Rawson)

1990
Letitia Baldrige's Complete Guide to the New Manners for the Nineties
(Rawson)

1990
Public Affairs, Private Relations (Doubleday)

1993
Letitia Baldrige's New Complete Guide to Executive Manners (Rawson)

As Clare Luce told me in 1956, "*Anyone* can get a book published who
knows how to apply the seat of the pants to the seat of the chair."

Letitia Baldrige's

MORE THAN MANNERS!

RAISING TODAY'S KIDS

TO HAVE KIND MANNERS

& GOOD HEARTS

RAWSON ASSOCIATES

Rawson Associates

Scribner

Simon & Schuster Inc.

1230 Avenue of the Americas

New York, NY 10020

Designed by Jenny Dossin

Set in New Baskerville

Manufactured in the United States of America

1 3 5 7 9 10 8 6 4 2

Library of Congress Cataloging-in-Publication Data

Baldrige, Letitia.
Letitia Baldrige's more than manners! : raising today's kids to have
kind manners and good hearts.
p.   cm.
Includes index.
1. Child rearing. 2. Etiquette for children and teenagers.
3. Social skills in children. 4. Children—Conduct of life.
I. Title.
HQ769.B3123   1997
649'.7—dc21   96-50980
CIP

ISBN 0-684-81875-2

THIS BOOK IS DEDICATED TO LUKE AND LILA—
AND THE OTHER KIND GRANDCHILDREN
YET TO COME IN OUR FAMILY

ACKNOWLEDGMENTS

I am incredibly indebted to Eleanor Rawson, my editor, publisher, grammar-corrector, moral-supporter, bucker-upper, repetition-deleter, and cobeliever that today's kids are *great*—just in need of a little more help than some are receiving from the adults in their lives at present. She has agonized with me every step of the way in getting this book finished, and jointly, we have talked and worried enough over the children of this world via long distance to enhance the P&L statements of the entire telephone industry.

I am most certainly indebted to my wonderful parents, who showed their children that the concrete results of kindness are friends, and, of course, to my husband, Bob, and offspring, Clare and Malcolm. And without those two wonderful combative older brothers of mine, I never would have been able to write this book, so I'm happy I had Bob and Mac in my life, too. As the Italians say, *"La famiglia è tutto."* (Family is everything.)

I'm grateful to all the kids who put up with my questions about kindness, including nieces and nephews, godchildren and godchildren's children, like young Michael Haft, who lives across the street, Katie and Alex Frank from Maryland, and the Northrop kids from New Jersey. I have chatted with children in all kinds of schools and marveled at their sense of fairness and justice. One of them proudly told me he knows what values are: "Values are when you've done something bad and you don't wanna do it again." I answered him, "Values are also when you've done something good and you *really* want to do it again."

CONTENTS

PART II

Practicing Kind Behavior Out in the World

PART III

*When Kindness Matters Most:
The Family Breaks Up, Regroups,
and Moves Ahead*

PART I

Where Kind Manners & Good Hearts Really Start

AT HOME

Before You Begin This Book

I have *written this book for everyone who loves a child.*

That's a pretty big number, because it includes married or single parents, siblings, grandparents, relatives, teachers, godparents, caregivers, cousins, coaches, next-door neighbors, housekeepers, and anyone who may be working so hard and going so fast just trying to survive that they may be letting some of the fundamentals slip by in the lives of children over whom they have some influence.

To me, one of the most appealing attractions about childhood is that everyone has to go through it. No one is excused; it's a universal experience—good for some, great for others, and, today, perfectly terrible for too many.

It's really too bad that today the term *family values* is being tossed around by political parties like a football being used to score points. This book is about *one* aspect of family values, but it is *not* about the political side of these values. It has nothing to do with Republicans, Democrats, entitlements, welfare, or other social programs. But it does concern human values of the spirit and heart— and a joint mission we should all have: *to do everything possible to help children grow up into the best human beings they can become.* That's a mission each of us should be actively sharing.

With the increasing erosion of human values in our society, it's time we stopped the hand-wringing and actually started to do something about our kids. If we adopt a mind-set of paying attention to what children are seeing, doing, and saying, and match it up with how we want them to be when they step from childhood into adulthood, and talk to them about it, and show them that high moral standards are not simply material for stand-up comics to make fun of, but for real people to live their lives by, we might succeed.

Never has our society seemed more inward directed and in need of real change in our relations to one another. But we can help turn that around. Each one of us whose life touches a child's has the potential to influence that child in an affirmative way. Each one of us can become a trainer of children's minds and hearts. As children grow up, the adults around them can have a powerful influence on them. We have opportunities to make points on character when the time is right, to store some values in their minds and show them how to reflect on the things we consider important. It requires dedication to the task, but it's a task worth all that we can give it.

Of necessity, a baby is born ego-directed, concerned with its own needs. As this child grows from babyhood into childhood, he or she is expected to begin to turn away from the self and out toward the world. It's a vast and serious undertaking, requiring basic inner strength in the child. That strength must be supported by direction, encouragement, and motivation from others. The child cannot do it alone.

Values are conclusions reached in part by closely observing other people from childhood on, and then deciding which ones are most worth emulating. A child who knows what is right and wrong ("Yes, I know I shouldn't have done that") has a good chance of growing up to be a civil, sensitive person. It's the child who can't see the differences between wrong and right whose future *un*happiness is almost assured.

Usually the first value a child understands and absorbs within the family is *behavior*. Thus, the three premises of this book are:

+ Kindness makes a child safer and happier in all of his or her worlds.

+ Kindness and natural civility are synonymous.

+ Kindness is taught by example, which means that every adult with whom a child spends any time has a great potential to shape that child's life.

When an adult accompanying a child sees someone being kind to another person, that adult can use this opportunity to point it out to the child, and explain why this behavior is so important. Even if the child forgets that incident until years later, but reacts to a similar incident with a similar act of kindness, the adult's lesson will have borne fruit. This is how character is built.

I am not a child psychologist (although I have a degree in psychology), but I am a practitioner of common sense who happens to have children, grandchildren, and many godchildren (twenty-one in all!). I am a student of behavior who has been observing it for several decades and from incredibly fine vantage points. I have lived and worked all over the world, with eyes watching and ears listening intently.

In my diplomatic career, I've seen the best of high-ranking manners on display (and also some of the worst!). In my Kennedy White House days, I witnessed the manners of America's politically powerful at close hand and saw the meanness of power society spotlighted most glaringly. In the years I have been in the business world, I've seen kindness and compassion balanced by greed and reckless ambition. It's a fascinating, always rapidly changing, world, but I also cannot fail to notice that today, many children are not being brought along by the hand through these changes. We adults are distracted. Times are tough. New worries, new diseases, more divorces, fewer jobs, more drugs, and less free time. How does the development of a child's awareness of other people fit into our burdensome schedules?

I think most of us would agree that civility has been eroding with an unfortunate acceleration in the late nineties. We're acting tired. We greet nastiness with greater nastiness. Our ears seem to be blocked when we hear our children using foul language (maybe because their ears are filled with our own foul language!). When our children are caught cheating at school, we blame the school system. On the playing fields of sports, we pretend not to see team members cheating, being bad sports, or showing terrible manners to the opposing team. The worst part of the sports world, however, are the young players' parents, who berate the coaches and game officials while urging their children on to win *regardless of fair competition.*

Most people are not unkind on purpose. They often don't even realize when they are acting that way. When young people are not even aware that something they're doing is thoughtless or just plain rude, you know there's a void at home. Someone has not been pointing out kind versus unkind behavior and guiding them to embrace the former.

Because of the fragmentation of family life and the distractions of our electronically fed world, kindness has been slipping away from us like an ignored visitor who feels he is no longer welcome and leaves. There seems to be a kind of desperation in our relationships, too. The former genial, relaxed, hail-fellow-well-met attitude, which used to be a common denominator in our society, has all but disappeared.

I come from the last generation where widowed grandparents lived with their children and their families—each one irritating the other but each one learning and profiting from the other. There was no alternative to adjusting to the arrangement. The young learned how to defer, the older how to tolerate.

I grew up in a time when we often trotted along with either parent when they went out to do volunteer service in the community. We children knew that when we grew up, community service was not an option for us. It was a certainty. We children lived in a complicated maze of rules and regulations, yet it was always possible to get through it, and particularly in the way my parents handled the maze, it felt good, not oppressive. There was no ambiguity about what was right or wrong, no gray area. It was an easy time in which to grow up, despite the national disciplines of a great Depression and a Second World War.

The family was always gathered around the table, every night and Sunday lunch. Mealtime was solid, dependable, nourishing in far more than food. The family members were like a flotilla of ships moving forward on an endless sea of support. It's ironic that a piece of furniture—the dinner table—became the symbol of family solidarity. It represented a time of innocence to which the world will probably never return. It was a time in which mealtime meant good conversation and sharing personal trials and tribulations.

In many households today no one sits down anymore at the dinner table. There is no way that an abstract lesson such as how a child shows deference and kindness to older people can be demonstrated. There is only the buzz from the microwave, signaling that an individual meal is now ready, and proclaiming that each member of the family can now pluck his tray and pursue his own interests. In place of a conversation with human beings who are also eating a meal, he or she now eats while shuttling around cyberspace on the computer.

I have written this book from the heart, because I feel so passionately that we must work harder with our children—and other people's children, too—to try to change this course of events. To illustrate certain points, I have told stories of my childhood and used snatches of conversations between adults and children. I have described other people's experiences with their children, which over the years were filed away in my notes and memory. (Of course, a *perfectly* kind child has never existed, and if he did he would be an obnoxious goody-goody!) But if some adults glean any ideas from the text that will help them communicate values to children, and if small connections of kindness are made, the entire book will have been worthwhile for you to have read and for me to have written.

Children are the most wonderful creatures in the world. They have a superb, almost magical vibrancy. (We all had it, too, as kids!) As they grow into adolescence, they create their own fireworks as they seek their generation's answers to society's problems. Listen to them. Engage them in conversation. Some of their solutions are preposterous, but there is *always* something there.

Creative thinking, new ways of unscrambling the status quo, fresh ideas to help us all get going—that's what we need. I'm convinced that the young have a natural desire to make the world kinder and more civil. But we need to nurture those seeds of civility and teach our youth how to express this virtue (rather than repress it, as some kids, who have been under terrible pressure, have been doing).

Come to think of it, it wouldn't be such a bad idea for us adults to do a better job of teaching more civility to ourselves!

Kind Manners Every Child Should Have

There are many rules of etiquette that have only to do with form and presentation, such as forks go to the left and knives and spoons to the right of the plate in a place setting. (It's efficient and it looks good that way.) Then there are manners and goodwill toward others, which have little to do with form and presentation and *everything to do with the heart.* I like a definition supplied by a high school junior, a young man who was also captain of the school wrestling team: "A kind heart and kind manners mean you don't hurt feelings and you make other people feel good." This was a philosophical wrestler speaking, perhaps a rare breed, but a hopeful sign for society in general.

WHEN SHOULD A CHILD BE TAUGHT THIS?

Many aspects of a child's development, like walking and talking, develop naturally when the child is ready. Training in kind manners, good hearts, and good minds can begin even before a child reaches the "terrible twos" stage, when every question and request he answers with a resolute "No." These qualities do not develop naturally *but are the result of the considerable effort, patience, and quality time expended by an adult with a child.* (To many young parents, that statement is "putting it mildly.")

At a certain point in a child's life, never totally predictable, he or she suddenly learns what "No," coming from an adult, signifies. You can almost see an attitude toward manners begin to develop in a baby in a high chair when he stops flicking his spoon of pureed spinach into your face, not because you're sputtering a burst of "No, don't do that!" in an increasingly displeased voice, but because he feels better when you smile rather than frown at him. He is on the threshold of kind behavior when he stops yanking a person's hair or wrenching the earring from a lady's ear. It's not just a question of obedience. He is becoming aware that his actions are not pleasing, and even causing great distress to another person. It's as though there's a sudden illumination in a dark room.

When a child finally understands that an earring-yank really hurts, he ceases doing it. He can now even receive a hug from Mommy's visitor without tugging at and possibly breaking that lady's tantalizing jewelry. He begins to conclude that he also makes Dad much happier and more smiley at feeding time when he keeps his food on his high chair tray rather than flinging it down onto the floor.

He even comes to realize, after months of throwing things in all directions and expecting them to be returned, that it gets tiresome for the adults and older siblings to keep fetching objects for him. He can even conclude that they will stop playing with him if he continues. His socialization progresses. The cadence of the rhythmic "No, no, no" begins to lose its charm. You can almost see and feel the toddler's transformation. A soon-to-be-socialized person is about to step into . . . well, if not "polite society," at least a reasonable facsimile thereof.

It's an adult's duty, not just an option, to teach children how to be kind and concerned for others. When a little girl makes a mess on the table at mealtime, she's excused by the guests because "she's such a cute little girl." When a grown-up daughter who's not been trained to eat properly with others makes a mess on the table while dining with her business client, the excuses no longer hold. No one regards her sloppiness as being cute anymore. Her career may even be in jeopardy because she detracts from rather than enhances the corporate image.

Somewhere in between being considered cute and entering her teens, she should have been taught by *someone,* who was not too busy with other priorities, how to eat properly. A working mother may say, "I don't have time for that, I can't possibly eat dinner with the children." But it's not a good excuse. If parents cannot take fifteen minutes a day from their schedule to teach their children, they should arrange for someone else (spouse, significant other, brother, father, mother, sister, housekeeper, cousin) who *will* eat with the young members of the family every so often and "teach them how to wield their cutlery," as an English book of manners once described it.

Self-confidence is something we should work to instill in every child. So is a behavioral comfort level as a future adult. There can be no comfort level when a young person does not know how to handle himself, when he doesn't know what to do or say in unexpected circumstances, and when he doesn't know how to treat friends and colleagues—in short, how to move with grace through life.

On a recent afternoon, I asked a group of teenage girls to write down some of the reasons they considered manners to be important to their futures. "Someone with kind manners," wrote one girl, "is popular and well liked. She is a credit to her family." Another stated that "she will attain greater success in her career than someone who shows a lack of civility." One girl wrote that "if she has good manners, she'll have more dates." A girl with her mind on her future security wrote, "She'll be able to meet rich and important men who will help her, whether she's ugly or beautiful." When I asked for a further explanation, she gave me a logical one: "If she's ugly, her good manners will help her career; if she's beautiful *and* well mannered, she also can end up being married to the CEO."

"Why not wind up *being* the CEO," I asked, "instead of just married to him?" (They would rather have been married to him.) Another added, "Someone with kind manners has a better sex life than someone without them." As I read this comment I found myself laughing, then realized this discussion had better stop right here. I accepted her logic as a legitimate point—without class discussion.

The rules of kind manners are really a simple lesson for a child to learn: Manners and kind behavior are *the same*. The heart of each is *thinking out beyond oneself.* This definition is an *excellent rebuttal* to those who think it's "cool" to refer to manners as elitist, archaic, artificial, foppish, irrelevant, anachronistic, intrusive, politically incorrect, and against the First Amendment!

When a Child Asks, "Why Do I Have to Be Kind?"

This question deserves an immediate, careful response. Such a query stems partly from pique, partly from real curiosity. "Just why is it important, anyway?" a child will ask and then accuse the parent of "making a big deal out of it."

Since you *do* make a big deal out of it, you owe your children an explanation, to be given at a time when everyone is calm and relaxed and no one is being disciplined or criticized. You need to help a child understand the logic and efficiency that is involved in being polite and considerate of others. Children should understand that:

+ *Kind manners and good behavior make you feel really good about yourself,* because, for example, when you are accidentally thrust into an unpleasant situation, you could just sit there and do or say nothing to relieve it. Instead, you make an effort to be helpful. In other words, your choice to act makes a difference in the way others are feeling.

+ *Kind behavior makes your world function better.* It becomes more orderly and efficient.

+ *Consideration colors the world in brighter, happier hues.* When people are kind to one another, wherever they happen to be—in school, on the playground, at home with the family, at work— the space they occupy becomes warmer and more comfortable.

+ *Civility and kind manners give you a strong sense of self,* a feeling of knowing what you're doing—in other words, the security of knowing you are "doing it right."

◆ *When you practice civility, people are drawn to you and you find your-self with lots of friends*—just because you're nice to be around!

MANNERS ARE BETTER TAUGHT
AFFIRMATIVELY THAN NEGATIVELY

It's easy to teach kind behavior and manners as a "don't" philoso-phy. We're always telling young people *not* to do this or that, or to *stop* doing whatever it is they're doing. For example:

"Jeanne, I said stop doing that!"

"But Dad, you don't even know what I'm doing. You can't see me!"

"I know I can't, but stop doing it anyway."

Jeanne's father would have much more success with her if he took a positive attitude on the subject of her actions. He could impress her with the good behavior of other children he and his daughter happen to observe—and not just criticize the bad behav-ior they happen to witness. They might see:

◆ a young girl voluntarily returning a grocery cart that had been left in the way of cars in the supermarket parking lot.

◆ a child automatically rising to give an older person his seat on the bus.

◆ a boy helping a disabled person cross the street when that per-son was caught by a traffic light that changed too fast.

◆ a girl in the library helping a stranger who has too many books in his arms to carry them to the returns desk.

◆ a child running in a sudden burst of wind to fetch papers that scattered from the hands of the person walking ahead.

◆ a teenager seeing that someone is having trouble handling heavy baggage on the escalator and rushing to help.

◆ a young girl asking, "May I help you?" and waiting until an impaired person gets into the car, and closing the door for that person.

◆ a teenager observing an elderly woman having trouble getting her coat on, getting up, and helping her with it.

NAGGING A CHILD IS A REAL TURNOFF

Adults who nag children all the time about their manners can really turn a positive into a negative. A child who is constantly told how bad or selfish she is will start to believe it and not care about the rewards of kind manners. I have heard people talking to children sarcastically, over their heads, using terms kids can't understand. They certainly don't advance their children's embrace of kindness and good behavior with that kind of rhetoric.

Instead, adults should seize a target of opportunity whenever one presents itself to remind a child that kindness and manners are one and the same. "Wasn't that great of him to do that?" you might say, not expecting the child with you to answer the question. You've made an *editorial observation*. When a child hears an adult say something like that, he understands. The "Enter" key has been pressed. The kind act has gone into the file.

If your child wonders aloud why you helped a total stranger, you've been given a perfect opportunity to toss out the Golden Rule (something that, like a winning pitch, should be tossed out whenever possible). "Think how you would have felt if you were in her place and a stranger had helped you—just like that? You'd be grateful!"

The opportunities to teach kindness are everywhere. When children respond and begin to act that way, they should receive proper recognition for it.

If you've finished lunch at a fast-food place with your son, for example, and someone seated nearby has just let a salt shaker drop to the floor, your son may instinctively go over to pick it up and hand it back. "That was kind," you say to him, immediately reinforcing his helpful behavior. If he didn't think of this all by himself, perhaps a small whisper from you, that it would be a "kind" thing to do, would work. Unfortunately, in many cases, the so-called gentleman seated nearby might not even say thank you to your son. He might just say "hum" and take the salt shaker, as though it's his prerogative to be helped. If that happens, you should say quietly to your son, "Don't worry, for every person who doesn't thank you for doing what you just did, there are twenty people who would. Forget him. Just keep on remembering the twenty others."

If you're fortunate, acts of kindness *will* become instinctive in the children around you, in the children whose lives you touch, whether you're a parent, a relative, or just a friend. You have so much power to influence them for good. And yes, there will be obnoxious, snarly people who will reject any child who does something nice for them, but those sad creatures are in a very small minority.

The great thing about important acts of kindness is that they often emanate from minor suggestions. Help a child understand that he or she should never think, "Oh, if I go see Jimmy when he's sick and bring him a present, it wouldn't mean anything." Instead, help the child conclude, "My visit will probably mean a lot to Jimmy. It's worth the effort. But what if they won't let me in to see him?"

That's when you say, "The fact that you went there, that's what's important. He'll appreciate it."

A very small gesture can soothe, comfort, and motivate someone who's having a hard time, for whatever reason—including death, illness, disappointments, failures. (Of course, the child or his parent has to be sensitive enough to be aware that a friend is having a hard time and could use a little kindness.)

Praise children whenever you can, and truly listen to their replies, because unlike adults, they usually don't know how to embroider stories and puff themselves up:

"Golly, I didn't know it would mean that much. I'm glad I did it."

"Did she really say that? I thought I hadn't really helped at all."

When a child realizes the extent of his power to help someone, and to make a difference in that person's life, the "thinking out" process becomes instinctive and the tendency to turn inward and think only about himself begins to disappear. And therein lies the solution to much of society's ills.

WHEN CHILDREN START
TO THINK ABOUT OTHERS IT IS NO MIRACLE

It may seem as though a miracle has occurred when the "thinking out" process begins to function in a child. Most likely, some adult somewhere has helped that child get to that point. A boy or girl who gets into the habit of thinking of ways to surprise and please other people—thanks to an occasional gentle prod from elsewhere—finds it rewarding. The child usually receives a great deal in return in terms of gratitude, recognition, or, as one little girl described it, "the pleasure of seeing someone smile just because of *me*."

Opportunities are all around us to demonstrate the meaning of "thinking out." This may be the moment to say to your seven-year-old, "Be kind to that little girl who's our guest, even if she's only three. Play with her, even if she's not much fun for you at this age. Show her your room, your fish, your books, whatever. She's feeling a little scared in this house, which is strange to her. You can make her feel better."

An adult should not hesitate to verbalize approbation. "We're proud of you, Louisa, for doing that." Children need to hear adults *say it, not just think it.*

Parents probably never realize the importance of what they do for their children when they encourage or comfort their child. The reward may come years later. One college student, a successful athlete, had a roommate who craved becoming a successful athlete. The roommate went into a deep depression when he was on the basketball team for an entire season but never made it off the bench and into a game. He resigned from the team and was ready to quit college, too, because he felt himself to be a total failure. Then his successful athlete roommate remembered an appropriately encouraging poem—an institutional United Technology ad—his father had torn out of the *Wall Street Journal* for him many years back, at a time when he was also sitting on the bench all season without the coach calling him into the game. Now, five years later, he called home and asked his parents to "take it off the wall [where he'd hung it, framed] and ship it to me, please." His father asked why he needed it.

"Dad," he replied, "you don't know how that poem helped me with what I was feeling about myself at the time you gave it to me. Now I know someone who really needs it on *his* wall. I want to loan it to him." So a father helped his son, and the son helped his friend. The circle of influence doesn't have to stop there.

Getting a Child to Agree that "Thinking Out" Is Cool

I'll never forget the instance in my own life when my mother—and fate—pointed out to me that you can be paid back later in life for your kindnesses of the moment. In eighth grade, just before summer vacation started, I gave up my precious place on a school camping trip to let a new girl go in my place. I'd heard she was fighting back the tears all the time because there wasn't room for her and it was her first chance to make new friends in a new town. So I magnanimously gave her my place. (My brother Bob said I did it because I knew there would be terrible mosquito and poison ivy problems, which it turned out there were, but he was just trying to make me look like less of a saint to my parents!)

The following September my great-uncle treated our family to a week in New York. These were the Depression years, so the excitement was pretty great. At the Rainbow Room the night before we went home to Omaha and back to school, Fred Astaire came into that glamorous place for dinner. He saw my parents, whom he knew from his Omaha days, stopped to put his arms around my mother's neck, said, "Hello, Jean—and Mac—!" gave her a big hug, and stayed a moment to talk with us. Later, he came over and asked me to dance! It was actually a dance contest, which he and I won— he in his dazzling English tailor-made dark suit, I in my cotton dress, white anklets, and loafers. It was a moment of such excitement and triumph, I almost fainted. My mother said, "You see what you get in return for giving up your place on the camping trip?"

Ever since, I've been searching in my life—unsuccessfully, of course—for a payback of equal glory and intensity!

The First Manners: Hellos and Good-Byes

If only all the moms and dads in this world would teach their children one of the most basic elements of manners—how to say hello and good-bye—the entire world would be a warmer, more welcoming place.

For example, a dad says, "Allen, when one of Mom and my friends—or when anyone, for that matter—comes into the living room when you're on the floor studying or reading on the sofa, or maybe you're in the family room watching TV or studying or playing a computer game, I want you to get up, put out your hand to shake theirs, and say, 'Hello, Miss, Mr., or Mrs. So-and-So.' Be sure to look them straight in the eyes."

"What if I don't know who they are?"

"Makes no difference. You still get up, greet them, and say who you are. 'Hello. I'm Allen.' When you put out your hand, they'll say hello back and tell you their name in return."

"What if I don't care who they are, and they don't care who I am?"

"If someone is in the room where you are, I assure you they want to know who's in the room with them. That's human nature. No one likes a mystery."

"You're always telling me to study more, to concentrate. How can I concentrate if people keep coming in the room all the time and breaking my concentration?"

"You know that doesn't happen, Allen. We don't have that many people coming to see us 'all the time.'"

"Dad, what difference does it make to your friends or to the . . . the exterminator, for example, if I say hello or not? I just don't see—"

"They are all people and they deserve to be greeted, each and every one of them. You've got to learn that *now.* Everyone deserves to be treated with attention and respect. Haven't you noticed that when you see someone in the street or in a store or even in the house, and you smile and say a bright hello to that person, he smiles back and maybe keeps that smile on his face? That's what you can do for people, just by making a little effort for them.

"Remember when you were ten, Allen, and you wanted to be an astronaut? Now that you're thirteen, you want to be a lawyer. Well, let me tell you, you'd never be allowed into astronaut training, and you'd never attract or keep legal clients without having people skills. And the first step in developing people skills is to know how to introduce yourself to others, to care about them, and to make them feel comfortable with you. It's not difficult—in fact, it becomes automatic with practice."

One Way Kindness Is Learned: Remember, Your Child Is Watching You

On the drive to school, if you become angry at an inconsiderate, dangerous driver, a child is an alert witness when you give that person the finger or use unsavory language. You run a great risk of having your child grow up to behave exactly as you do in similarly stressful situations.

It took only two weeks of school in September for a fourth-grader, the grandson of a man I know, to pick up the bad habit of mouthing obscenities, most of which he didn't understand. The older man had a strong reaction. After he delivered a sermon to the boy on the evils of bad language, and after having muttered more than once "How could a thing like this happen at such an expensive private school?" the boy answered, "Granddad, I was just copying the way you talk. The kids in my grade talk like that, too. I figured since you do it better than anyone, it was okay for me to do the same."

The grandfather (who, by the way, paid for the tuition at his grandson's school) related a happy ending to the story. They talked the problem out together and ultimately settled on a fine, to be put in a pot and donated to a community project, each time one heard the other using this language. Early on, the project made out well, but after four months it earned nothing.

Ironically, children can make excellent teachers of manners to adults! I remember years ago when, tired and cranky, I was driving my fourteen-year-old daughter somewhere. A speeding driver on my left cut over to the right lane in front of us without signaling, and we narrowly missed a collision. Both cars were now stopped for a red light. Crimson-faced with fury, I pulled up alongside the other driver and gave him a none-too-gentle reprimand. When I had calmed down and the traffic moved forward, wise young Clare commented, "You know, Mom, that wasn't very nice." When I think of all the years I had spent using that same phrase with our children, it was embarrassing to be reminded of it by a fourteen-year-old.

"You're right," I admitted. "It wasn't the best way to handle the situation."

Her reply was incredibly appropriate. "Mom, I think you'd better read a book that's on the first shelf in our library."

"Which one, Clare?"

"The latest one you wrote, Mom."

Our son, Malcolm, passed on another lesson in manners. We were having lunch one day in a restaurant, a reward for his having suffered through two hours of hated shopping for school clothes. Unaware, I sat down at a table that had already been taken by another woman who had left some of her things on a chair and had gone to make a telephone call. We ordered our lunches, and when she returned, she was surprised to find us there, deep in conversation. I should have risen immediately and vacated the table. Instead, she was the one who removed her things and went in search of another table.

"Mom"—Malcolm's voice was the voice of my conscience—"you didn't apologize to that lady and leave. It was *her* table."

Then I realized what I had done. I'm always telling people to "be aware" of others around them. I had not been the slightest bit aware. "You're right, Malcolm, we should have left, not she."

He studied me as we sat there talking. "Well, aren't you going to do it now?"

"Do what?"

"Give her the table."

Really embarrassed now, I got up, went to the woman (who was now at a table next to the kitchen door), and apologized. She smiled and said it was all right. No need to change now. I was mortified at my lack of attention to what was going on around me, a common error in human kindness of which I was continually chiding my own children to be aware.

Young people can be direct, even curt, without meaning to be unkind. The roads that lead to understanding virtues must first be pointed out to them, like routes on a map; then children come to know them and can travel along them safely by themselves. They often don't want to understand why obeying and being kind is a great plus in their corner. The subject is abstract, difficult to comprehend, and sometimes counter to what they feel like doing and saying at any given moment, but explaining it is also worth any amount of energy you, as an adult, put into it.

Modesty Is Intrinsic in Good Manners

One of the nicest aspects of good manners is that they are taught and practiced modestly, not noisily and self-praisingly. Mom doesn't say to a child, "You're so wonderful, you're such a good girl because you showed everyone today what I've taught you. It's too bad the other kids don't have any manners."

Instead, mom says to her child, "I was watching you today. You made me very proud."

A young person who has been taught good manners doesn't lord it over his peers. He doesn't boast about "knowing about manners, and the rest of you don't know anything." Anyone acting as though he or she is better than anyone else has removed the adjective in front of the word. The "good" is gone. Just plain manners, without the adjective, are lifeless, selfish, without meaning.

Good manners are quiet. There is no sound to them. They are simply there, a kind way of moving through life. There is no feeling of superiority intrinsic to them, or inferiority either. You don't hear them, but you see them in the way people treat one another.

Teach Your Kids Respect for Authority Figures in Their Lives

We live in a free society that is nevertheless based on taking orders from higher authorities and performing acts of obedience. (Too bad that in many schools today this philosophy is considered unnecessary and old-fashioned, and doubly too bad is the fact that many of the kids who denigrate this philosophy end up either in prison or dead from an overdose.)

The child who grows up unable to accept reasonable authority figures guiding him toward what he should be doing as a civil, caring individual and what he shouldn't be doing, in turn may very well become an adult who can't shoulder responsibility or take orders and therefore can't successfully hold down a job—or worse. . . .

A kid who sounds like a broken record, saying, "*I* don't have to do that," and "That doesn't apply to *me*," messes up not only his own life but the lives of those around him:

+ Remember the kid in your grade who cheated on an important test by getting hold of an advance copy of it, so that your entire class was penalized?

+ Remember the kid who mocked and obstructed the fire drill in school and then was injured years later in a fire he had decided was just a test?

+ Remember the kid who was told by the nurse to go home from school at once because he had chicken pox, but then went to a classmate's birthday party instead and gave it to many of the guests?

Kids who grow up behaving that way—in a smart-ass manner, to use the vernacular—are usually the product of uncaring parents. *So what is the definition of a "caring parent"?*

+ A parent who knows how to delineate right from wrong in terms a young child can understand—and who praises the right behavior.

+ A parent who remembers his promises and delivers on them.

+ A parent for whom a child willingly turns off the TV and puts away games in order to hear what his mother or father has to say in a serious family discussion.

+ A parent who makes certain that his child understands the importance of the decent, well-meaning authority figures in his life.

Even a three-year-old can begin to see the logic of a hierarchy of command, or the need to have *someone* in charge. Consequently, one of the most important lessons we can teach a young child is that as he grows up he is going to be increasingly surrounded by authority figures, not just his family members but also the families of his young friends, teachers, sitters, religious instructors, doctors, nurses, coaches, policemen, bus drivers, volunteer road-crossing guards, firemen, and store clerks.

I remember one summer in Quogue, Long Island, when my father caught me, age ten, sassing the high school student who handled the ice-cream cone concession at the beach.

"But Dad," I protested, "he's a kid, he's only a freshman in high school."

"He is the manager of the ice-cream stand at this part of the beach," he answered. "He's the boss here at this moment. It doesn't matter who owns the concession. He's been left in charge. He has authority over you, and you must obey him when he says 'no more napkins, no more sprinkles.'"

I had to go apologize to him, which embarrassed him even more than me. I remember that incident to this day. It was so many years ago, but I can see all of his freckles and his sunburned, peeling nose; the jaunty little cap he wore; and the bow tie with his dad's white shirt and the ice-cream-splashed apron over his pants. I realized later that my father had caught me being fresh, probably flirting, as a ten-year-old would do (i.e., not very artfully), and that he had forced me to realize that as long as that boy was in charge of that stand, I was to obey his authority or depart quietly, without an ice-cream cone.

One of our primary jobs as adults is to help children to follow fair rules in life by respecting those in charge, taking instruction, and adjusting with grace instead of conflict. Those rules can be as serious as, "Don't ever even think of touching the fire alarm in fun," to a less serious, "Stop popping your bubble gum in people's faces."

When a child asks Why not? always give a reply, even if you're exasperated. You can keep your answer short. If your child demands to know why *not* pull the fire alarm, explain how a false alarm prank can pull precious fire equipment away from a real fire, and can result in injury, death, and serious damage. When a child wonders why popping bubble gum in general is wrong, explain that chewing, smacking, and making a big ugly pink smear on his face when he pops it is an unattractive and offensive gesture to anyone who has to look at him. It may be fine to pop-pop with your friends, but it's disrespectful to those who are forced to view it.

"Is it that bad, Mom?" your child might ask.

I hope your reply would be, "It's *that* bad."

In defining the word *respect,* the dictionary says, among other things, "the sense of worth or excellence of a person."

The first people a child learns to respect are, of course, his parents or any other adults in the house. Among those I admire most are single parents who, regardless of personal feelings toward the divorced spouse, teach their children to respect the absent parent. It takes a lot of character and skill to overcome one's personal animosities for the good of the child.

A child will obey a person he respects. But it takes an older person to sort all of this out for him, to demonstrate the logic of it, and to explain that, the older the child gets, the more people he will meet in life who will deserve his respect. "You obey an older person," you might explain to a child, "because he or she has experienced a lot, learned a lot, and will use it as a responsibility to keep you safe and happy."

A longtime friend and I were reminiscing recently. She grew up in a big old house where her parents and three grandparents lived. She told me that one day she confronted her parents in a twelve-year-old's rage.

"I've been putting up with this too long," she complained.

"Putting up with what?" interrupted her maternal grandmother.

"The fact that everybody in this house bosses me, and half the time it contradicts something somebody else told me. Just who is the real boss here?" she asked grumpily.

Her grandfather intervened at once, looking over the top of his newspaper. "I'd say it was God, but since He chooses not to let us see Him today, you're going to have to take orders from whoever happens to be the oldest person in the room, and right now, the oldest person on the whole block is me." Her grandfather was a tall, majestic-looking bearded man who'd been told once he looked like Moses and had been quoting the Bible ever since. He also had a sense of humor.

A child should learn right away that respect is owed to all the elders in the family. It is a universal truth, something that has been passed down from generation to generation.

My friend said she felt a wonderful sense of security—the first time in her twelve years of existence that she had figured it all out.

"What I had learned was how the relationships in our family worked. I was sure it was different in each family, but a child has to learn how it all works in his own. I learned that a smart kid lets everyone in an authority position in the family think they're the ultimate boss, for whatever reason they find themselves in that position. You figure it out. Don't hurt your grandparents' feelings by telling them they can't tell you what to do, because they deserve deference. You don't play off the parents against one another, or you can get in big trouble. It's called 'getting smart.'"

Teach Children the Rules of "Deference" to Older People

This means that a younger person:

+ stands up when an older person comes into the room

+ sits down at the dinner table *after* that person does

+ passes the food to an older person first

+ much as it hurts, gives his grandfather the sports section of the newspaper first or, when watching TV together, lets grandparents or parents discuss their program preferences first

+ helps older guests with their coats

+ opens the door when an older person leaves

+ offers to do all the "running upstairs" to fetch things grandpa and grandma may have forgotten

✦ doesn't make fun of them in the house in front of his friends

✦ doesn't make fun of them out of the house in front of anyone

✦ doesn't tease them by whispering if they're hard of hearing

✦ doesn't point out or make note of anyone's obvious signs of aging—forgetfulness, hair loss, and increased wrinkles

✦ asks older people to talk about their past, helping them relive memories of which they are proud; even if the younger person is bored, he should act fascinated, because an older person often believes no one wants to hear what he has to say (which must be one of the loneliest, most agonizing feelings in the world)

✦ realizes that he has so much yet to learn in life that in listening to the wisdom of an older person, he is taking advantage of a rich opportunity

In fact, young people today would do the twenty-first century a great service if they were to take down their grandparents' oral histories in some form. In this electronic age, individual histories are simply evaporating in a puff of smoke.

A Father Teaches His Son to Respect Women, and Both Parents Show Respect for One Another at Home

A boy grows up without properly respecting women if a father's conversation leans heavily toward the discussion of women's bodies, and women are judged primarily by how good those bodies are and by how sexy their language and movements are. A father should realize that he is seriously trivializing women when he jokes with his men friends in the presence of his son about "the boobs and buns on those babes on TV and in the magazines." He should remember from his own youth what a deep effect all of that has on the psyche of an adolescent boy. In a family where women are in the minority, where men's athletic shoes and socks seem to be strewn across the entire floor space, the conversation often turns to rollicking jokes about women or gays ("jock talk"). These jokes sound hilarious to the male household members, but they are not funny to the objects of their derision. They are demeaning and they hurt.

There is too much frank talk among boys and girls in school and on TV these days about the size of a boy's penis or the size of a girl's breasts. Sex talk and bathroom talk—subjects that used to be confined to Las Vegas nightclub shows and stand-up comics—are now a regular part of prime-time TV. These subjects have become as common as a discussion of what's for dinner in many households.

If a son asks what possible harm there could be in his joking suggestively about girls ("*Everyone* does it, you realize that, Dad"), tell him that the more he does it, the less regard his own mother, sisters, and future girlfriends will have for him. This is not an era in which women want to adorn pedestals and be worshiped like Aphrodite, the goddess of love and beauty. It is an era in which men and women are meant to share—responsibilities, joys, and problems alike. Whether a woman works in an office, drives a truck, teaches a class, or pushes a pram all day, she deserves respect for what she contributes to the family and to her society. When a father and son make snickering jokes about women, as they do incessantly on television sitcoms, or when men on the job engage in any kind of sexual harassment they can get away with, one hears the sound of respect for the female sex being chipped away. It can lead from unkindness to criminal acts. It's very predictable that a boy who grows up in a home environment where it's amusing to put down women will have trouble in his relationships with women when he's older.

But it's not just fathers who should teach their sons respect for women, it's mothers, too, who should discourage their teenage daughters from discussing boys only in terms of the quality of their bodies. A mother should keep repeating, "How about his mind? His intelligence? His manners and kindness? His sense of humor? His imagination? You are going to live with those qualities long after 'the great bod' has slipped into rounded shoulders, flabby arms, and an undeniable paunch."

If we're lucky, we might yet return to a much more idyllic era in which teenagers (and their parents, too) discuss their contemporaries in terms of who's the most caring, decent, brightest, best read, wittiest, best sport, most articulate, and most trustworthy person among their friends and colleagues.

Why Complimenting Your Spouse Will Help Your Kids Have Kind Hearts

When children hear their parents praising each other, it makes them feel good and secure, and they may very well grow up to compliment their spouses, too. When a woman appears dressed for a party she likes to hear her husband say, "Wow! You look terrific tonight. Kids, do you realize what a good-looking mother you have?" A husband likes to hear his wife say to the children, "Did you notice what a good host your dad was at our dinner party tonight? He was by far the most interesting man there."

The children may react to this kind of conversation by giggling and throwing furtive glances at one another, but they usually take it all in. Mom and Dad have said kind things to each other and their words seemed to have had a happy effect on all concerned. Perhaps saying those lovey-dovey things isn't such a bad idea.

As they develop into mature adults, children who are accustomed to hearing compliments passed around are in the process of becoming successful human beings. You have taught them to look at the world in a *positive,* not a negative, way.

THE WEDGE-DRIVER BETWEEN PARENTS AND CHILDREN

It's the responsibility of both parents *not* to belittle each other in front of the children, and thus drive a wedge between the offspring and the other parent. In the heat of an argument, a husband or wife can undo their children's respect and admiration for the other parent in the matter of a minute! Accusations, the big "put-downs," can be devastating for a child to overhear. A parent who *must* talk against his or her spouse should go *far* out of earshot of the children. Regardless of whether a quarreling couple stays together because they have to, or whether they divorce and go their separate ways, and regardless of whether one spouse has been terribly wronged by the other, *for one spouse to cause the children to lose respect for the other is unforgivable.*

The Treasure Chest of Praise for a Child

Praise is a great gift, but it's most effective when you know how and when to give it. It can work miracles. For example:

+ Children who are praised by the adults around them, when it's truly merited, grow up to be straight, proud human beings. When a child *earns* praise that is properly articulated, that behavior is reinforced and his or her self-assurance grows.

+ Children who receive an extra bonus of praise for those tough moments when they're feeling down—and when they may not deserve it all that much—can forestall feelings of a lack of self-worth and depression.

+ A child who has been praised adequately while growing up will instinctively know when and how to praise his own family, work associates, and friends. It is a gift that is almost always passed on.

+ Praise is part of the formula for a successful marriage and better-adjusted kids. Even the family dog is a happier, better-functioning animal if it is praised often for good behavior.

+ When you point out and praise your child's kind acts toward others, honesty, or good sportsmanship, he won't forget them. Those good behaviors will have their own importance and priority in his mind.

+ When a child has tried hard and failed in a particular subject, project, or goal in school, praise him *for his perseverance* and *for having tried so hard.* Motivate your son or daughter to continue, not to lose heart. Tell him about your own disappointments when you were growing up, and your eventual successes. Keep reminding her that no one has to stay a loser, that losing is temporary—because courage, determination, and willpower can drive it away.

And reaffirm that winning isn't everything—in most situations, only one person or team can win at a time. What's more important is *Did you give it your best effort?* If you did that, you won a victory, within yourself, no matter what the outcome.

Teach Your Children to Give and Receive Compliments with Grace

The ability to give compliments to family, friends, and employees is a most effective form of creative kindness. Show a child how to praise someone who deserves it, particularly someone who is down on his luck and needs it. If it all sounds like unnatural, saccharine behavior to your child, don't be discouraged. Learning the art of giving sincere compliments is a goal that can take years to accomplish. But put it on your child's wish list. Make it something he strives for.

In order for your child to give compliments naturally, you must teach him to look at others with eyes that see the good, not just the bad. If you're a person who often compliments adult friends, relatives, and others in front of your children, they will learn how to do the same.

Show your child that a person who compliments or praises him or her deserves to be thanked: "If someone—the pizza cook, the bus driver, anyone—says, 'You look very nice tonight, young lady,' always smile and say, 'Thank you.'" It's as simple as that.

Teach your child *never to throw a compliment back in someone's face.* It's a boomerang that hurts when it returns. For example:

"What you said tonight to Emily was just plain rude."

"What do you mean, Mom?"

"When you both tried on your prom dresses in your room, she said she had never seen a prettier dress on you. She said you looked really nice in that color green. You shot back at her a list of ten reasons why you looked 'awful,' to use your own words, including the fact that green was unbecoming to you, you looked terrible with a pimple on the end of your nose, you had gained three pounds since yesterday, your shoes were wrong, and your hair looked gross."

"Well, it was all true."

"Do you mind if I tell you what you should have said when Emily paid you such a sincere compliment? You should have said, 'Thanks, Em. That's really nice of you!'"

"Isn't it a lot better to soften some of those exaggerated comments? I mean, Heather Locklear doesn't even look that great."

"No, it's unkind and awkward for the person who says something nice to you to start downgrading the praise. Just be grateful, smile, thank the person sincerely, and feel good about what was just said."

The Bad Habit of Bad-mouthing People

Constantly criticizing people can quickly become a habit in a child's life if it is not brought to his attention. It can make him feel big, bold, and powerful, and can take his mind off his own failings. But when you hear your child being caustic with friends, or making a nasty crack about someone who has just been praised in the conversation, *act fast!*

After explaining why knocking his or her siblings or friends is unacceptable behavior, teach your child *why*. (*It's mean; it smacks of jealousy; people will start thinking you're talking about them behind their backs, too; it makes everyone around feel uneasy.*)

It becomes uncomfortable listening to someone who is unable to talk about a schoolmate, teacher, sister, or anyone close without being critical. It can creep up so pervasively that the child who's doing the slamming is probably unaware of the pollution he is throwing into the air and the damage he is causing. If repeated often enough, an untrue or exaggerated criticism can become a truth.

A catty child may have peers clustering around him or her "to get the dirt," but he eventually becomes an unlovable, unpopular person whom no one trusts. The whole family and the others around the house, like a grandparent or a sitter, should be made aware that this is something the child needs to cure. "Please don't be so critical!" is a request that perhaps needs to be said often. It's more effective when it's said gently, not as a harsh command. When it's a brother or sister saying it, the admonition may be doubly effective. For example:

FAMILY CRITIC: She's *really ugly.*

DEFENDER: I don't think so at all. She has beautiful eyes. I'd feel lucky to have eyes like that. So, frankly, should you.

FAMILY CRITIC: He really messed up in today's game. He's the reason they lost. What a geek!

DEFENDER: Not right! He played very well. You're forgetting those great passes he made.

FAMILY CRITIC: She's really dumb. Incredibly stupid.

DEFENDER: She's a lot smarter than most of the kids. Try listening to her sometime.

FAMILY CRITIC: So that's his jacket. He's too skinny for it.

DEFENDER: I think it's great-looking. Maybe you need to get your vision checked.

Of course, there are reasons why children become overly critical:

+ They hear it at home. They become accustomed to their parents or caregivers making unkind remarks about people, and therefore look upon it as acceptable behavior.

+ They feel threatened by a newcomer on the scene at home or at school, so they believe they're boosting their own position by making the newcomer seem flawed. They seek relief from their own insecurities by accusing someone else of their own inadequacies.

+ If they're witty about their people-bashing, they draw laughs and attention from their audiences (witness the success of the TV comedies when both generations get laughs because of verbal assaults on one another).

As a parent, it's up to you to make a child realize the harm critical comments can cause, to himself most of all:

+ A critical tongue betrays the speaker's own lack of self-confidence. ("If you're feeling insignificant, you can make yourself noticed by making someone else look bad.") Self-assured people don't behave like this. They have better things to do.

+ It's cowardly to criticize someone who's not present to defend himself from what may be completely false allegations.

+ Don't think that what you said won't get back to the victim! It will.

+ The victim may decide to get back at you and give you some of your own medicine.

When you lecture your child for making mean remarks about others, you might be confronted with a retort like:

"But Mom, *you* do it all the time. You're always saying things like that about your friends. How come you get to do it, but when I do it, it's the end of the world?"

It may be time for you to confess to your child that, yes, you do make some cutting remarks, but you don't do it all the time, and when you do, you're sorry for having done it. Then suggest the two of you make a pact: "You stop speaking negatively about people, and I'll do the same. We'll either be kind when talking about others or we'll keep quiet. Deal?"

Back in my Omaha days, my mother noticed I had developed a lamentable habit when I was thirteen and in the throes of adolescence. I guess I'd decided that since I was a physical disaster myself in those days, everyone else had to be, too. One Saturday, Mother took my best friend, Anne Gallagher, and me to lunch at the Aquila Court Tearoom in Omaha. Not only did they serve fantastic creamed chicken in a potato basket (in those days, that was considered royal banquet fare for a Saturday), but they had beautiful models walking around the tables, showing off the latest fashions. Anne and I knew we'd never own those dresses nor have the bodies to wear them, nor have invitations to the kinds of places where such clothes were meant to be worn. Through lunch I noticed my mother using a small notepad that sat in her lap, but I didn't think anything about it. We were too busy talking. Later, back home, we had a private chat.

"Tish, I've noticed how critical you've become of everybody lately. I thought I'd measure how serious this habit is, so I counted the number of cracks you two girls made against your friends during the eighty minutes we ate lunch. I made check marks on my pad."

I thought this was kind of a dumb thing to do, but I asked politely, "And so?"

"The score was three unkind remarks by Anne and twenty-eight by you."

I was stunned. "You know," my mother continued, "when you talk that way about your friends, they'll eventually hear what you're saying and they'll turn away from you. And they won't come back. To make and keep friends, you have to like people and think the best of them, Tish. You're doing exactly the opposite. Besides, you sound so jealous all the time!"

It was all she had to say. Mother knew how to hit home when she was reining in one of her brood. My friends were the most important thing in the world to me, next to my family and my dog. So from then on I checked myself and greatly reduced the number of catty remarks. One is never totally cured, but even today, whenever I make a remark that stings, I'm stung back. It's probably my mother up in heaven, reminding me not to do that. Ouch!

Gay Bashing

Homosexual jokes are crude and cruel, but they become more loathsome when young ears are listening. With gay bashing such a serious national problem today, an adult should explain that he or she is not asking the child to embrace or even praise a homosexual lifestyle but only to be tolerant of the fact that others have chosen it. Even the fact that one may be morally and ethically against homosexual relationships does not give one the right to be violent in condemning them. If your teenagers question you about this subject, teach them that what does not concern them should not turn them into emotional advocates against the choices of other people. What should concern your children are their own actions and their feelings about marriage and family, which hopefully you have instilled as values in them.

A gay man with whom I used to work in the home furnishings industry once stated that verbal taunts hurt him every bit as much as if stones were being tossed at him. This is why it's so important for parents *not* to make gay or lesbian jokes in front of their children. When they do, children react by thinking such behavior is "an okay thing to do," and copy the adults.

If there's one type of person you do not wish your child to grow up to be, it's a person who advocates violence against any group. Peace!

Bigotry and Prejudice

Just as a child develops his or her best character traits and kindness at home, so, too, can he or she learn the worst there.

Prejudice falls into the category of the worst of the contagious diseases, since it is spread to a child at home by his parents, then carried to school where the child infects his friends. A child can also contract the disease from other children on the playground, when nasty, taunting remarks are made about people who are of a different color, nationality, or religious faith. These mean-spirited "spit-balls," as a teacher friend of mine calls them, are tossed around with force, some not aimed at anyone in particular, others aimed very deliberately at specific members of specific groups. For example, it's one thing when adults talk to each other about their fears that certain groups are taking all the jobs in the area. Everyone understands the emotional influence of economic pressures on our attitudes, but to hurl unfounded, nasty, discriminatory remarks in front of the children is very likely to turn them into unreasonable, prejudiced adults.

A child making a racial slur and proudly admitting that "I learned it at school" is a bad enough indictment of our society. It's worse when a child boasts to his friends, "That's what my dad said," or "That's how my mom feels about 'them,'" or "That's my older brother's newest joke."

"You are what you hear at home" sounds like an advertising slogan gone awry, but it's true. If you want your child to grow up to be a fair person, you first have to teach him that we are all alike, except that some of us are more fortunate than others. A parent should find creative ways to keep repeating the thought that *no one is better than anyone else* (so the children don't think that their parents are obsessed with it).

Explain that the real differences are not in the way people look or in the money or education they have, *but in the way they are inside.* There are good people and bad people in every group. There are mean people and kind people in every age group and socioeconomic class.

A friend of mine took her young niece to lunch one Saturday and gave her, as she described it, "the lecture of the day," this time on the subject of religious bigotry.

"My sister works all the time, and my niece has been living in a fatherless home for five years, so I welcomed the chance to spend some quality time with her. I think I managed to drive home the points my sister doesn't have the time to take up with her."

"You're a great aunt," I said admiringly, "but how does your niece feel about all that lecturing?"

"I only do it for five minutes, usually right after we've ordered the food. She claims it's worth sitting through in order to have a really good meal in a nice restaurant. She tells her friends she has 'lofty lunches' with her aunt."

If you catch your child making a racist or any kind of antiethnic statement, jump on it immediately. This is no time for an attitude of "Oh, well, I'll address that subject at a later time." *Now* is the time.

"I'm just trying to tell you that not only are the teasings and smart-aleck remarks against other groups cruel and unkind, but they're not permissible in today's society. When you get out of school and start to work, you'll find that no decent boss will permit that kind of talk, and you'll be out of a job."

An adolescent should be made to understand that meanness goes hand in hand with immaturity. "After you leave school, you're supposed to be able to qualify as an adult, and that means you don't show your own insecurity by slamming ethnic groups. It becomes a very tough habit to break. It's the kiss of death in the workplace, because intolerance—in any business worth your time and talent—isn't tolerated. Bigots at first sight might be considered witty and amusing, but people later figure out that they're really very unintelligent and untrustworthy."

STRENGTH AND DIVERSITY

A wise parent teaches his child—even a young one—that diversity is a good thing, that having different kinds of cultures, backgrounds, and talents commingled makes for a healthier, happier society. In spite of America's problems, diversity is one of its strong suits.

When someone from another country joins your child's class in school, inject your own welcoming enthusiasm into your child's mind.

"So you have a new student in your class who came from Togo? Great! Perhaps she would like to come for lunch with us next Saturday and stay to play? Why not invite two other classmates. It's a good way to welcome her. She must feel very strange in a new country, so far from her home and her friends. . . . I'm sure that if you were in her place you'd be pleased to be asked."

The more we learn about the world outside our own, the more tolerant and interested—and interesting—we become. Learning about other people and cultures is an adventure—and the basis of a lot of good conversation. When someone who is well traveled or well read comes to your house to visit, teach your child:

- ✦ to listen and learn

- ✦ to ask that person questions about his customs or country or religion

- ✦ to show an interest in matters outside their own narrow world

I congratulated a father who to me was an inspiration in the way he had instructed his children about the world outside. He had traveled extensively with them, made them dabble (even to the point of proficiency) in a couple of foreign languages, and arranged for them to go abroad with the American Field Service program, where they lived with foreign families during the summer or midterm vacation period. Every year he and his wife also welcomed one or more foreign students to their home for six weeks. He'd been an exchange student himself in his high school days. He gave me his list of "To Dos" to assure that your child won't be "a blindsided bigot":

+ Encourage the instruction of foreign languages.

+ Take your kids to foreign movies.

+ Welcome foreign students and racially diverse students to your house for weekend activities.

+ Have a globe or atlas in the house to teach children something of immense importance that's missing in many schools today— international geography. (Have geography quizzes that are fun, with prizes for the children who have learned the most.)

+ Take your children to a variety of church services of different faiths and cultures.

+ Show your kids how to find out about other cultures and religions via the Web pages on the Internet, as well as at the public library.

+ Invite a foreign student from your child's class to dinner, and cook a dinner indigenous to your guest of honor's culture— with the culinary guidance, hopefully, of the guest's parents. (Even if the guest does nothing more than bring some of his country's local spices, it will add great luster to the occasion.)

+ Discuss the great artists, performers, writers, and athletes of other countries around the dinner table. Get to know their names and what their accomplishments are, in accordance with the interests of your own family, which could be anything from sports to cooking, from architecture to art, from science to fashion and design.

This is really the adults' responsibility—to inspire the children to stretch their minds, and to give them something worthwhile to listen to at family gatherings.

How I wish that I had had some children with me on a recent

Sunday night when I entertained by myself five Chinese business-men and educators fresh off the plane from Xiaogan, Hubei, in the People's Republic of China. Only one of them spoke English or had ever been in this country before. They arrived punctually to the minute and presented me with gifts (I realized I had none for them, which was appallingly bad of me). They each gave me a busi-ness card, held by its corners, presented with a courtly bow. Our instant bonding was the subject of all our respective children. They had come to see me about teaching manners to the Chinese who will be working with American business and travel people.

My husband was away. I had prepared for them what I thought was a typical Chinese meal. A Chinese friend prepared the rice for me—the one sure thing—and I made soup and a huge panful of stir-fried chicken and vegetables. When I asked them to come out into the kitchen, friendly American style, to taste the stir-fry (I was worried about the amounts of soy sauce, sesame oil, and stir fry sauce I had used), they politely explained, "Men do not enter the women's kitchen at a party in our country." A Chinese friend had made an authentic Chinese dessert for me and left it for me in her covered pot, with instructions to heat it well before serving it. I for-got about it, having left it simmering on the stove, but soon the smoke through two sets of doors informed us that something was really amiss. The pot had melted, the dessert was all over the kitchen in a scorching, odiferous mess. Having been through many social disasters in my life, I knew that action, not panic, was called for. Windows were opened to rid us of the smoke, ice cream with hot fudge sauce was unearthed as a substitute dessert, there were many toasts to "the future manners of the children of China and the United States." As they walked out, I gave each of them an unwrapped gift (another gaffe): a mouse pad with the United States Capitol painted on it. They were delightful, and in spite of all my errors, they were so thrilled to be in a private home, they could barely contain themselves. I bought a new pot the next day, to make amends to my Chinese friend.

The stories of each parent's encounters on trips abroad or in international business or social contacts in this country should be told to the children, recounted with enthusiasm, admiration, and respect for the other country. Children take in that enthusiasm and will feel affirmatively toward that country. I am certain the gentlemen from Hubei told their own children about their Chinese dinner in Ms. Baldrige's home with much laughter, too.

The desire to know about another culture and to work together results from warm personal contacts, regardless of gaffes.

Kindness Around Us

It's heartening to watch selfless acts of kindness become a natural part of a child's character—like the actions of these children:

+ *A teenager* reacts to the flood devastation in a neighboring community by organizing a collection of clothing for children who are flood victims.

+ *A fourth-grader* sees a TV news story about some dogs that have been mistreated. He collects dog toys, food, and treats from schoolmates and their parents to bring to the Humane Society for the recuperating animals.

+ *A high school sophomore* learns that the elderly man who lives nearby has not been out of his house since his accident, so he sets up a schedule to take him out in his wheelchair for a half hour every afternoon after school.

+ *A ninth-grader* whose father is a florist decides that the neighbors need cheering up after eight weeks of unrelenting winter weather, so she asks her father for some fresh violets, and makes a small bouquet, each tied with a violet ribbon, to give to each family on her street, with a card that reads, "Just to cheer you up and make you feel that spring will come someday!"

+ *A seventh-grader,* without prompting, asks the teacher if he can take the weekend homework to a classmate who is not even a close friend but who's in the hospital.

+ *An eighth-grader* was seated next to a much younger child whom she didn't know at a birthday lunch. The little boy accidentally dropped his half-melted ice-cream bar on the host's carpet. The other children began to tease and laugh at him, so the eighth-grader swung into action. Knowing the child was miserable with embarrassment, she grabbed the ice cream with her paper napkin, rushed to the kitchen, deposited it in the trash, then returned to the table with a fresh ice-cream bar for the boy and a wet towel with which to clean the mess on the carpet. It was all done in a flash. She was kind to console the child; she was also polite, because she assisted the party host by correcting the problems at her end of the table. She put harmony back into the party scene. But someone taught her how to react like that; it was not divine intuition.

There are kind things done to us all the time of which we are not all that aware. Consider a compliment that someone gives you about your child. Your dinner guest may whisper that he has just met your son for the first time. "That child of yours," the guest adds, "is so poised and well mannered. I enjoyed talking to him. You must be proud of him."

Hearing those words makes you feel great. Even if you know that your child *is* the most perfect, wonderful, brightest person in the whole world, it's nice to hear it from someone *else*.

There can be nothing more relevant or important today than the quality of our personal relationships. We *need* to have little kindnesses shown to us to feel appreciated, which is what acts of kindness accomplish for us. They lift our spirits! And we need to return these gifts in kind to others for the very same reason.

Preparing Young People to Handle Hostility and Anger

Since our present world is a violent one, your kids will probably get used to seeing guns, metal detectors, and security guards wandering around school, and attend required violence-prevention training meetings in the school auditorium. (Some schools today look like the old movies of Nazi youth camps.)

I always used to hope that we'd see instruction on civility and manners in school assemblies, as part of a new curriculum. Instead, that time is taken up with necessary violence prevention.

Yes, it's important for a parent to teach a child to beware of trouble, to walk away from it quickly, to find an adult to help, and all the rest, but it is even more important for that same child to learn from a very early age to handle *his own anger and hostility*. The first warnings of a person who gets "out of control" too quickly is usually when a child is abusive to a sibling (or a pet) when angry about something. Be aware of it, establish good communications with your child, and make him aware of how serious you consider the charges. Be sure that if you work, your child-care giver supplies complete information on anything that happened during the day connected to this kind of violent behavior against siblings. If it continues, seek psychological counseling for the child.

Make time, in a calm moment, to talk with your child about the ways of handling one's own angry feelings. You might say to him or her: There are some things we can do to keep ourselves from blowing up at someone and striking out, even if we very much want to, among them:

+ Tell yourself to calm down and "chill out." Your being in control of yourself makes you respected by your peers. They see you in charge of your emotions and you will look strong and like a leader, not cowardly.

+ Take some deep breaths. Visualize all that oxygen flowing around inside your brain. It will relax you.

+ Count to twenty-five while looking down at the ground, not at the faces of the people toward whom you feel aggression at this point. There's something psychologically calming when you look at the ground. It is not confrontational, like a glare or a stare.

+ After the counting and deep-breathing exercises, remind yourself that giving in to violence is not grown-up and cool; it's dumb, juvenile, and unimaginative. Since only people without brains resort to violence, remind yourself that you have a plentiful supply of brains to help you work out problems. If reciting numbers to yourself is boring, start counting the brains in your head instead! It's a satisfying activity, and remember, too, you will want to keep all of them for as long as you can—and not lose them in a fight.

A Parent's Heartbreak: When Someone Says, "Your Child Lies, Cheats, or Steals"

It has to be one of life's worst moments, to hear bad things about your child—that human being in whom you had such confidence, for whom you had such hopes, and of whom you have always been proud. At first you think the tales are only rumors. Later, when the source of the complaints becomes one of authority, you know you have to accept it—and act.

The two worst parental reactions to a child's being in trouble are (1) *complacency* ("Oh, what he did wasn't so serious; I used to do things like that when I was his age") and (2) *denial* ("What? You must be kidding. My daughter couldn't have done anything like that. What a crazy idea!").

Then someone says to you, "Your kid is in real trouble." Later, that warning becomes more ominous. It's no longer that your child is in real trouble but rather your kid *is* real trouble. The supports have been pulled out from under the structure of his character. It's time to meet the emergency head-on and seek every kind of help available to you. It's time to devote all of your energies and creativity to the task. You want to save this child of yours.

+ *First, talk to your child—calmly, coolly, unemotionally.* Show him (or her) that *you* are in command of this conversation, not him. But make him talk to you, too. This needs to be a conversation, not an interrogation. You can ask him questions without trying to cut the answers out of him with a knife. Strike through any sullenness, defensiveness, or sarcasm he may be showing you. If he tries to defend himself by saying he didn't do any of these things, tell him, "This is denial; don't go there with me."

+ *Keep talking about "trust." It's a great word.* Show him that you trust him, that you want him to trust you, that he can trust you to keep things confidential and not to pass them on to the rest of the family. Make him believe he can tell you anything, that it is safe with you.

+ *Show him he is your first priority.* Scare him with how important you feel this matter is, how both you and your spouse are going to drop everything to get him through this mess, to be by his side—to get to the bottom of these accusations and to cure the reasons that lie behind them.

✦ *Show him that he must take his punishment—and learn from it.* Whatever he has to do, the whole family will be behind him, but *he must do it.* It doesn't matter whether the punishment is juvenile detention for selling drugs or expulsion from school for serious cheating. He must accept it. You're not going to try to get him off for something of which he is patently guilty. This whole experience can be beneficial—if he learns from it. (One of my brothers, about twelve at the time, shot out a streetlight from his bedroom window with a BB gun. As punishment, my father "arranged" not only to have the court order him to pay for the expensive repair of the lamp, but also to serve on the municipal garage truck detail. My brother learned a great deal from that experience.)

✦ *Get your child the very best help there is—legal, psychological, spiritual—whatever it takes.* Talk to him, talk to him, keep on talking to him. Keep those lines of communication open.

✦ *Convince him that this is not the end of the world, that he will rebuild his life.* Show him how you grieve over the wrong acts he committed, not the fact that he got caught doing it. This is a time for building character. Even small lies, when they are constant, need quick treatment, including a verbal and perhaps written apology if they have hurt someone, and financial reparation if a financial loss was involved. The most important aspect of all, of course, is the resolve never to do it again.

The family that sticks together when something like this happens is a family grown stronger because of it. A child learning to own up to his wrongful deed, apologizing for it, expiating it, and then showing others how to avoid doing it, is a great example of building character. Lots of American kids today have to learn that it is *the bad deed* that is wrong, *not the getting caught.*

A Conscience? What's That?

It's difficult for a child today to be upset by a guilty conscience, because most don't have a clue as to what that is. In fact, it often seems most adults don't have a clue either. Our society is too often driven toward pleasure and success, "and forget the consequences." Children who are guided by their consciences are usually the ones who spend a lot of time with their parents (or even one parent)—not just playing computer games, viewing a video, or munching tacos, but actually quietly talking to one another about their feelings, their actions, their hopes and disappointments. A wise parent makes a child understand what a conscience is—that inner voice that tells you what you're doing wrong, that stops you in your tracks when you're about to do something that's unfair or unethical, that loud click in your head and the sickening feeling in the pit of your stomach when you've been unjust or not owned up to some misdeed or have taken credit for something that wasn't yours.

I attended nine years of school in a very strict convent, the kind that is not around anymore. The Mesdames of the Sacred Heart at Duchesne in Omaha, Nebraska, talked incessantly about conscience, and although they put the fear of God in their students, they also made us strong in our resolve. Our consciences governed us like straitjackets. As a result we didn't spend a lot of time "wiffle-waffling" about our sex lives when we were old enough to have them. God, Heaven, and Hell loomed over our decisions—such as whether tonight would be the night we'd lose our virginity because the gorgeous man we were dancing with on the darkened dance floor was what we'd been waiting for since we'd seen Clark Gable in *Gone With the Wind*. But, no, our consciences told us that if we lost our morals that night, we would:

+ kill our parents; and if we got pregnant, force our families to leave town because of the shame of it

+ bring down the very wrath of God upon us (see *Dante's Inferno*)

✦ ruin our reputations forever and find our only future employment in whorehouses

Naturally, we committed overkill in the sharpening of our consciences. At the age of eleven, when I saw a homeless man begging on the corner of Farnam and 17th Streets, I told my mother I was going immediately to the bank to withdraw every cent from my minuscule savings account to give to him. My conscience was hurting because he was so unfortunate and I so lucky. My mother deterred me from this rash gesture by informing me that she knew this panhandler very well, that his was a clever act, that he drove a Cadillac and was worth more money than my father. At times one has to rein in the conscience.

In my childhood, there was a clear understanding of right and wrong. We confessed all over the place when we were bad—to our parents, teachers, and priests in the confessional. The mea culpas were plentiful. It helped pass the time of day, and the exoneration always felt good. We didn't have to consult our consciences, wondering about right and wrong. We just knew it—*pow!* There were no movies or TV programs showing that children have the right to enjoy themselves, regardless of at whose expense, that people have the right to follow their desires of the moment and to lie, steal, and plunder if they feel like it.

Parents might consider making a child's conscience a major project in the coming years. Children need help in learning how to confess and apologize when they have done something wrong. Children deserve being praised to the skies when they are strong enough to say "no" and follow a righteous path, which may be a very lonely one.

This is also an important point to discuss with a child-care giver who is with your children during the day. Make sure the caregiver knows what you believe a conscience to be, and that she give your children a prompt reminder when it is needed.

A Child's Conscience and Drugs: A Personal Philosophy

I believe that a child's conscience is a particularly powerful weapon in his battle against drugs and that it should be used. Any weapon at hand should be used. Hopefully, you've talked to your children about this subject from the time they were old enough to understand what drugs are. Hopefully, you've frightened them with the tragic consequences of taking drugs. Once won't do it. Keep it up. You might hear rumors that your child's classmates are experimenting with drugs. You realize it won't be long now. You'd better take action fast. For example:

+ Get a drug counselor to address your child and friends.

+ Take him or her to a drug rehab program residence that allows visitors, where your child can see addicts going through the program.

+ Ask your child point-blank if he or she has ever taken any kind of narcotic—whether it's inhaling, injecting, smoking, or swallowing something. Tell your child he must tell you the truth. If the answer is, "Oh, gee, Mom and Dad, we don't really take drugs. No one does in our class. Once in a while someone fools around a little, but it's not taking drugs," zero in, put the fear of God in your child, and forbid him to touch the drug culture, with direct punishment to befall him if he does. In other words, get *tough*.

+ Talk to your child about his conscience, and remind him that if he does drugs he is denying his family, his birthright, and his future. He is lying to his parents in the most serious way. He is throwing away his life.

+ Keep talking. Don't let up on her. Ride her, hound her. Make her see that your number-one priority is to keep her away from drugs. Keep in contact with the school. Watch her like a hawk.

+ Appealing to a child's conscience and preaching about how the brain is fried on drugs, like breakfast eggs (very understandable to the young!), are good practices. But if a parent doesn't even realize his child is taking something—ingesting, inhaling, shooting up, swallowing pills, whatever—the preaching is all for naught. A parent should know his child well enough to be able to detect if he or she is "on something." A parent should feel the slightest change in his child's behavior. Perhaps the basis of this entire problem is *to know your own child* before dealing with him.

✦ Of course, there is no conscience in a child when he sees a parent using drugs, including overindulging in alcohol. The devastating legacy is passed on, and any conscience the child may have developed atrophies into nonexistence.

If only the thousands of kids who get hooked on drugs every year, because they can't stand the pain of their lives and because they demand instant relief from any troubles . . . if only those kids could have had *my* parents, they would have known how to fight the enemy. And if only all parents would realize the power they have to teach their kids to take it on the chin and not be deterred in going forward, we would not have some of the teenage problems we have today.

A friend of mine told me how he became a mentor to one of his son's friends a year ago at the boy's request. "It was as if he asked me to take over his life. He even made an appointment to come see me at my office. I was really impressed by that. He said he wanted a 'confidential chat.' The kid was scared, he was getting more into drugs at school, and his widowed father didn't have the time to even notice what was happening to him, much less talk to him. He told me his grades were down, he was depressed, and his father was either busy on court cases all the time or spending the rest of the time with the young woman he was obviously falling in love with."

"What did you do?" I asked, wondering how this incredibly busy man seemed to be able to make time for another man's child.

"He became like my own son. Our house became his house, and instead of worrying about this situation, his father relished it. It gave him more time for his lady love."

A Young Person and the Question of Character

When a parent first starts thinking about building a child's character, it may seem to be a formidable task. But it really is a shared responsibility, for the child himself will also mold his own, according to his priorities.

When I was growing up, my constant battles with my older brothers were definitely a character-building exercise, which makes me return once again to my philosophy that everything bad that happens to you has a kernel or even a large residual of good that comes out of it.

When I was five years old, my brothers' "beastliness" to their little sister had reached a climax as far as I was concerned. (I didn't know the word *beastly* in those days, but if I had, I would have used it.) Our parents were in Washington, D.C., for the closing weeks of a session of the U.S. Congress. The Baldrige kids stayed behind in school in Omaha, in the care of our wonderful Irish nursemaid, Reggie Struble.

Mac and Bob realized that with our parents absent, they had a much better chance of terrorizing their brat of a sibling. They knew my deepest fear was of the dark, so one night they managed to dismantle the hall lamp right outside my bedroom, which emanated a warm, comforting light through the glass transom over the door, and kept me feeling safe. The two boys then made horrible, scary noises in the dark outside my room. After a few moments of sickening panic, a cool calm encased me. Action! I did not have to take it anymore. I could be mistress of my fate. I packed my doll's suitcase with her nightgown and one dress—and incidentally, her, too. I got dressed, took a streetcar token from my bureau drawer, put on my plaid coat and beret, and slid out of the house to the corner, where the Farnam streetcar stopped at 39th Street. The conductor was nonplussed when I boarded, quite alone.

"And where are you going, young lady?"

"To Washington," I replied bravely, "to my mommy and daddy."

He decided he couldn't leave me, so he took me all the way to Union Station, which was the turnaround point for the streetcars. When we got there, he called the police, and within minutes I was back on 39th Street, in the arms of a hysterical Reggie.

My mother immediately came home on the train from Washington (no planes in those days) and left my father to tough out the last weeks of the congressional session alone. My brothers were properly punished for their persecution of their little sister, and I felt enormous happiness and pride—first, because they were in parental hot water (and how!), and second, because I had been self-reliant enough to almost transfer myself to Washington all by myself. I was proud for not having panicked out there in the lonely night air of the city.

Strangely enough, that same pride of self-reliance came back to me when, as a nineteen-year-old student in war-ravaged Paris in 1946, I felt myself in grave danger. Our boat train had arrived in the Gare St. Lazare very late (two A.M.); the people who were supposed to pick me up didn't know where I was and had called the police, but I had no telephone number or address to go to. Dragging a footlocker and a suitcase, unable to find a porter or a taxi or any means of help, I wandered through the unlit streets of Paris on foot, trying to find a hotel. I stumbled into the only place open on the street. A dirty neon sign looked very good, and so did the dimly lit, smoke-filled bar inside, but it was frequented by ominous-looking Algerians, mostly men. Clad in my camel-hair, double-breasted, Brooks Brothers polo coat with pearl buttons (the typical American college girl's outer layer in those days), I gave only cursory importance to the fact that I could be robbed, murdered, or raped (I hardly knew what the latter meant in those days). No one in the United States or the Republic of France had a clue as to where I was. So I addressed the entire bar audience with a lusty "Au Secours!" (Help!) Everyone in the place jumped out of their chairs, startled beyond belief. I was a six-foot-one apparition from another life (they averaged about five feet four). They had never seen anyone dressed like me before. The war was just over; there were no tourists. They had never seen anyone so tall, so young, so American, and so out of place. Having heard me say I had had nothing to eat since a seven o'clock breakfast, when the boat docked at Cherbourg that morning, they gave me a piece of bread and a bitter-tasting aperitif. Then four men escorted me gallantly to the nearest hotel—thank heavens, including my footlocker and suitcase. It was l'Hotel Louvois, where they rattled the shutters, woke up the concierge, and forced him in his pajamas and bathrobe (under threats, I'm sure) to give me a room for the night. The gallant Four Horsemen from the Algerian Apocalypse saved my life.

In spite of my cry for help (which I had made in the bar to elicit attention and sympathy, and which worked wondrously well), I managed a tough situation skillfully. I felt very self-reliant, and before I fell into exhausted sleep that night, I remembered back to Omaha when I was five, fleeing from my brothers after they had shut off the night-light. I very definitely related the two incidents. I wasn't scared. I just felt in charge.

Helping Your Child Build His Character

Toughing it out. People tend to misinterpret what really builds character. If a woman refuses a high-calorie dessert at lunch, others at the table will say, "She's in her character-building mode." A father will tell his high school senior son, "No, you can't have a convertible as a graduation present. It builds character to drive an economy sedan."

The process of a child shaping his character is probably the most important thing that happens in his life—after being born, of course! It is the basis of his present and future happiness and all his relationships. It results in his becoming a mature, sensitive adult whom other people want to be around.

When I was in grade school, I once asked my father what the term *character* meant, because although we often heard grown-ups use the term, we didn't understand it. It's the kind of topic you can ask someone else to explain, but to which you never receive a comprehensible answer. But my father did have one. "Simple," he said. "Character-building means toughing it out." That was it.

If he were alive today and were asked the same question, he would probably say the same thing, but he probably would also add, "I'll tell you what 'toughing it out' means. It means *not* taking drugs and alcohol to make you forget whatever is upsetting you."

I remember all the times in my life that he used the "Be tough" exhortation in comforting me in his own way. When trouble came to one of us children, Mother's soothing consolation was coated with pretty, comforting words. "It's going to be all right, you'll feel better soon, everything's going to be just fine." My father's vocabulary choices were very different—"a guy sort of thing," which my brothers proceeded to carry with them through their lives.

When I broke my arm—the first time (in two places)—and the pain was almost unbearable, Dad took me to the Clarkson Hospital in Omaha. Mother was working as a volunteer that day at the Christ Child Society orphanage and was spared the details of my accident until that evening. If she had been with me at Clarkson, she would have been soothing my brow, grimacing with pain on my behalf, begging the Virgin Mary to send me immediate relief from my pain, and whispering, "I'm so sorry, Tish, I'm so sorry." She would have been murmuring sweet phrases of comfort in my ear, like a lullaby of angels. She would have rocked me in her arms, like a baby yet again, which is how she always treated her children when they were sick or hurt, no matter how large or how old they grew.

Instead, my father was with me at the hospital, giving me the "guy thing." But it worked beautifully. My father winced when I winced, but repeatedly said, "You're a brave, strong girl. You're toughing out this pain like a soldier who's been wounded in battle, like a guy who's been clobbered by Joe Louis in the boxing ring. I'm proud of you. You're accepting the pain and you realize it's at its worst now. No one will ever call you a coward."

The Baldrige family was well known in all of the Omaha hospitals, not as big donors, alas, because that was not possible, but

because we accident-prone children were the most constant users
of the emergency services. We could have furnished the plot for a
very lengthy major network TV series. Just to illustrate, we were
once all in the same hospital at the same time: my oldest brother
Mac with electric shock suffered from putting Mother's hairpin
into the electric wall socket, my brother Bob with a double mastoid
operation, and I with both hands crushed when I pulled over on
top of me a five-hundred-pound fern-filled cement urn from the
porch railing. Our numerous accidents and operations provided
many opportunities for *all of us* to build character—the Baldrige
kids because of the pain we suffered, our parents because of the
bills they paid.

I don't think my brothers or I could have said whose parental
comforting style was more effective, Mom's or Dad's, but certainly
our mother was the one who got the biggest workout in this area.
Kindness is a family tradition that children learn from parents, and
then pass down to their own families.

I well remember a high school freshman dance at Omaha's
Chermont Ballroom, where I towered over every boy in the room.
In those days, tall girls were practically nonexistent, and it was all
cheek-to-cheek, body-to-body dancing. No one asked me to dance.
(As high school humor went in those days, the saying was "Confu-
cius say that short boy who dance with tall girl get bust in face.")
The boys didn't want me to muss their careful coifs any more than
I wanted, after dancing with them, a residue of their hair oil streak-
ing under my chin and on the dress. I was miserable, so I called
home to ask my parents to come get me. (My father was there in his
car in ten minutes, having changed from his pajamas.) My pain had
become their pain. My mother told me that "the boys *will* grow
taller one day, and then you'll see how many will be dying to dance
with you, and it *will* happen." My father said, "It won't always be this
way, Tish. Just tough it out and wait." (They were both right.)

WE NEED TO TALK TO KIDS SO THEY WILL LISTEN AND WE NEED TO LISTEN SO THEY WILL TALK

If we talk a lot to our children, if we explore and discover what's going on in their lives in and out of school, we know when to put out a strong hand of support and some words of wisdom, too. The following constitute a small sampling of what kind of trouble there might be:

+ when a teacher is being unfair to the child

+ when he doesn't make the team

+ when she misses by one word in the spelling contest and isn't the student who goes to Washington to meet the President

+ when he has a terrible time at the party because no one would talk to him or agree to dance with him or even acknowledge he was there

+ when she was mugged and lost her savings from her after-school job

+ when he was hurt in an accident or got sick and had to miss what he considered the most important event of his life

+ when she worked harder than she ever had in her life, did a superior job, and then got a bad grade

+ when someone called him fat and wimpy

+ when someone told her she had skin like a spotted leopard

+ when he tried out for the leading role in the school play and ended up being put in charge of the curtain

+ when her dog was run over in front of her eyes

+ when he was promised six weeks at summer camp and then the parents' finances wouldn't allow even one week

+ when her best friend's parents are sending their daughter to Stanford, but her own parents can only afford a local community college

+ when a bully beat him up on the school playground

A parent, or any adult who is close to a child, can and should help him get through what must be gone through. To instill in a child a feeling that he or she is master of his or her own fate is essential. Say to a child who needs the reinforcement, "Hey, you're going to be okay, you're going to be fine. You're strong enough to take this, you will take it, and you'll be even stronger afterward. You have a lot of strength and willpower. Not everyone has. You're going to get through this!"

A kindhearted adult friend who doesn't even know the child well can also have an enormous influence over him by giving him a pep talk. Show the boy or girl how to create his own personal credo when he's troubled and hurting.

Here is one such, for example:

+ No drugs. They're for losers. I'm not one.

+ Ditto alcohol. It makes a person lose control of his life.

+ I don't need tobacco either. It's a symbol of weakness, not of sophistication.

+ In fact, I don't need any artificial anything to help me run my life. This is not being a wimp. This is demonstrating leadership to my peers.

+ I feel great because I can handle most of what comes along. Toughing it out is ultimately much easier to do than running away or giving in and drinking or taking drugs to erase whatever anguish I may be feeling. (You'll have a long, hard time recovering from the latter. Each instance of "toughing it out" and saying no is another step toward becoming stronger.)

Giving Your Kids Spiritual Values

You may not have a particular religious faith yourself, but if you feel spiritual values should be instilled in your children, give them the chance to have exposure to a religion. Whether they accept or reject it will be their decision. There are very good reasons why having spiritual values will help them get through life:

◆ It gives a child an added measure of happiness to know that a superior force knows of that child's existence, is responsible for that existence, and *cares* about him.

◆ It can give a child courage to survive the sadnesses and disappointments that life brings.

◆ It sharpens a child's conscience, so that he will more clearly understand right from wrong. (He may still choose to do the wrong thing, but at least he'll know it's wrong!)

◆ It brings consolation in times of sadness.

Faith is a great helping hand out there. If you have no congregation of your own, you might suggest that a relative or friend take your child with him or her to a service. Let your child try out several kinds of services, if he shows some interest. A teenager might become attracted to one specific faith by going with someone else, and then attend services on his own.

You can give a child a young person's book about faith. If the family of the child you're helping comes from a particular faith (Episcopalian, Catholic, Presbyterian, Baptist, Christian Scientist, Jewish, Islamic, whatever), find a child's book from that religion. In other words, never upset the parents by trying to move their child away from the faith in which the parents were brought up. If the parents were brought up in no faith, your task is easier. You have a *tabula rasa.* You can tell those parents about what you've seen with your own eyes through life—how spiritual values can make a child strong in character, console him in times of grief, and make him a happier person.

All the work you might do to give a particular child some spiritual values in his life to help him grow strong doesn't necessarily mean that it will "take," like a successful vaccination. It's unpredictable. Faith works for some people and doesn't for others. At least, give your child a crack at it.

My mother was one of the most devout people I have ever known. A Roman Catholic, she said a daily rosary for every person she knew who was in trouble. We kids counted that at times she had eleven going a day. My father was a Baptist, and when I was a young child and had that accident with the cement urn that crushed my hands, my mother sent Dad to every convent and church in Omaha to get all the communities of nuns making novenas nonstop for "little Letitia, so that she'll be able to use her hands again." (The surgeons had told my parents they doubted I would ever have the use of my hands again.) He drove all night around town, waking up the nuns and priests wherever he went, begging for their prayers. Shortly after this incident Mother Callahan, a tiny pistol of a nun (four feet ten) at my school, the Duchesne Academy, ran up to my father in her black habit. She looked, as he described her, like a fast sailboat at full sail. She elicited from him a promise that one day he would become a Catholic like my mother—in thanks to the Almighty for saving my life and my hands.

Fifteen years later, on their thirty-fifth wedding anniversary, my father disappeared from our apartment for most of the morning. When he came back at noon, he informed Mother that his anniversary present was a fulfillment of his promise to Mother Callahan. That morning he had received several sacraments of the church and was now a full-fledged Roman Catholic. It was a present my mother never forgot for one day the rest of her life.

When I asked Father Burke of Georgetown University how my father, Mac Baldrige, had done in his religious instruction, and in learning his catechism, he laughed and said, "There will probably never be another conversion like it. Your father and I, both old football players [they were stars from their days at Yale and Notre Dame], met at your residence on afternoons when your mother was doing her Red Cross volunteer work and was away from the apartment. The two of us spent our time on the floor, recalling and practicing various winning plays with an actual football in our hands."

As the ball went flying around the living room, Father Burke told me, they prayed "they wouldn't break anything and that Jean [my mother] wouldn't come in and find us, thus ruining the surprise."

"But Father Burke, what did Dad learn about Christian doctrine in those sessions? Does he understand and know his catechism?" I asked.

"Your father," he said, laughing again, "didn't need to learn all that stuff. He's been a good, holy man all his life. God knows how good he is. Forget about the rest of it."

And so my father attended Mass every Sunday the rest of his life, a full-fledged Catholic who really didn't understand the Mass. It didn't matter. He knew how to thank God for his family. That was, in essence, his religion. And in my eyes, he was a saint.

Cultivating the Art of Leadership in Kids

What's leadership? To me it's that mysterious, ethereal energy that motivates a person to rise above others, to assess a situation, and then to act and take charge. (There are those who just watch the parade, there are those who join the parade, and then there are those who lead it.)

Leadership begins to sprout at a very young age. Leaders and followers show their colors early on. If, in the presence of children, you use every opportunity to point out examples of leadership and good sportsmanship, you may feel that the children are not listening or understanding, but it's amazing how positive tidbits of someone's actions will be remembered by children and become a permanent part of their memory bank.

Children like to remember good things, such as times when their own actions deserved special praise, or even how when someone else's deeds were praised it reflected glory on them, too. They want to be like the people who merit that praise.

Although a child is not going to understand leadership unless it is explained, a young mind quickly absorbs the fact that a leader is a person who makes things better for the world. An adult has to drop that seed of wisdom in young minds and keep reminding them of it. The concept may very well be enough to keep a child strong in the face of peer pressure. The idea of being of genuine use to his world can seize a child's imagination and help him cling tenaciously to moral values when the resolve and values of those around him who are less motivated are fraying.

It is important to make a child feel excited about life's possibilities, about the roles of leaders and even the possibility of leadership for him in his own life. If you hear enthusiasm about this in a young voice, *stop and listen!* Then encourage the passion you hear.

Unfortunately, the press today emphasizes the sleazy, scandalous, gory, ugly, and depressing events of the day. Good news is not prime-time news. Therefore, our nation's leaders, heroes, great entertainment figures, sports personalities, and other high achievers are not ordinarily presented in the media as very good role models. Frequently, it's not their achievements that get them space, it's the scandals in which they're implicated that make news.

Not long ago, when I was conducting a discussion with a group of kids from the inner city, I told them that George Washington, our first President, a great general, smart businessman, astute farmer, and convivial host, was my favorite role model. And he had such beautiful manners! I asked the kids who their favorite role models were. A fourteen-year-old girl immediately answered, "Anyone who isn't in the slammer!"

It was cynical, brash, but a very good answer.

A good alternative for helping kids find role models is the hero- or heroine-a-month family study project. Our world is full of heroes past and present. The public schools don't teach children much about the Founding Fathers anymore. In this politically correct world, George Washington, Thomas Jefferson, and their peers have been excluded from many history books. But there are thousands of books on past and present role models. Any librarian can show you a wealth of material. A good family project is to take out a library book, a tape, or a CD-ROM on a hero or heroine once a month, to digest and discuss as a family project. That's twelve role models a year, twelve more than your children would have known about otherwise. Let the older children choose the subjects of the biographies. Make it fun. Let them contribute their own summaries on the subjects, or start a scrapbook, for leading the discussion. One child reported to me that his parents have been doing this for two years now, and that they have a hero dinner discussion once a week.

Libraries have excellent tapes, CD-ROMs, and films on the lives and times of great leaders and important periods in history. And many cable and public radio stations run excellent individual shows and series on these subjects. Some even provide transcripts and study guides that make a great basis for family discussions and reports.

Siblings: Kindness, Competition, and Mayhem

The present American obsession with marrying, divorcing, and repeating the cycle once or twice more upsets the support that brothers and sisters used to bring to one another over a period of time.

I remember a friend's admission that when she married for the third time and took her two children out of her second husband's house to join her third husband, the ones who suffered the most from the switch were the *children of her second husband and his first wife.* "They had become attached to my kids," she said ruefully, "in an incredibly strong way. When I married someone else and took my children away from them, they didn't get over the shock and loss for several years. It never occurred to me that stepsiblings could be that important in their lives, but then I realized that it is the power of brother-sister love that's involved here. It didn't matter who the parents were. To the children, all that mattered was who *they* were."

It's a miracle to watch a maturing older sister consoling a sobbing baby brother who has hurt himself. A short time before this, she may have been bedeviling him by stealing his toys and being generally obnoxious, knowing full well, of course, that he is too small to fight back. Now she is all heart. He has a cut finger, and she is truly solicitous of his welfare, a brave nurse to the rescue.

Until recently this sister may have watched her little brother without emotion, busy with her own preoccupations, none of which concerned him. Today she has a maternal arm around him, is patting his hand and repeating, "It's going to be all right, you'll see." She is growing up and beginning to feel compassion.

Jessie and Jamie

As a child matures and experiences life more fully, his reservoir of sympathy for others should expand commensurately. (The happy truth is that it can expand forever.) If he has brothers or sisters, he will be able to feel empathy at an earlier age than an only child, for there are opportunities all around him to witness his brothers' and sisters' sorrows and pain. An adult who witnesses a child's sudden understanding of someone else's pain should acknowledge it and praise that little burst of sympathy: "Yes, go on, tell Jamie how sorry you feel about his upset tummy. He'd like to hear you say that."

You are encouraging kindness in your child by urging him to reach out to his sibling: "Look, you may be feeling real sorrow right now, but it doesn't do your sister any good if you don't show what you're feeling inside—either in words or in actions. Express what you feel. Show Jessie how you feel about her dog's having been run over. Give her a big hug. She'll know what you mean by that. Or tell her in your own words how sorry you are that Brownie is gone, because he was such a wonderful dog and everyone loved him so much. . . ."

WHEN EVERY ONE OF THE KIDS IN YOUR FAMILY IS A STAR, EXCEPT YOU

It's not fun being the odd person out in a family of stars. It's no fun to get poorer grades and to be clumsy instead of agile, and to be not so beautiful when compared to your older sister, or not so bright when compared to your younger brother.

Christopher

The middle child in a family of three children often feels the odd person out, even if it's unwarranted. I remember a friend telling me about being asked to speak to her son Christopher's fifth-grade teacher, Mrs. Ryan. Christopher, it seems, was having a tough time in class.

"Tell me," the teacher asked, "does Christopher's older brother keep lording it over him? He constantly refers to him in class, as though he's in awe of him. Is the older boy the 'perfect child' in the family, while he, Christopher, is the failure?"

"No . . . I mean . . . I haven't been aware of this," my friend reportedly said, feeling quite stunned.

"Mrs. Butler, Christopher recently has such a sad, woebegone face on him, I just had to see if there was some way I could help."

"He has a sad face?" his mother asked in disbelief.

"Have you looked him in the face recently?"

That's when Christopher's mother realized she had not seen all this because of the short amount of time she spends with her children. She was unaware of the suffering Christopher was enduring. His teacher had to point it out to her. She immediately began to attack the problem, and she showed me her list. She had written:

+ Her ex-husband should be made fully aware of the problem and pay Christopher more attention, which he immediately did.

+ Her oldest, "star" son was asked to spend more time with his younger brother and be supportive of him, which he immediately did.

+ She stopped spending so much time on the reading materials that she would take from her briefcase and attack every night before going to sleep. She turned the extra time over to Christopher.

+ She canceled weekend meetings and tennis games, and turned that time over to Christopher, substituting activities of his choosing, such as art projects. He began banjo lessons and she checked his progress every other day. She helped him raise some baby chicks and got to know what a sensitive, fine young boy he was.

She was encouraged, she told me, because Christopher was "blossoming." When I asked her what all this did to the baby of the family, a three-year-old, her mother replied, "There's no neglect there, I assure you. She gets her proper due, although she's so independent, she could easily skipper a boat by herself. She takes no nonsense from her brothers. They call her 'Slugger.'"

Then my friend said, "You know the most important thing I learned from this experience? I learned to look in the faces of my children, carefully, *every day of their lives.* Even though my job keeps me away from them, no one can read them better than *I.*"

BUILDING A FEELING OF SELF-WORTH

Just as there is a tremendous bond among siblings, so can they be victims of one another's teasing. A younger brother who gets good grades can decimate an older brother by calling him "Dumbo" after the older brother brings home a less than good report card. An older sister with a beautiful body and a large supply of willpower can obliterate a younger, pudgy sister when she discovers her sister has hidden a forbidden bag of chocolate chip cookies in their shared closet. A tall son in the family, a natural athlete, can drive his unathletic brother into deep envy and despair by the way he performs on the baseball field in front of the family. *Adults and children who show kindness to children who suffer from feelings of inferiority are a strong antidote for this problem.*

✦ *A father can say to his daughter, "Help out your sister. I'm not asking you to tell her a lie. I'm asking you to find one of her attractive features and to comment on it. She needs something nice said to her this very minute by someone. She's pretty low."*

"And if I can't find anything at all that's attractive about her, Dad?"

"I'm asking you to use a magnifying glass, if you have to, although that's not necessary. I think that if you try, you can easily come up with a list of ten things about your sister that are very appealing. Please, I'm begging you, compile that list, will you?"

The girls' father was using an intelligent ruse. By putting his older daughter to work, by giving her an intellectual exercise to reflect on all the attractive points of her sister, his elder daughter will probably come to have much more respect for her sister, even to see her in a new light, and to be able to support her much more easily. We often label someone as a "total nerd" when there are only one or two bad points in that person. When one child honestly and carefully assesses the good points of another one, the result is usually pretty fair, even substantive.

✦ A kind parent points out to any child who suffers from periods of feeling inferior that *he or she has a unique, valued position in the family structure,* as well as a great potential that needs only nurturing and developing. A child needs to be told that his personality makes him as satisfying to his parents as any of his siblings.

✦ *A parent should never forget to communicate to the children: "I love you kids equally.* I love you all. No matter what anyone does, I still love you, *in equally huge amounts."*

✦ *Wise parents who recognize insecurity in one of their offspring should motivate siblings to empathize and lend a helping hand.* Brothers and sisters who bicker at home are usually their siblings' most ardent and effective defenders in school or on the playground. (My brother Bob, who would refer to me with endearing names around the house like "scuzzbag" one minute, would grab a boy who was annoying me outside school ten minutes later and yell in his face, "You can't talk like THAT! That's my SISTER!")

✦ *Children should be made to understand why they should feel sympathy for a sibling who needs some support,* and not only feel it but know how to translate it into action. Parents might hold a family powwow to consider the problem, and elicit the suggestions of the children, who usually know better than anyone what steps should be used to help their sibling.

Sean

The five children of one family I know are much admired because they always seem to be cheerful, outgoing, energetic, and happy. Their father told me that by the time he was fifteen the middle son was, in the words of a younger sister, "a nerd and a complete and utter mess." The father added, "Other than that, he was a great kid."

He and his wife held a family conference without Sean, the middle son, who was off on a rafting trip. The parents explained to the other children how sensitive Sean was about his bad complexion and "endless bad hair days." His younger brother said at this point, "If I looked like him, I'd go hide in a Tibetan monastery." Everyone laughed and told their favorite stories about their brother, but then the serious discussions began. The parents explained how Sean's physical appearance (in a large family of good-looking kids) had made him lose out with the girls. He therefore didn't know how to talk to them and none of them would go with him to a game or a movie, much less a school dance. The parents went on to say how Sean was suffering over this, but of course he would never let on to his family what was going on inside him. It was affecting his school-work and even his sports performance. The parents asked the four brothers and sisters to do their best to buck him up, not tear him down by teasing. It was time for action.

Two years later, Sean's father reported, the crisis was past. His siblings "had really done a job on him." His skin was almost totally cleared up, his grades were up, he was on the track team, and he was going out with girls. At times they went too far, such as the day his eight-year-old sister accosted the prettiest girl in the high school and asked her if she wouldn't like to come to the house to meet her brother and then go to the movies with him. Amused by the little sister, the prettiest girl in the school did join the family for burgers, then she went to the movie with Sean, and his social success was confirmed.

IF YOU THINK YOUR CHILDREN FIGHT TOO MUCH, JUST REMEMBER THE BALDRIGE KIDS AND INSTANTLY FEEL BETTER

Every time I hear about brothers and sisters fighting, I immediately think back to my youth, when the three Baldrige kids "had at" one another all the time, so much so that my father, very worried, spoke to my mother one day.

"Jean, I'm embarrassed to bring this up, but are they—our children, that is—quite normal? Should we consult a psychologist about them?" (For my father to say the word *psychologist* in the 1930s, at a time when he compared them unfavorably to voodoo practitioners, shows the depth of his despair.)

"What do you mean?" my mother had asked in as indignant a tone as she could muster.

"They never do anything but fight. There might be a homicide one day."

My mother assured him that there would be no homicide (which there wasn't), that we would grow out of it (which we did), and that it was perfectly normal with three very competitive, noisy kids (which we were). My mother had grown up in a large family; my father was an only child. My father loved his children completely, but I'm sure he was delighted when Monday mornings rolled around and he could retreat to the safety of legal squabbles in court, away from the sibling squabbles at home.

My two older brothers resented me. First, I was the baby of the family, and second, I was the only girl and the obvious apple of my father's eye. They embarked upon a plan of intimidation and revenge, which sharpened in intensity during the years commensurate to the amount of telling on them that I did. I always went to my father first with my stories of their abuse, because he never saw through my exaggerations, as my mother did. Second, the leather razor strap hung in my father's bathroom. It comforted me to know it was there, because it was the symbol of the punishment on my brothers' behinds that could take place if warranted. As far as I was concerned, Mac and Bob warranted it constantly, but no one else thought so. Since my crimes against them are not recounted in this book, only their crimes against me, some might consider this historical account slightly unfair.

+ Both brothers began their campaign with a certain flair when I was about two. They gave me a push on my kiddie cart at the top of the stairs on the second floor. Mother called an ambulance and then the doctor, who said, "Is that Letitia making all those screaming noises?"

  "Yes," sobbed my mother.

  "Stop worrying," he said. "She's all right." My brother Mac later commented that I had a cement head and no brains, and that is why I went all the way downstairs on my head without hurting myself.

+ Santa gave Bobby a baseball bat one year, and in a practice session in the family living room, he just happened to be swinging too near me. I was knocked unconscious for three hours. My brothers called it the best Christmas so far.

+ When I would go flying by on my balloon-tired bicycle on our front sidewalk, Mac had a very annoying habit of sticking his foot out to catch mine in the pedals. One of his punishments was having to buy me a new bike from his allowance for the next year.

✦ Both brothers managed to take a running jump one Christmas day and land on my new, long-awaited dollhouse. The world's worst tornado couldn't have done a better job. This happened during the Depression, and it was not possible for my parents to buy me another one. I am still waiting for the day when I can buy the most grandiose dollhouse in existence.

✦ The pièce de résistance happened when I was twelve and my brothers and their friends were holding a meeting in our big living room of the "older, cool high school guys" in Omaha—the Les Hiboux Club. (My family allowed all of us the use of the house for our friends, and there were always giant bowls of popcorn, Cokes, and glazed doughnuts for our guests.)

I arrived in the hallway outside the living room this Saturday afternoon in time to hear my prized, secret little green leather diary being read aloud. My brothers had picked the lock with one of my mother's hairpins. The diary was full of passionate yearnings and professions of love for several boys, all of whom were now sitting in our living room, listening to the burning words. The hilarity of the Les Hiboux Club members had never been so pronounced, and my mortification matched its intensity. Luckily, we moved to the East Coast from Omaha soon after!

When World War II started, my father went off to war, and my two brothers subsequently did, too. By now, we three Baldriges had become fast friends and allies. I cried over my father and brothers every night. I wrote them letters daily and sent them many boxes of Hershey candy bars, which was rewarding, because some of the handsome young officer friends would write me appreciative letters in return. (My brothers made them do so.) They sent me snapshots of themselves, too, which I would swoon over while listening to Tommy Dorsey records. I would, of course, pretend those soldiers were madly in love with me, too.

It's hard to realize that siblings can fight so much, be so competitive, and yet be such great friends by the time they finish the angst of adolescence. My brothers returned from the war and were smart enough to marry superior women (I would not have forgiven them if they had not). My father returned from the war, arriving ahead of time as a surprise, and I realized he was home because I saw a beautiful nightgown Mom had just purchased lying in wait on the bed in their Washington apartment.

All of this is just to say that you shouldn't be morose if your quarreling offspring are not yet showing any signs of improving their relationships. As long as there is no money to fight over, with the passage of time, brothers and sisters usually become what they should be to one another—the most trusted and loving of best friends. That is fortuitous, because parents die and siblings stick around for a long while. They're worth any amount of tears shed over stolen frosting and picked diary locks.

THE PLUS SIDE OF A GIRL'S GROWING UP WITH BROTHERS

+ She will never suffer sexual harassment on the job. She's been through it all already, and knows how "not to tolerate it."

+ She learns to give back verbally to the opposite sex exactly what she got. Her vocabulary is consequently a plus point.

+ She learns not to have any romantic illusions whatsoever about the opposite sex. She knows exactly what she's getting into when she marries—she marries a brother of sorts.

+ She learns how to become a teacher of manners. Brothers do fall apart when they begin to date, and sisters become excellent resources on how to please a woman; how to apologize to her effectively when he messes up (without having to spend too much money on the "I'm sorry" gift); and what kind of manners he is supposed to display in front of his date's parents.

+ She learns sharp male negotiating styles. It really helps a woman in business to remember how her brothers' cunning minds worked when they were talking their parents out of something they didn't want to do but that their little sister wanted to do, and how to talk their little sister out of almost anything by using threats, innuendo, and tricks.

+ She learns how "to be at home with the guys." A girl with older brothers can walk into any situation where she's meeting men for the first time and feel comfortable, whether it's a business or a social event. She learns to be breezy around boys, picks up on what they consider "really cool" in the female, and then usually unconsciously absorbs it into her personality.

+ She has probably seen the male body unclothed on more than one occasion in her life, never found it particularly impressive on those occasions, and therefore has no prudish hang-ups about it. Whenever I went into the Baldrige children's bathroom by mistake when a brother was there (no locks on bathroom doors), I always retracted quickly, happy and delighted I was born female.

THE PLUS SIDE OF A BOY'S GROWING UP WITH SISTERS

A brother's list of what he learns from growing up with a sister would be different, but equally important to him.

+ He will probably never sexually harass women in the workplace. He has already got it out of his system with his sister(s), and he may be just a little bit afraid that someone like his sister might be around in that workplace to haunt him.

+ He has learned how to engage in and occasionally win a verbal duel with the women in his life. He should be experienced at it after all those years with his sister, when verbal duels were part of everyday life. He already is many points ahead of a man with no sisters.

+ He has absolutely no romantic illusions about the opposite sex. Any beginnings of such illusions in his adolescence were knocked out of him by his sister. He knows women far too well to be surprised or deluded. When he ultimately falls in love, he will be much more sure.

+ He is much better prepared in the field of manners than a sisterless man. He's been told all through his life how rude and unfeeling he is to women. He's heard his sister's relentless criticism not only of his own manners but of those of all his friends as well. In self-defense, when he begins dating, he seeks to acquire social savviness. He knows that a degree of civility will give him an edge his contemporaries do not have.

+ He doesn't have to learn female negotiating styles. He already knows them. He has witnessed his sister wrapping her father around her little finger and gaining unfair advantages, so he is well aware of the power of feminine wiles in the workplace.

+ He knows how to relax in female company because he has had so much practice with his sister and her friends when they were hanging out at his house. He meets women easily, judges them expertly, and the more he has fought with his sister growing up, the more likely he is to marry someone just like her!

+ He has probably seen the female body of his sister unclothed on more than one accidental occasion in life, and if he is like my brothers, never found it particularly impressive on those occasions. Whenever one of my brothers or their friends would come into the children's bathroom by mistake when I was there, that person would always retreat quickly, happy and delighted he was born male. He would therefore have no prudish hang-ups—or great expectations—about the female anatomy. If women without their clothes on look like a sister does, what's so special?

When I asked my mother how she and Dad had stood us during those trying years of our growing up, she answered, "We kept a sense of humor about it." That seems to be a key to many kinds of survival.

The News About How Parents' Jobs Affect Children's Attitudes

The vice president for human resources at a business lunch was nervously tapping his water glass with his spoon. He was far away from the conversation at our table. At a certain moment, I asked him, an old friend, "Why are you so uptight today? I haven't seen you glass-tapping like this in a long time."

He laughed, immediately relaxed his long frame in the chair, and apologized for being as far away as I thought he was. "I'm pre-occupied," he said, "because I'm blamed by our employees for everything: wages too low for them to live on; bad water in the pipes in our building, which is supposedly making people sick; dis-crimination against Latinos in hiring; overpriced food in our cafe-teria—would you like me to go on?"

"You make me want to come to work for you immediately!" I answered.

"The latest thing is that our senior management is now accused of making our employees' kids' grades sink in school." He held his head in mock exasperation. "Our personnel policies are supposedly making some employees unhappy, and those parents then make their kids unhappy, who then get bad grades." When pressed for details, he said employees all over the country had been reading the results of students as reported in the *Wall Street Journal* and other publica-tions, stating that children reflect their parents' frustrations and unhappiness on the job. They also, on the other hand, reflect their parents' happiness and feelings of success in the workplace—when that occurs—in which case the children benefit from it.

"Happy parents on the job make better parents who then have better children," he said wryly, "and the company is supposed to be responsible for this entire chain of events."

I later asked the wives of two pairs of dual-career parents (both in their mid-thirties) how their children reacted to their jobs. They both said the children asked two questions frequently: Why do you have to work so hard? Why can't you stay home with me? They both said that their older children sometimes took delight in trying to layer a load of guilt on their working parents. "Mother A," who hated her job, said the children succeeded in the mission of mak-ing her feel guilty. "Mother B," who loved her job, would have none of that. They felt completely different about their careers and their children's reactions to their careers, although they did share some similarities. For example:

Both sets of parents have to work for financial reasons. Their careers do not represent a capricious decision to "have a job" in order to be considered important and be "part of a stimulating environment." They need the money for the children's schools, and both sets of parents have the care of their own aging parents on their minds as well.

Both mothers, if given a choice, would have stayed home with the kids until they had finished grade school. Parent B probably would have worked even if she could have stayed home during her children's high school years, because, as she said, "Your children are already on their own by then, and all you can do is touch base whenever you can and keep trying to insert your values into their 'antiadult' minds."

Mother A is probably depressed about her status in life. And she

---

$\mathscr{T}$HE DIFFERENCES IN ATTITUDE TOWARD WORK BETWEEN MOTHER A AND MOTHER B

MOTHER A	MOTHER B
✦ Doesn't talk about work, so the children know little of her job. When she does mention her work, it's to belittle it and complain. Doesn't know anything about her coworkers' home lives or their children.	✦ Talks about her job with her children. Is very proud of what she is learning and accomplishing. Gives her children a full report on her day, once she has learned what happened in *their* lives that day.
✦ Doesn't have any personal relationships with others in the office and doesn't care.	✦ Has made a whole new set of friends—her coworkers—and knows all about their weddings, christenings, bar mitzvahs, first communions, and graduations.
✦ Just wants to do her job and collect her pay.	✦ Has a well-thought-out set of goals for advancement in her business. Tells her children all about friends on the job, so that they're eager for the news of Mom's life at work.
✦ Doesn't want her children to become involved with her colleagues.	

may take out her frustrations on her husband—and certainly on her children. Since they only hear complaints from her about her working life, they will not only reflect her depression now, but they will have a tough time in the future engendering enthusiasm about entering the life of work themselves. They will automatically feel that a mom can't work and raise a family properly and be happy, which is a tragedy, because that will be the lot in life of a majority of women in this country, whether they like it or not. A positive attitude toward one's job has an uplifting effect on everyone around the person, including the family.

AN ANTIDOTE TO THIS NEW PARENTING PROBLEM

✦ Both parents should talk with enthusiasm about their jobs with their children. *They should make them understand what they do.*

✦ *Both parents should talk about the helpful, considerate things* they and their coworkers do on the job—as a kind of celebration of humanity.

✦ When parents react to the good fortune or bad fortune of their colleagues, they should make their children aware of the reasons for their emotions. *They should make the children understand how grown-ups feel compassion for their coworkers* and congratulate them when they've done something wonderful and mourn with them when tragedy strikes. When an adult is sensitive to and caring about others, he also helps his child to be that way in her own world.

When a parent returns home from work too sapped to be able to notice signs of trouble in his or her child's voice and face, it is a serious matter. If mom's having a very difficult time in her own working life, she often doesn't have enough emotional strength to turn her attention and therapeutic love toward her child, who needs it so desperately.

There are many solutions, including these:

✦ *Parents should realize that their sense of satisfaction with their jobs brings happiness into the home,* which then acts like a magical nutrient that comforts and even inspires their children. If they're frozen by habit in a job that is unfulfilling, they should consider trying to get into a new situation.

✦ *Senior management needs more education on this subject.* Successful executives who are parents can impress a hardened CEO with the need to do something about helping employees whose children are facing difficulties because of their extended absences from the home. A senior executive who has no home life of his own should realize that his less privileged employees cannot spend their lives fulfilling his wishes and working his hours to the detriment of any personal life. If they do, they will lose efficiency and productivity.

✦ *More flextime in the workplace might help parents cope.* An executive who is stressed out over his or her children is going to contribute very little to the bottom line. An executive who gives extra time to his children when they need it and who feels he is not shirking his parental responsibilities will do a better job as a result.

✦ *Some parents may need to examine the quality of child care their children are getting.* They may need to investigate what's happening in the present arrangement or in the day-care center, and reach out for better help.

✦ *Women or men who don't have to work* so hard, and can now sacrifice a few years out of their lives, might return home part-time for a number of years, while their children mature.

✦ If fate decrees that a parent can't be around that much for children's important events, *perhaps relatives and friends could fill the void and serve as surrogate parents* . . . at a baseball game or a ballet recital or a speech on "Our Founding Fathers" at the school assembly. It takes planning on the parent's part—and caring, too.

✦ *More denial of your own free time—giving up the things you love to do on weekends, such as playing tennis or golf—*is not always pleasant. But spending that time with your children will reap enormous benefits in their lives—and what's more important than that? The tennis and golf can wait. Your children can't.

✦ *Becoming more sensitive to how your children are doing in school is fundamental.* You'll never know how much your own mind-set is affecting your children unless you keep in touch with their teachers. Talk to them more often. (Call them at a time convenient for *them,* not you.) Once you have established a good rapport with a teacher, ask those questions that are tough to ask: Does Tommy ever talk to you about my job? Does he ever say I'm not home enough or that I work too hard? Could my own unhappiness with my job be affecting him, do you think? Does he sound as though in his mind I'm neglecting him?

Square with those teachers, make them feel your concern about your child, establish a good basis of communication, so that they will become energized to help you with your problem.

Find a way to enjoy what you're doing in your professional life. Maybe your child sees more unhappiness in you than you feel in yourself. Maybe it's time for you to do something about it. And if you have a success on the job, tell your children all about it—every last detail. Make them proud of you, just as you long to have them make you proud of them: "Hey, kids, Mom's proposal was accepted by the boss! Tonight we celebrate. You pick where we'll go to dinner. Mom's feeling good!"

PART II

Practicing Kind Behavior Out in the World

A Young Person Out in the World

When your child begins to deal with people outside the family, he or she is "out in the world," even if only at a play date with a friend, visiting others with the family, or greeting neighbors. Interacting with the outside world is a whole new experience. Adults have two major responsibilities here:

- ✦ To make sure the children know how to behave with consideration "out there."

- ✦ To make sure young people know how to handle themselves in a safe way.

You show a child how to be a good citizen and how to behave out in the world, first, by your own excellent example, and second, by gently pointing out the kind—and the thoughtless—behavior of the friends or strangers around you. If children were always accompanied out in the world by their well-mannered parents, they would always be well mannered, too. They would, in fact, know nothing other than a well-mannered world, but that is obviously a utopia that will never come to pass. So we should rejoice that somehow the majority of children grow up regardless to be caring, attractive, considerate, well-behaved adults.

Today's parents certainly deserve our admiration and credit. With their unbelievably busy schedules, they still find time to worry about all the junk targeting their children on video, TV, and computer screens and monitors. They worry incessantly about the advent of drugs and rampant crime. And even many day-care centers are trying to stem the tide of rudeness by having children turn to one another in the morning, shake hands, and exchange a good morning greeting. Some public schools have put manners sessions into the curriculum. Some expensive "manners schools" are flourishing in conjunction with banquet departments of posh hotels. No matter where on the economic or social scale they fit, a good number of people are noticing and starting to care about the behavior they see around them.

What is sad is that when children turn into teens and are under their peers' influence in junior high school, manners are often no longer a major factor in their lives. Those who do have kind manners sometimes don't know how to stand up to the teasing this causes. They're called "wimps" and "muffs," which is anything but flattering. So they change. They toughen up. Observant parents who see this happening and know how to talk to their kids can give them pep talks, keep tightening the sails, making their offspring realize that kind manners are going to be one of their greatest assets as they grow up. Kids need continual reinforcement of this idea.

As my Francophile grandmother said once, when I was brooding over a fellow student who had called me "Miss Priss" and made people laugh at me, "Remember, Letitia, don't waste your energy on such a person. Save it for better things. *Il faut toujours aller en haut, jamais en bas.*" (Always go in the up direction, never the down.) My brothers would always help, too, giving me their brand of pungent advice when I was feeling hurt. Mac, feeling enraged that anyone would publicly call his sister "Miss Priss," said that "the next time that girl in your grade says something like that to you, just slug her and she'll stop." Then he added, "Of course, Tish, I know you never will. And even if you tried, you'd miss, knowing you!"

As children begin to mature and take on responsibilities and become more independent, they sometimes need to be taught how to stay joyous, spontaneous, and able to feel the excitement of the moment. This is where not only the parents and siblings but relatives and friends of the family can help.

"Hey, Tanya, I hear you rode your bike to school today for the first time. That's great!"

"George, your mom said you're on the honor roll! Congratulations!"

In my opinion many of today's kids often seem to be overly blasé. It's the super-razzle-dazzle of our electronic age that makes them that way. They're overstimulated by it all, so anything any of us can do to wake them up and *make them feel passionate about something of simplicity in their lives* is a great contribution. We adults should remember that when we reveal our own passion and enthusiasm about something while we're with our children, it becomes contagious and they pick up on it.

Kindness and Safety Out in the World

Your child's first trip to school alone may be traumatic for you, but then he will start going alone to the store and other places, and you'll soon find yourself having to let go. He will start taking a public bus downtown to meet friends at the movies or to his music teacher's studio. The fortunate child who's been shown what to do, how "to be kind but careful" out there, how to be aware of others, and *how to be safe,* is acting within a framework you have built to protect him.

A CHILD'S PREPARATION FOR THE DANGER OUT IN THE WORLD

In today's unsafe world, adults must teach their children to sense danger and know what to do about it, without making them paranoid. You also don't want to cut your children off from interaction with other people, because that's the key to a happy life. It's a difficult line to draw, this alliance between wisdom and fear, safe measures and paranoia.

As a parent or caretaker, you should make a serious study of the physical conditions of the place where you live. Learn from friends and neighbors what to watch out for—anything from tips on how to keep bicycles from getting stolen to the stores in the neighborhood that offer a safe haven to children. In a large city, ask about the prevalence of auto thefts, break-ins, and muggings in your neighborhood—even incidences of child molestation in the last five years. *Have these discussions out of the earshot of your kids.* Drop by for a chat at your local police precinct when they're not extremely busy, so they can tell you of any problems that may exist in the area. Any crack houses in the area? Houses of prostitution? Sometimes the police give seminars at the local precinct on neighborhood safety. Ask for tips on what you should do to keep your kids safe—and, incidentally, yourself too. In other words be aware, but not panicked by every strange thing or person you see—just be aware.

A Child Deals with Strangers

Caring parents used to teach their kids to answer politely, even enthusiastically, any questions put to them, even by strangers. I remember my mother teaching this behavior to the Baldrige kids. If I was stopped by a stranger, for example, looking for a particular place when I was walking home alone from school, I'd be forthcoming.

"Green's Drugstore? Just go straight up Farnam Street three blocks, and you'll see it on the corner. You'll really like it—they have *great* ice cream!" Today, a mother would probably teach her child to say, "I don't know. Ask that person up the block."

Teach a Child to Walk On, If Necessary

When your child's alone and a stranger says, "That's a pretty dress" or "You look nice today," teach the child to say "Thank you," but to walk on and add nothing further.

"Don't start a conversation with a stranger," you might instruct your child, "unless you're with me." In other words, *teach your child to answer questions put to him when he's with you or another caregiver but not when he's with his peers or alone.* Let's say you and your daughter (holding her doll) are standing in the elevator and an elderly person says to her, "What a pretty doll! What's her name?" your daughter should answer. Even if she gives only a one-syllable answer, "Jane," she has been agreeable. But if she should be alone in the elevator for some reason, she should *not* answer.

Teach your child that if he or she is alone, on a quick errand or on his or her way to and from school:

+ He or she should never get into someone's car, unless she's being picked up by a friend's parent, she knows the person, and it's been prearranged.

+ She should never accept a gift of money, candy, or food from a stranger.

+ If she sees a crowd forming on the street, because something has just happened, her curiosity about the scene, with police and ambulances on hand, might drive her to find out what's going on. Instead, she should run *away from* it, not *toward* it.

✦ She should never converse with a stranger who begins to ask her questions about her name, where she lives, or who's home. She should be taught to say, "Sorry, I'm late," and to continue walking on quickly, without divulging any information as to where she's headed or who will be there. If the stranger follows her and she is now really frightened, she should head quickly, even run, for a "safe haven" shop in the neighborhood. (The more noise, commotion, and conspicuous behavior she shows, the better. If safe havens exist in your city, your children should be made aware of where they are.) Or she can go into any store and whisper to someone who works there that she's frightened, that there's someone following her.

The keystone of a child's sense of safety is that he or she has someone to talk things over with at home. A good rule to establish in your household is that no child goes to sleep at night without having told an adult care-giver anything that may have frightened him or her during that day. (Mom and Dad, your evening social plans may have to be delayed because of this conversation with your child, but it will be worth it.) Your child should be taught to confide in you about anything that happened that was strange or worrisome—such as seeing curious-looking strangers near the school, people exhibiting unusual behavior or trying to get kids into cars, or strangers of any age or description offering lures of candy, cookies, or toys. When a child reports this, the adult should reassure him, "You were right to tell me this right away. We'll take care of it *immediately*. Don't worry!"

"Taking care of it" means immediately reporting it to the school authorities and perhaps also to the police. It may mean accompanying the child to school for a while to make him feel safer, instead of allowing him to take his usual route alone.

It's not easy to teach a child the nuances of care in talking to strangers, but with patience they can be absorbed. It's unfortunate and unfair that families today must spend such a large amount of time and energy keeping their children protected from possible harm, rather than being able to devote that time to enriching their lives and preparing them to become caring members of the community. Somehow, the busier we become, the harder we are going to have to work to keep a balance at home.

Compassion, Yes, but with Safety

It is very hard for a young person to discern whether a strange adult who seems to be in trouble out in public is really having an emergency, just pretending to need help, or suffering from alcoholism or a drug seizure. If your child passes a person who is alone and in obvious distress, has collapsed, and is lying on the sidewalk, instruct your child to say to the person in trouble (if the person is conscious) that he or she is going to get help, then "run like crazy" to find an adult to handle it from here on. If this scene happens near home, then the child should run home for help. If it's near school, he or she should find a teacher or a shopkeeper, a bus driver, or, best of all, a police officer. Your young child should not try to help strangers by himself. Let an adult do it, but your child can play a very important role by *getting* help.

The optimum is to teach your child ways to exhibit safe behavior but not to be one of those people who never help anyone, who are either so terrified or so lazy that they never involve themselves in the slightest aspect of another human being's predicament.

Correcting a Young Person's Behavior Out in the World

- ✦ *Watch your own behavior first and foremost, of course.* It's impossible to give an effective lecture to the kids one minute while you, a caregiver, behave like a shrew the next. The child under your influence will take after your good points and bad alike.

- ✦ *Timing is important* in the correction of a child's behavior outside the home. The time to talk about it is at the moment something of importance takes place—or, at least, soon after—but always privately, if possible, so that siblings and other children will not hear the criticism and tease the child you're correcting. (There are times, of course, when it's impossible to correct a child afterward in private, such as when he or she is smacking a young sibling who's been annoying him in the backseat of the car!)

+ *Don't waste your ammunition by pointing out others' petty mistakes.* When someone pushes in ahead of you in a line, don't react with open anger in front of your child. Stay in control. Primarily, you want him to be sensitive to a person's serious rudeness, and he won't be if you're not. (This is a lecture I have to give myself quite often!)

+ *If a person does an unexpected kindness in the presence of your child, respond rapidly to that courtesy,* so that someday your child will automatically follow suit when someone shows him consideration. "Remember," keep reminding him when the occasion warrants it, "you really can't thank someone too much." My daughter, Clare, then about eight, was with me the day I slipped on the ice on Madison Avenue in New York. I ended up in a most ungraceful heap on the sidewalk, every shred of dignity having abandoned me, but with only a bruised thigh, a cut knee, and hurt pride to show for it. A young teenager, who was near us when it happened, rushed to cover me with her coat, then into the Baccarat Crystal store in front of us to seek the manager's assistance. She then went into a nearby pharmacy and came back with a box of Band-Aids, three of which I applied to my bleeding knee. She wouldn't let me pay her back. Clare watched while I thanked the girl and got her name and school address. The next day Clare helped me select a book as a thank-you present for my young rescuer, and I showed her the note I wrote to the principal of the teenager's school, pointing out her kindness and helpfulness. Hopefully something from that incident has sunk into my daughter's memory. As for the teenager, I'm sure she has grown up to be a wonderful woman.

WHEN YOUR CHILD'S GUEST IS THE TROUBLEMAKER

If your child's friend is the one being rude, don't try to make that child understand how badly he is behaving, unless his parent has given you instructions to do so. A little girl's mother, for example, might say, "Michele's being very negative these days for some reason, so please feel free to discipline her if she gets out of line." Even with this kind of carte blanche approval of pulling her daughter into line, it's unwise to try to discipline someone else's child. Establish law and order, so to speak, in your house, automobile, yard, apartment house court or lobby, or wherever you have jurisdiction over the group of kids playing there. *Tell them the rules at the beginning of their play period, so that they understand what's expected of them (which is half the battle):*

"Remember, it's just as I said last time, only none of you were listening. We don't scream and yell around here, because it upsets the neighbors; we don't tease the dog, because that's being cruel to her; we don't climb on the fence, because that's what pulls it down and costs a lot to repair; and we don't fight with one another. You kids can fight with your brothers and sisters at home, *not here.* Anyone who can't follow the rules must go home."

Any talk about your child's bad behavior should take place the minute his or her friends are no longer present. Stress the role of *kindness* in his or her actions:

"You ignored Sam. He tried to play with you kids, and you wouldn't let him—you kept shoving him away, calling him a 'little squirt' and in general making him feel miserable. You wouldn't let him play, *not* because he's not a nice kid but because he's smaller than the rest of you. Do you feel good that you made him miserable? No? Well, then let's not have that happen again. The next time you kids get together again, like next Saturday at Dave's house, go out of your way to make him part of the group. If you tell your friends *that's the way it's going to be,* they'll follow your lead."

If one kid sticks up for someone who is being wronged, he is usually listened to, because the seeds of compassion in the other children are usually there. Someone has to articulate them and believe in others' sense of fairness. And if your son does what you asked him to do, to help Sam, "the squirt," you should congratulate him and then yourself. Your child is a *leader.*

If one of your child's friends misbehaves in your house, explain why it's unacceptable. If your daughter's friend, let's call her Joni, keeps sliding down the banister again and again, after you've told her not to because it is very dangerous, you have the right to take her home. Explain why you could not allow it to continue. Mention to one and all that it's much better for Joni to be going to her house rather than to the emergency room of the hospital. Always explain *why* you do something this drastic when it concerns your child's friends' safety.

If Joni comes over again to play with your daughter, give her another chance—and a courteous warning. Don't expect her to misbehave. Take it for granted that she *will* behave, and she probably will.

If you make sure your children understand why you forbid them to do certain things, when they're older and when you tell them to stay away from the kids who use drugs in school, they may very well listen to that message. If you've taken the time to explain the cause and effect of drugs, and warned, "Don't experiment, don't try drugs *even once,*" they might remember all the times you warned them about other things, too, like sliding down the banister and getting hurt.

Many would agree that the absolutely worst kind of parent is the one who says, "*My* child would never take drugs." Just keep in mind that everyone's children are capable of doing anything.

At first, a child may copy a kind act just to seek your approval and praise, but in time he will come to enjoy the pleasant inner feelings that result from helping someone. Knowing that people like him for something he's just done leaves a feeling of warmth inside that can't be described in mere words. He's made a *difference* in his world. There's no better feeling.

Your Child at School

The first major rite of passage for your child is the electrifying process of starting school. (Many parents feel *they* are the ones who need treatment for the trauma of starting school, not the child!) Some children fall right into it with glee. Others take longer. But whatever a child's reaction, parents can quietly and unobtrusively do a lot to help children successfully make this first giant step of moving out into a real world of their own. It's a comprehensive goal—that of adjusting to this new world and getting along with their peers and all the authority figures they now must heed for a long future ahead.

Being Likable at School

School is a laboratory for adulthood, so it's important to instill in children at an early age a certain wisdom about the behavior and character traits that will win them friends, mentors, and respect in school.

"Mom" Talks to Her Child Before He or She Starts School for the First Time

It's smart to talk to your son or daughter about the friends they'll make well before the school year starts. It's a mistake to talk in terms of their having the responsibility to "make friends with the brightest, smartest, richest, or most athletic kids in school." Talk instead to your children about "making friends with boys and girls who are happy, fun to be with," and who "like to do the same kind of things you do."

Have your child join you in composing a list of the traits that help a child make friends. Help him articulate what he likes in another child, and that another child would like in him. By making the list and focusing him on it for a short period of time, he'll remember parts of it at unpredictable times when he starts school (neither of you can predict when, but he *will* remember segments like this):

+ *Get to know the names of the children sitting around you.* "I'd like to give you my name and then will you give me yours? I'm Harry Jones. What's your name?"

+ *Be interested in who he or she is.* "I'll tell you about my family. I have a big brother and a little sister. I have a dog, too. Do you have a brother or sister? Do you have a dog or cat?"

+ *Show that you know how to share.* "I have some interesting games. I brought one to school. Would you like to play with it, and share your toys, too?"

+ *Learn how to extend an invitation to a new friend.* "Would you like to come over to my house next Saturday? I have games we can play. You can decide which one we'll play first. We have juice and cookies and you can play with my dog, too." (Of course, parental permission is needed for both children, so there are logistical details to be settled between parents before the "social engagement" can be made firm.)

+ *If you look like you want to have friends, you'll draw them to you.* Have a smile on your face, and other children will smile, too. Always look like you're happy, because that makes others feel good.

+ *You can never talk about sharing too often.* Tell the children seated at your worktable you like sharing things, including crayons, paper, paste, and the other art materials that are handed out.

+ *Be agreeable about doing what the teacher asks you to do.* Follow her instructions right away, because it makes things run better in class, and other kids won't be mad at you for holding up the activities.

+ *Remember that other kids really like the kids who act like they like them.* That's what it's all about.

Respecting the Teacher and School Authorities

Teach your child to respect the school principal, his or her teachers, assistant teachers, school nurses, coaches, gym instructors, music instructors, playground supervisors, safety patrol members, and any others in authority at school. If some of them aren't so great, if some of them are a little unfair, you respect them anyway and tell your child, "They are in charge. It's your job to work with them." This trains your child to respect the hierarchy we all encounter in adult life, no matter how highly placed we become. It's a lesson that must be learned and certainly is more easily learned in childhood.

MAKE YOUR CHILD AWARE OF "SCHOOL MANNERS"

✦ Teach your child the procedure for greeting his teacher. "Good morning, Ms. Trimble or Mr. Page," or whatever the name is. Teachers should be addressed by their titles and family names. At the end of class, children should say good-bye in the same manner: "Good-bye, Ms. Trimble," or "Thank you, Mr. Page." If the teacher says, "Everyone call me Al," the children should obey, but that doesn't mean they should adopt that kind of informality with other adults, unless the adults insist. *My children and all of their friends were never allowed to address an adult by a given name, even when the adult insisted. "Sorry, Mr. O'Brien, Mom and Dad won't let us call grown-ups by their first names. They say it's disrespectful."* But this is a decision for each parent to make, and to instruct their children accordingly.

✦ It goes without saying that you teach your children to follow the teacher's orders without "smart-aleck back talk."

✦ Talking in class, reading comics, throwing guided missiles, taunting other students, making nasty comments, teasing students who aren't prepared or who aren't as bright as the rest of the class are all examples of rudeness and arrogance that should never be committed by *your* child. If you question him as to the general class behavior, he will probably tell you about it with some candor, particularly *since it's easier to answer questions about other students' behavior than personally directed questions.* Talk over with his teachers any serious information you glean from these conversations. Guide and support him on proper behavior:

"I don't care if all the other kids make gestures behind the teacher's back. *You're* not going to do it."

"I'll be called a sissy or something gross."

"For one moment, probably, yes. But show leadership by refusing to defy your teacher. Tell the other kids, 'Since we're all pretty obnoxious and give her a hard time, maybe we're cowards to do things behind her back, when she can't see what we're up to. Maybe we just ought to give her a hard time when she can see us doing it.' I promise you that even if they tease you, your words will sink in. Most kids are fair, after all. The ones who aren't, aren't liked."

✦ A student should learn to say certain phrases automatically:

✔ "May I" when asking permission of the teacher.

✔ "Please" when asking a favor of the teacher.

✔ "Thank you" every time a teacher fulfills his request.

These simple phrases are the basis of all manners.

✦ Adults should keep using those phrases when talking to a small child if he or she carries out an order. Even a two-year-old will parrot those polite phrases back to an adult when they are constantly said to him. Ultimately, he will have learned them and can use them at the appropriate times. One day when he's a grown-up, he will make a wonderful impression on those around him.

One father I know was so upset by what he found to be the general behavior of the students in his son's freshman class in high school that he invited the whole class to his home for a Saturday lunch. They were given a strong lecture on behavior by a brilliant but contrasting pair: the local university's football coach and the leading ballet instructor in the region. The coach pulled no punches about "what a lack of discipline I've seen all around school," and said, "I'd never allow any of the kids presently in my math class onto the football team. They could never take it."

The ballet instructor went after the girls' tough behavior and smart-aleck attitude, and said the girls ought to be studying hard, learning their lessons but also exercising their bodies and eating properly so they could become "beautiful, healthy adults." She swung her leg up, using a high table as a barre, and stretched like a beautiful bird in flight. As she finished, she simply said, "Discipline, discipline, discipline."

One of the girls remarked wryly, "No one in this room except Ms. Gregorivitch can do that stretch." The ballet instructor heard the remark and said, "Thank you for the compliment. I started doing that exercise when I was eight. I've now been doing it for forty years. Perhaps you girls can start doing it tomorrow. There's still time left for you."

The coach and the ballet instructor told the young students that if they were serious about their high school years, respected their teachers, and followed their advice, it would start them on an exciting adulthood, culminating in a good college, a good job, and a good life ahead.

The freshmen were impressed. These were mature role models inspiring them. One of the girls whispered, sounding incredulous, "They sound just like my parents."

The boy's father is the one who impressed me. He was the one who had been creative enough to arrange for the two "stars" to appear at lunch, proving that parents who merely wring their hands and cry "Woe is me" over the behavior of their kids in school and don't take action are just treading water. Action and initiative are called for, ideas need to be tried out, creative minds need to ignite with enthusiastic ideas, and adults need to get going with trial-and-error plans instead of just complaining about conditions. A community or block group could do the same thing.

Blaming the Teacher

If parents do not intervene, a child might learn at an early age to blame any setback in his or her life on someone else—most conveniently the teacher. A common complaint from kids is, "The teacher doesn't like me," or "Our teacher is unfair." This lament might be heard at any stage in a child's life, from kindergarten through medical school. From there it's a quick step to laying the blame on the boss at work.

If your child returns from school someday stating, "I hate my teacher," before you offer sympathy, act quickly to offset the potential hostility of the situation. "Just say you don't like her, Annie. Don't say *hate*. That's a really ugly word to use."

"I don't like her," the child replies.

"Tell me just what happened in school today. Let's talk about this." At this moment, Annie's mother stops what she's doing and asks Annie to turn off the videocassette. She is signaling her daughter that it's time to talk seriously, and that it's a two-way street.

The Importance of Listening

Both mother and daughter should now listen to one another without distractions around them. When her parent is listening with total dedication, a child tends to compose her thoughts with greater care than usual. She *wants* to communicate properly. She *wants* to persuade her parent to take three steps:

+ Accept her side of the story, not the teacher's.

+ Take action to clear up the problem.

+ Forget it ever happened, so that it will all go away.

Why worry, you ask, about your child's relationship with the teacher—someone who will be in the classroom with your progeny for only one year? Next year's teacher in English will be different; so will next year's teacher in math. Why worry if your child blames part of his school troubles on teachers during any given year?

The answer is: The teacher is the child's first symbol of authority outside of the family and baby-sitters. To make fun of the teacher is to make fun in later years of the clergy, the police, judges, and bosses. A child who comes home from school boasting of having sassed the teacher and earning laughs for his efforts exhibits a behavior that spells trouble. Sassing is unkind, for one thing, but it is also using a symbol of authority as the scapegoat for one's own failures.

There's a fine line between sympathizing with a child who has done badly in a school subject and helping him realize that he *has* merited the bad marks. If he's smart, he'll ask for your help. "What should I do about it, Dad?" you might hear from him. (Be sure to tell him you're *glad* he asked.)

Your answer could be threefold, the same advice a kind manager would give you when you've "messed up" on your job:

+ Admit your failure to do good work.

+ Apologize for it.

+ Vow to do much better.

Perhaps your daughter has just returned home from school bitterly complaining about her "unfair" English teacher, who returned her composition with a low grade attached.

Don't rush her; don't show disdain for anything she says. Don't disagree. Don't make noises of sympathy or cluckings of disapproval. Tell her you want to hear it all; you'll react to it afterward, but you first "want to hear her side." It may mean that you have to cancel or be late for an appointment to have this conversation, but a chance to drive home a lesson in values to your child is more important than most appointments any day. First of all, listen to your child's accusations, and if they are serious, follow up on their accuracy. If they prove to be exaggerated, talk seriously with her.

"You have the right not to like Ms. Larkin, but watch how you talk about her. Your friends will hear you saying these things about her, and they'll repeat them. Word gets around fast. You'll hurt her feelings, and you may hurt her career as a teacher. Do you want to be the cause of that?"

"But Mom, she's unfair!"

"She's the one who was appointed to judge your work, Cyn, so you have to accept her evaluation."

"She's a big slob."

"I hope you don't talk about me like that when I criticize you. You have a natural talent in English, but you didn't spend a lot of time on that paper, I noticed. Whether you like it or hate it, you have to accept the mark. It was your teacher's judgment call, not yours."

"But it was a good story even if I didn't spend a lot of time on it."

"Do you think you're a better judge of composition than Ms. Larkin? She has been teaching English for over a decade. She's highly respected."

"She was unfair."

"She has given you good marks before, because you did a good job on other compositions. She gave you a bad mark this time because you did a hasty job of writing. Accept it, tough it out, and resolve to do better the next time. She—and I—want you to do work that represents the best you're capable of doing."

Unfortunately, today it's often the parents who rise in defense of their children, who don't check out the child's complaints and who rush to the school principal to blame a particular teacher, who may well not be at fault. Naturally, among the many teachers who interact with a child as she grows up, there are bound to be those who are not quite fair, but the majority of them are overworked, underpaid, and unappreciated for their efforts.

A child needs to be heard loud and clear when she voices accusations of unfair treatment that seem authentic. Parents need to check and recheck what is going on in that classroom. Your child may have a special behavioral, physical, or developmental problem of which the teacher is unaware (perhaps even *you* are unaware of it). Instead of complaining to the principal, the parent should communicate with the teacher and then communicate with the child. Some parents are so unreasonable they won't allow a teacher to make any criticisms of their "little darling" on any occasion. If there's anything easy to predict, it is that such a child will not learn the values of kindness and discipline and will not have an easy time in life.

The young person who *does* accept the authority figure in charge will grow into someone who accepts the hierarchy of management on the job, and who consequently becomes a good team worker.

The child who accepts authority becomes a leader, too, for a leader is someone who listens before taking charge. *He is someone who has accepted direction before becoming the one who directs.*

IF HIS OR HER TEACHER IS BEING UNFAIR

Meet privately with the teacher and, without making any accusations whatsoever, explain:

+ how upset your child is about his relations with his teacher

+ how he really wants to succeed in her class

+ how disappointed he is in himself that he is displeasing her, but he simply doesn't understand what he's doing wrong

+ how determined he is to rectify whatever it is he's doing wrong

+ how much he hopes at the same time that she can be more understanding or patient with him

+ how both your child and you, his parents, are determined to solve this problem

Ask a school peer of your son's or daughter's if your child truly is being mistreated by the teacher. If the answer is yes, and if, after your personal interview with the teacher, the unfair treatment of your child continues, go to the principal. If the unfair treatment continues, go to the superintendent of schools for the district. (Don't tell your child about these rather drastic measures, and be sure you have full, careful, written documentation of the nature of your complaints and the dates of the incidents with this teacher.)

If Your Child Is Falling Behind at School, Find Out Why!

Get help right away for a developmental problem. Don't waste time, because even information on the problem might take considerable time just to locate. There is a bureaucratic maze to be mastered at the local, state, and federal levels. Programs designed to help specific problems differ from state to state and city to city, so you will want to research every avenue of help.

The Individuals with Disabilities Education Act (IDEA), enacted in 1990, establishes guidelines for your handicapped child and guarantees him an equal opportunity to benefit from free, appropriate, public instruction. He also has the right to be educated in the "least restrictive environment," which is another way of saying that the government is pushing for inclusion in the schools—the integrating and mainstreaming of children with mental and physical disabilities. If your child has a disability, ask your local school district to evaluate your child and let you know what services might be available for him. If you don't like the decisions made regarding your child, you have the right to "equal access and due process" to get them changed.

The secret to helping a child who's suffering because he or she is "different" in some way is to *realize* he or she is suffering. Talk to your child's teachers, his coaches, the school nurse. Talk to your pastor or rabbi. Talk to other parents who are going through the same experiences you are—for comfort as well as advice. (I'll never forget the renowned pediatrician who once told me that the perfect person to whom a worried parent should go for advice is a well-adjusted mother of six!)

Parents should compare notes on their progress in finding the appropriate programs for their children, and exchange helpful information. Every year there are great new books and publications on the subject (a smart reference librarian can cut through the mediocre list to the really good ones). Adults need to support one another during this tough time, too, and certainly it's necessary for the family to act in concert. As one friend put it, "This is the time when it's really important for the kid's whole family to be on the same page."

On the other hand, there are many reasons why a child who is *not* physically or learning disabled might be troubled at school. First of all, he or she may be exaggerating in order to get more attention at home (which he or she may need) or to excuse his own inattention to his work. But then again maybe not. It's up to the parent to find the truth.

A child feels victimized when he or she is criticized, teased, or accused, because:

+ he's of a different race, color, nationality, or religion

+ he is poor or even homeless

+ he can't speak English well enough to be understood and to understand

+ he may be athletically challenged

+ he is too smart in class

+ he is perhaps too "dumb" in class

+ he is perhaps too fat or thin

+ he wears clothes that are considered tacky and unstylish by his peers

+ he's considered too goody-goody—trying to be teacher's pet

+ he might be accused of cheating on tests and in sports by jealous peers

+ his parents are so "different" from the other parents

+ if he is older perhaps he's moralistic and critical of kids who have unprotected sex and who abuse drugs and alcohol

+ he is too quick with his hand up in class to answer the teacher

+ he is decidedly too pretty or too unattractive

+ he is rich and accused of taking unfair advantage because of it

This list could go on forever. When I was a child in school, the list was almost identical (except for the temptations of sex, drugs, and alcohol), but there was one great difference. Some of our class may have started out being cruel on the playground to newly arrived classmates who were "different," but the teachers soon stopped it. Classes were smaller, and teachers saw what was going on. (Punishments in those days were swift, effective, and definitely unchallenged.)

Show Your Son or Daughter What Kindness Really Is

+ Listen to what he says and keep listening, rather than lecturing. To get an overall picture of what's bothering him, it's smart to listen to his complaints and beyond them for clues as to what's really happening inside.

+ Sympathize.

+ Investigate.

+ Tell him how much you love him.

+ Tell him again.

+ Watch how he's progressing with the problem.

+ Return to his teacher or counselors for more advice if it isn't working out.

+ Initiate new programs if the old ones don't seem to work.

+ Talk to his really close friends and seek their help—to keep you informed as to what's happening with him. Ask them to give him an assist whenever they can. (Kids have good hearts but sometimes just don't think about ways in which they can help.)

+ If there's a student who's causing the main problem with your child, have a personal intervention with him or her *if* the teacher or counselor deems it advisable, and if his parent agrees to be present, too.

+ Buck up your child at home—cheer him up, tell him he's wonderful, that he's going to get over the problem, that things will get better.

Presents for Teachers

Parents are saying that in many schools holiday presents for their children's teachers have become a serious financial burden. It becomes very expensive, year after year, to keep buying gifts for your child's most important teachers. Class mothers will call the other mothers to collect anywhere from ten to twenty-five dollars apiece in contributions toward the purchase of a nice present.

If you can't afford it, you don't have to do this. You can say to the class mother, "Thank you for organizing a class gift to the teacher, but we're going to do our own thing this year." Your own thing can be sending a holiday card to the teacher with a thoughtfully composed note, written by the child or, if he is too young, by his parent, stating the child's gratitude "for being so helpful and for being such a good teacher this year. I learned a lot, thanks to you!" Warm words for a teacher to hear.

Another way to say thanks to these teachers is with handmade gifts either mother or child makes, or make together—socks, useful crafts, specially potted plants, kitchen gifts of cookies, preserves, family specialties.

One fifteen-year-old high school student I know realized that she owed a great deal to a person who had spent an inordinate amount of extra time that year helping her compensate for problems caused by her dyslexia. The young girl explained to me that she felt really bad that her family had no money for presents that year. "But then," she said, a big smile crossing her features, "I was able to give my teacher a Christmas present that meant a lot to her. I baby-sat for her two kids on some Saturday nights so that she and her husband could go out on the town."

"What a great idea!" I said. "How did you think of that nice gesture?"

"Oh, my aunt always used to teach me stuff like that. She was always telling me things I could do to 'spread a little cheer around'—particularly things people weren't expecting."

The Importance of the Team: Sharing Blame and Credit

One of the most difficult lessons a child must learn in life is to be a team player. School is where he or she learns a lot of this—to share the credit even when it might belong to him alone and the blame when he had almost nothing to do with what went wrong. When your child comes home, jubilant about his or her victory in an athletic game, a successful play produced at school, a TV game show of schools competing for the "right answer" to history and current events questions, whatever it is: Greet that victory with joy and jubilation. Then gently introduce the fact that his teammates or the other players in the enterprise also deserve to be praised.

It's time to teach your child a fact of life, that there will be times when he deserves to be the only one praised and applauded, but he should valiantly keep mentioning *"We* did it, hooray!" and people will respect him for it. There will be other times when his group is praised and applauded for an accomplishment, but his involvement was little or nothing. Yet he is justified to stand up with the group when it takes a bow for that feat.

"It all comes out even in the end," you might say. "But in the meantime you have been kind to your friends by letting them take a bow with you, and they have been kind to you when they let you take a bow with them, even though your contribution was small. This is how we all get along better in life."

Your fifteen-year-old son, we'll call him Bill, bursts into the room—breathless with excitement from having successfully competed in a weekend civic project—and says, "Dad, I won the treasure hunt! I was the one who figured out all the clues and found the treasure." As his parent, you react with justified pride in his accomplishment. You have been hearing all year about this city-wide, difficult treasure hunt sponsored by local businesses. You congratulate Bill. After a while, you ask him, "Weren't you on one of your high school's teams for this hunt?"

"Yeah, I was on Central's Green Team."

"Then Central's Green *Team* won, Bill, not you alone."

"I did most of the work, Dad. I found it."

"Look, you were part of a group in the search. Everyone was pulling together, weren't they? You might have been smarter—and luckier—than your teammates, but you should talk about this victory in terms of 'We,' not 'I.'"

There are examples all around today of kids showing good teamsmanship—not all on the playing fields or in science lab projects. There was Gretchen's girls slumber party, for example. The girls were all roughhousing. One of them, Marilyn, in a display of overexuberance, broke a valuable antique porcelain lamp on the piano. When Gretchen's parents arrived home later and saw what had happened, their daughter immediately and abjectly apologized without mentioning Marilyn's name. It was: *"We* broke it, Mom, I'm so sorry." This fact made it easy for all the girls to step forward and apologize to Gretchen's parents for the broken lamp. The next day the girls, as a group, took the broken pieces to a repair shop to try to have the lamp reassembled. It proved to be impossible. They then tried to buy a similar antique, way beyond their financial capabilities, of course, and Gretchen's mother at this point stepped in to say it was not necessary to replace it. The fact that they had tried so hard to make amends and were remorseful erased every bit of resentment over the incident.

Can Homework Be Considered "Kind"?

Since I like relating everything in life to kindness, a high school junior challenged me recently. "Just show me what's so kind about doing homework," he said sarcastically. Here goes.

+ First of all, it's kind for members of the household to be sufficiently quiet during the time when young people are supposed to be doing their homework so they can concentrate. This entails the strict adherence to the rule of "no noise" during study hour from mom, dad, or a child-care giver. (This also means that the sitter, or whoever is staying with the kids, is not watching television, playing the piano, yakking on the telephone, or playing barking games with the dog.)

+ Second, when a young person faithfully does his or her homework, it's a kindness to the teacher. When students are prepared, the class flows well and the teacher loves the job more and is more effective in leading her students ahead.

+ *Mainly, a young person should look on doing his homework as a kindness to himself.* He is the major benefactor.

+ He's going to have an easier time at school when he does his homework.

+ He's going to get into good work and responsibility habits that carry on through adult life.

+ He's going to enjoy learning more.

+ He'll keep up with his classmates more easily—maybe even lead them.

+ And he won't be full of remorse and guilt. He'll feel justifiable pride (one of the loveliest feelings in the world) for having done his homework and done it well.

+ The material goes into the right file in his brain. It's a total win-win situation.

If you can get this across to your children, homework will assume a priority in their lives when they return from school. They'll do it before telephone talking, mall visiting, sports, TV, and all the other distractions of their lives. Just like brushing their teeth at night, they'll realize they'll feel a lot better to have it nicely finished—over and out—before going on to another activity with a free mind and a good conscience.

Being a "Good Guy" When There's a New Student in Class

Recently, I talked with a married couple who have been good friends of mine since childhood. We discussed the meteoric career of their daughter in the business world—a young woman who became an electrical engineer and is now managing a division of two thousand people for her corporation. Her mother reported that the CEO had made her a division head "because she had a better way with people than anyone else with her qualifications." Apparently her promotion had been greeted with cheers down the line, because she had so many friends and supporters.

I reminded her parents of a conversation we had had many years ago about their daughter's first day back at school. It was a good example of how parents can instill compassion in the hearts of the next generation. The conversation went something like this:

"Is there anybody new in your class this year?" asked Cameron's mother. Cameron had just begun third grade.

"One girl."

"Is she nice?"

"Dunno." Cameron continued studying her soup bowl.

"Does she have any friends in school?"

"Guess not."

"Where does she come from—another school? Another city?"

"Dunno."

"The teacher didn't introduce her and tell the class about her?"

"The teacher gave us her name."

"I bet she felt scared and strange being in a new school."

"Probably." Cameron continued concentrating on her soup, disregarding the intensity of her mother's questioning.

"Did it occur to you that she might be sad to be in a new school where she knows no one? Didn't you think *you* might be able to do a couple of things to make her feel much better?"

"Mommy, it was the first day of school!"

"You could make such a difference in her life, just with a couple of things."

"What things?"

Everyone around the table then entered into the discussion. We even made a list for Cameron of "kind things" that could be done for the new girl. We included suggestions such as:

+ Ask her to talk about her family, her old school, and her best friend. She's probably feeling hesitant about coming forward with her own life. Show you're interested, and then she'll answer. Predict that she'll soon have a new best friend (not necessarily you, but someone).

+ Show her around. Sit with her in the cafeteria at lunchtime and introduce her to your pals.

+ Tell her how nice you've heard the teacher is. Talk about the fun times you have in school, so she'll look forward to coming to school tomorrow and the next day, instead of dreading it.

+ Invite her to your house when you're having other friends over.

+ Bring her a new, especially favorite book of yours, wrapped as a gift. It will give her something fun to do when she's home after school and maybe feeling lonely. It will also make her feel special, to be singled out by you with a present, particularly a book that is one of your favorites.

+ Make her feel glad that she's come to your school and that she's in your class. She will never forget you—ever. You have shown her what a real friend is even if she doesn't remain a close friend (because she has found other girls who share more of her interests).

What the dinner table group was doing that evening was helping Cameron develop the "people skills" that helped carry her successfully into adult life. Cameron's parents really cared about what was going on in her life.

If Your Child Is the Recipient of Ethnic Slurs from Classmates

+ Again, be aware of what's going on and stay on top of it.

+ Notify his teachers if the situation worsens.

+ Encourage your child each evening when you see him—tell him to be brave about cruel remarks and to be proud of who he is and where he comes from. Educate him in his own religion, history, and traditions. Celebrate your traditional religious or national feasts. If your child is knowledgeable about—yes, and *proud of*—his heritage he can defend himself verbally and even fascinate the other students with his stories. Teach him not to fight with his fists but to fight instead with the weapon of knowledge about his origins.

+ Teach him to stay calm when he is being insulted, to keep control of his emotions, and to come home at the end of the school day to the comfort of his family. (It goes without saying that the parents of such a child, even though hard at work all day, have the child's troubles on their minds, too, and they are 'eady to support and sympathize with him the minute every-one is home from work and school.)

+ The perfect put-down to a bigot who is discriminating against someone from another race, nationality, or religion is to say, "I can't understand how you can be so un-American. That's not the way we Americans behave."

What to Do If a Bully Strikes

If your child comes to you complaining about being the victim of a bully, listen carefully and collect every bit of information possible on the aggressive behavior from the child, his teachers, and his friends. Have someone in authority at the school discreetly observe what's going on during the periods the child is being persecuted and report to you. Let the school authorities deal with the bully and his or her parents. In the meantime, tell your child:

+ The family is behind him all the way and will do everything possible to help. The use of threats and meanness to stop a bully's meanness is not the answer (something that needs to be explained to an older child or older sibling who just might be ready to take on the adversary).

+ The victim must be assured that he or she does not merit any of the insults hurled at him by the attacker.

+ The victim should realize that only insecure, unhappy, and jealous people resort to abusive behavior—and are, therefore, to be pitied. They know no other means of gaining the attention they crave.

Keep building up your child's self-esteem. His positive points far outweigh his not being able to handle the bully himself. In the long run, other kids who can't stand this kind of behavior may well gang up and take care of the bully themselves.

If this doesn't happen, report it to the school authorities. It is always better when children themselves take care of this situation, but if it's impossible, go to the top and report it.

Moral Buck-Ups

Parents, grandparents, aunts and uncles, older brothers and sisters—anyone who is mature and close to your child—can sense when there's trouble in that child's life in school or with peers. It's important not only to sense it but to act quickly to ease the stress the child is enduring. Any child who has a close relationship with many adults in his life is fortunate, because he or she has somewhere to go to find answers and get help. This makes it imperative for concerned adults to have their ears open and to be aware of what's going on in the child's life, so that when there's a need for a "moral buck-up"—as my parents used to call them—one will be forthcoming.

When a child gets into the habit of confiding in an older person and seeking his or her counsel, it's something that will carry him through life. He will always seek counsel, and be helped by it. Then, when he reaches adulthood, most likely he will find himself the dispenser of "moral buck-ups" to the younger generation (what goes around comes around).

When a child faces a tough situation caused by others in his school who are betraying moral precepts you have taught him, there are three types of action he can pursue, according to his age and maturity. When he faces the wrongdoing of peers in his school, he can:

+ ignore what's happening and not become involved

+ tell someone in authority about the offense

+ talk to the wrongdoer himself, say he knows that person is doing this incorrect thing, that he's not going to say anything to anyone, but that the offender had better stop doing it and shape up

A child who is capable of following this latter course of action is already showing that he or she is a born leader.

Regardless of the course of action taken by the child whom you are trying to help, console him if he made the wrong decision and is regretting it.

After an experience where your child or his friends have been caught cheating or doing something morally wrong and are punished in some way for it, convince him that "everyone learns when something like this happens." If there's even a kernel of good that results from a nasty incident at school, it's an exercise in learning. It's a step up in maturity, so convince the child that the fears he has faced up to and been open about will always accomplish some good.

A young person is put in a really difficult position when he or she knows that a classmate is cheating or bringing alcohol or drugs to school or cutting classes, or doing anything that is morally wrong that hurts others or is illegal.

Dilemma: Does he or does he not turn in the offender to the teacher or someone in administration? If he does, he may incur the undying wrath of the offender and his or her friends. He might be branded a "squealer" and disdained by his classmates.

Solution for the Adult

+ Get the child to confide everything to you in detail so that you can decide how serious it is and help him decide what is the wise thing to do—before he does it!

+ If he relates to you a classmate's *minor* infraction of the rules, tell him to put it out of his mind, and not to tell anyone. Tell him to feel sorry for petty rule-breakers, because they are show-offs, weak, and gutless—and must be suffering from pangs of guilt. Conclude that in these circumstances it will come out in some other way.

+ Convince your child that other kids don't like children who are goody-goody (to use an archaic term), so he should never ever adapt a holier-than-thou attitude at school.

+ If the child should be in a quandary about a friend (who has been in trouble and punished in school) and wonders how he should act with that schoolmate in the future, tell him to act in a friendly manner, just as before. He should go up to that kid and say, "I'm sorry about what happened. I hope you're okay."

The other kids will note that and follow suit. It's another sign of leadership.

✦ If it's something really serious, such as schoolwide cheating or drug-pushing, find out if it is true, and if so, notify the principal yourself, so that the child won't be seen as a squealer. You can remain anonymous much more easily than your child.

✦ Always praise the child for having confided in you, and urge him to report to you if something like this happens again. (If something truly serious develops, then you will be aware of it and can take action.)

We are an overly busy society, and our children are often the victims of the lack of time we have to give to their development. *Be ready with that moral buck-up when a young person needs it.* Make him feel he's a good kid and a survivor, and that *you have faith in him.* Our country needs more adults who will say to the kids they know well, *"I always have time for you."*

The Goody-Goody Charge

It's pleasing and rewarding when your child carries out (without your prompting) some of your lessons on how to be a good friend, how to be respectful of authority figures, and how to assist people who need it.

But sometimes kids can be victimized by peers and at school for practicing the lessons taught them by caring parents about kind behavior and goodwill. It can break your heart when your child returns from school one day and informs you that he's being criticized for being a goody-goody and for doing the very things you, his parents, have trained him to do. Selfless behavior is sometimes a magnet for abuse in a class full of scrappy I-I, Me-Me kids intent on poking fun at anyone who lives by the Golden Rule.

That is a tough experience for any child to endure, and always reminds me of Clare Boothe Luce's cynical but accurate remark, "No good deed goes unpunished." If you're faced with this situation, stop whatever you're doing and supply the support needed at that very moment.

I remember my father's pep talks to my brothers and me whenever one of us was criticized by peers for being decent to an underdog. My father, an excellent public speaker, always used visual symbols when he talked. He would admonish any one of us when we were demoralized to "build some more flying buttresses on your cathedral. Don't let those kids get you down. Make the buttresses around your beliefs strong enough to withstand an earthquake!"

So, tell your child:

+ This is a world where goodness is often rewarded with cruelty, but that does not matter. The "long run" is what counts. Your child's kindness will help the recipient for a long time, maybe forever, as well as set a much-needed example for his peers. The taunting of a few people does not eradicate your child's courageous actions. *His peers will come to realize that eventually.*

+ There are a lot of jealous people in this world who resent someone else being kind and helpful, because they would like to be that way, too, but they just don't know how. They take out their frustration by attacking those who do know how.

+ Almost everyone in the world respects someone who "has enough guts" to stand up to the crowd in order to help someone or to uphold a law.

+ Your child should have some retort ready for tormenting peers, for example: "If standing up for someone is being goody-goody, then I'm proud to be called that. Go ahead, keep on calling me that. It's the opposite of being called a coward."

When my brothers were in high school my father decided to provide them with weekly boxing lessons. He engaged a professional boxer in Omaha who used to be a Golden Gloves champion. The lessons were held in our basement, but the shadowboxing went on all day and night, it seemed to me. When I finally went to my father and reported I was being victimized by this constant boxing, he told them to cut it out around the house, except during the lessons, but he also gave me an explanation. He said there were several kids in school who were being victimized by tough guys, and he wanted his sons to know what to do about it. They did! They never had to fight (at least in high school), but they must have exuded a sense of confidence that showed they knew what to do if forced to. And I suspect that some of my brothers' friends danced with me solely because they were afraid of what the Baldrige brothers would do if they didn't! (Mother later told me that was just a myth perpetrated by my brothers.)

Growing Up in the World

I'm glad I'm not a child today. Every time I think of all the conflicting orders and warnings a child gets in the early stages of his or her sorties into public life, it boggles the mind. I'm surprised that kids—and their parents—aren't all driven crazy by the conflicting commands given and received.

- ✦ On the one hand, a child is told not to talk to strangers, but on the other, she is told to be friendly to everyone she meets.

- ✦ She's told to be charming and talkative with Mommy's friends at a grown-up party, and in the next moment she's told to move off and not bother anyone.

- ✦ He's told he's being taken to a "terrific treat" lunch for having been so brave at the dentist, and in the next breath he's criticized for ordering the only food he *really* wants for a treat, because it's not healthy enough.

- ✦ She's told to use the public library often, and in the next minute she's criticized for spending too much time there.

- ✦ She's firmly ordered by her mother to help out the mother of the friend she is visiting for the weekend—with preparation of the meal, setting the table, and the cleanup—but the minute she tries, she's ordered by her friend's mother out of the kitchen once and for all. Whom does she obey?

And so it goes, with one step forward and two steps back, as a child matures and learns how to behave out in public. It's hard for parent *and* child.

I was paying for my lunch in a Lexington Avenue coffee shop one day, standing behind a nice-looking man who was also paying for his. In the other part of the coffee shop a child was throwing a terrible tantrum, down on the floor, screaming.

"The kids today," he said disgustedly, "don't know how to behave in public. No one's taught them *anything.*" His words were barely discernible in the midst of the high-pitched noises. "I just can't imagine how anyone could stand having a child like that around," he continued. "He's a menace to society."

With that he picked up his change, put it in his pocket, went over to the corner of the coffee shop, picked up his young, screaming son, and strode quickly out. He managed to throw me a wry glance and a smile as he did so.

A Child's Physical Appearance Out in the World

When a child is very young, he has little choice in how he appears—he starts out being dressed by someone else. It's fascinating to watch a child mature and begin to develop taste and to choose his own clothes—usually simply a reflection of what "everyone else" in his school and his particular part of the country is wearing at that particular moment.

A young child should be dressed as comfortably and as attractively as the family budget will permit, which, of course, is subject to wide interpretation. I know a hardworking pair of dual-career parents who spend sparingly on their own clothes but buy the most fashionable and expensive imports for their grade-school daughters; I know a wealthy widower lawyer who is so miserly that although his son keeps growing taller, the father refuses to keep pace with the growth, so the boy is mocked in school because his trousers are always too short and his shirts and sweaters too small. I know a young girl who committed suicide because her parents refused to give her the money to buy a senior prom dress after the money she had saved from baby-sitting was stolen from her school locker.

"Ridiculous!" you might say in response to all the above examples of how important the way a young person dresses may be to her or him, but the pressure is there. Most people desperately want to be attractive. Girls want to attract boys, boys want to be at ease with girls, parents want their children's good looks to coincide with the status the parents believe they have achieved in the community, and emotions on the subject are undeniably powerful!

When I was young, we didn't have as many hang-ups on how to dress. (The "young" age category lasted a long time in families in those days, until a child had finished college and was out in the working world or married.) Like today's kids, we wanted to dress like "everyone else," but our mothers were dictators with dressing power over us. I spent two decades of life having to "go back to your room to change." My mother's sense of what was appropriate motivated her to send me back to change out of a suit I had planned to wear at age twelve to a wedding, "because it isn't dressy enough." Then she would send me back to change out of a black dress I had put on at age seventeen to wear at a Saturday birthday lunch party, "because it's far too dressy." One of the most frequently recited questions raised in our house was "You're not going to wear *that*, are you?" (My brothers got it, too.)

I still remember having my first real "ball gown" made in Paris when I was an impoverished student. (I possessed a large bolt of fabulous satin brocade without having to pay for it, thanks to a friend whose family owned BUCOL, the most successful luxury fabrics house in France.) It was a heavenly shade of pale blue, off the shoulder, with a sweeping skirt that would take up an entire sofa if I were to sit down on one while wearing it (I never did). I picked out the fabric, I chose the design, I had it made by an accomplished dressmaker in Paris, and I felt very liberated and sophisticated in the process. My mother finally saw the Cinderella ball gown two years later, when I was home for a short vacation from my American embassy job in Paris. Her reaction was immediate and, as always, frank.

"Tish, a huge, full, bunchy skirt with a crinoline beneath? With *your* hips? And being so gloriously tall, did you ever think when you chose this—er—conspicuous fabric, that there might be too much of you to behold?"

Talk about a downer. We always talked frankly to one another in our family. Yet Mom was usually right as well as frank. I looked at myself in the mirror, turned around for a full view, front and back, and decided I did indeed look just like a walking sofa with deep cushions, upholstered in pale blue satin brocade. It was a fashion lesson I needed to learn. No more Marie Antoinette skirts for me. Straight and narrow from now on, I told myself, having seen the light, but it was also humbling for me to realize that when my wise mother wasn't around to help guide me in my wardrobe decisions, I could still make major mistakes, even if I was occupying a very responsible job in the world of international diplomacy.

Mom is still in my closets today—I can feel her disapproval when I take out something that is "not right" for the occasion. How I resented her authoritarian power over my wardrobe, but how right she always was. Her training was invaluable, and today, when I wear something outrageous to a dinner party, for example, I whisper to myself, "Mom, I'm old enough to have some bravado in my fashion now. I can be a little eccentric. I'm old enough and I'm not in the White House anymore."

If someone you know who *loves fashion* and *understands what the kids like to wear* advises your child on what clothes to buy and how to put them together, it's an invaluable service. Children from the age of seven up are taunted when they're not dressed in what is considered up-to-date by their peers. They need to be gently guided, cajoled, and taught to look at themselves in a mirror—so that they learn to stand up straight in their clothes, and wear things that are appropriate. They should sit down and lean over in pants and shorts that they are trying on in the fitting room to see if the garments are big enough and look attractive from all angles.

Today, "kid power" prevails. If looking "just like the other kids" means that girls buy fluid, flowery dresses worn with work boots, thick ski socks, and floppy black chiffon garden party hats, so be it. If being just like the other guys means work boots, long undershirts, underpants showing beneath the top layer of clothing, and shaved heads (except for a crew-cut strip of bright orange and green hair), so be it. Parents should breathe deeply and exhale when this happens, but at a certain moment it's a kindness to step in and keep a child from getting the body completely tattooed or allowing the face to be studded, or permitting one's beautiful daughter to emerge for an evening of hanging out with friends sporting a newly pierced navel in her bare midriff.

The era of the hippies, flower children, free love, and "commune chic" took over in the late 1960s. The Woodstock music festival and the drugged-out Haight-Ashbury district fashions were in vogue. It was a "Don't shave, don't bathe" era and the beginning of true individualism in dress. It was to become the badge of youth. For the first time probably in history nine- and ten-year-olds began to decide what they would buy, what fashions they would follow, and what fads they would promote at school. It was youth power at its youngest. It's still here.

SOME THOUGHTS ABOUT
HOW A CHILD DRESSES OUT IN PUBLIC

There's a happy medium between the strict maternal control over dressing that my generation endured and the laissez-faire, do-what-you-please philosophy of today. Because frankness is prized in modern society and because fashion is so overly important to teenagers and preteens, parents should be aware of what their children are wearing to school, to the mall, to church, and to sports events. Here's a short list of things for a parent to keep in mind as his or her child goes out the door—out in public, on his own:

✦ Explain to your child what narcissism is (i.e., excessive self-love, being self-centered and smug). Someone who constantly gazes at himself or herself in mirrors is narcissistic—one of the most unlovable traits any individual can develop. Self-obsession does not allow a person to think of anyone or anything but himself.

✦ But urge your child to check out how he or she looks before leaving the house. Teach him to make sure his grooming is perfect, from the condition of his hair to the condition of his shoes, and then to forget about how he looks until the next time he finds himself in the rest room in front of a mirror. (Kids who are constantly whipping out their combs every time they catch sight of themselves in a mirror or their reflection in a store window are just plain unattractive. When I asked one fifteen-year-old in a fast-food place how he could comb his locks so carefully without benefit of a mirror, he replied, "I comb my hair using a Braille technique.")

✦ One way in which an insensitive child can hurt another's feelings is to say mean things, even if they're true, about another person's clothes. A parent should warn, "If you can't say something nice to her about what she's wearing, just don't comment." The reason a child may not be wearing the "in" thing may be a lack of funds. To criticize can be to hurt, hurt, hurt.

✦ Teach your child to pay compliments to friends about the way they look, if praise is warranted. Boys should compliment girls and girls boys without embarrassment. There is no sexism in saying, "You look really nice tonight," or "That's a great-looking sweater!" Tell your kids not just to *think* compliments about their friends, but to *say them*.

A Couple of No-Noes and Yes-Yeses for the Kids

Help your child learn the difference between what is proper to wear in school, at play, and in a public environment. A child usually needs advice. Discuss what he or she is going to wear well ahead of some special event, so there won't be an emotional scene over it. We have become such an informal society that we often cross the line between informality and downright sloppiness. But there's a difference between dressing for a religious service and dressing for a baseball game. We need to point this out to our children:

"No, Betty, you may not wear those pants and a sweater to your cousin's wedding."

"Why?"

"Because you're not properly dressed for a religious ceremony in a house of worship. You're not showing respect for what's happening in that place. You're not even being kind to the bride and groom, because you look like you're dressed to do yard work."

The baseball cap worn by many boys for what seems like twenty-four hours a day, and which is probably one of the dirtiest items of clothing in any boy's closet, is *not* meant for the classroom or a restaurant or inside someone's home. If a boy wears the cap visor turned to the side (which tends to make him look mentally challenged), or if he wears the visor turned to the back, it flashes a sign of disrespect for authority, which is probably what he wants to do.

"Why?" your child might say.

"Because it's unkind to the teacher in the classroom. It's an act of defiance that says, 'I don't have to look respectful in your class, because I'm more important than you.' Wearing the cap in a restaurant is unkind, too. It's saying, 'All the rest of you can get dressed up to have a nice dinner in a nice place, but I don't have to worry about how I look. I can look as grungy as I please, and if I detract from the atmosphere of the place, I don't care.'"

GIRLS NEED TO UNDERSTAND THE SIGNALS THEY GIVE BY THE WAY THEY DRESS

A girl deserves some help about why "appropriate dressing" is a good thing. She needs to be taught, for example, what's a "come-on" to men—such as when, for example,

- ✦ she's overly made up and decked out with too much jewelry
- ✦ her skirt or slacks are too tight or her shorts are too short
- ✦ she's showing too much décolletage
- ✦ she's wearing see-through tops or sweaters that are too tight
- ✦ she is sporting visible, sexually related tattoos
- ✦ she's wearing a T-shirt printed with a sexual message that she and her friends may think is terribly funny but others will misinterpret

The women's movement has editorialized for twenty years that it's not a woman's fault when she shows a lot of bare skin and then is raped. Of course, it shouldn't matter how a woman is dressed, but to many men *it does matter,* and ominously so. It's especially serious when a young girl—age twelve and up—puts on a provocative show of skin. It's like choosing to jump into a snake pit with your eyes open. If a teenager lives at home, her parents should have enough control over her not to allow her out of the house improperly dressed—to keep her safe.

A young New York woman was talking about her mother the other day.

"She was an absolute ogress," she said, "and I kept saying to myself why was I so unlucky to have a mom like that? And then, since I've been living in New York, I've seen so many things that have happened to girls my age, just because they weren't smart enough to foresee trouble, they just hadn't been warned. All of a sudden, my mom wasn't the ogress anymore. She was smart, caring, and my protector. I just hope that when I have my own kids, I can do half as well."

Mothers have traditionally stopped attempts by their daughters to grow up too quickly. A child putting on makeup and nail polish too early may amuse her friends, but when she wears it every day in grade school, or even early junior high, it is too much too soon.

Wearing makeup and sexy clothes too early may give a young girl's friends and relations a laugh, but it is the wrong way for her to define herself. It can even draw her into a circle of kids who drink, take drugs, and have sex before high school. This "much-too-soon" trend is growing in popularity all over America. Many parents seem to be unaware of it.

The boys in school are all cheering her on for making herself up like a young hooker, and thinking it's smart and grown-up to drink alcohol and to smoke. So you've got tough competition when you lecture her not to do this.

Your child might say, "You can't stop me from doing this. Don't be such a hypocrite. You did this, too, when you were a kid."

At this point, one mother I know interrupted. "Wait a moment," she said. "I was several years older than you before I started all that, and more important, I didn't have a mother like me to keep me from doing it. I've always regretted that."

I'll never forget our son's coming home one day at age eleven from his conservative private boys' school and offhandedly telling us that two of his classmates arrived at school drunk at eight that morning—and were then "taken away somewhere." They had "got into the old man's booze" and evidently had been helping themselves to it for some time. "The corridors reeked of boobon," he said, not even pronouncing the liquor properly. I told our son that if *he* ever pulled anything like that, his parents would deal with his punishment in a way to make what his uncle received for shooting out the streetlight from his bedroom window (giving up Saturdays to work on a city garbage truck) seem minor in comparison.

Your daughter may characterize you as "the only mother in the entire school who won't let her kid wear really fashionable makeup and cool clothes." Give her some kind of a treat to compensate for it, but hold fast. It's worth any effort and exercise in creativity on your part to keep your child *a child* for a reasonable period of time.

ONE GREAT SOLUTION: UNIFORMS

The lack of understanding of what constitutes appropriate apparel is causing a groundswell of parental and teacher approval of school uniforms. Many think it's a great idea, because then the children without the money to buy the really hip jeans, footwear, and jewelry would not be so separate from the ones who can afford them. Uniforms have a lot going for them. For example, they:

+ help discourage the glorification of gangs by removing the visual clothing symbol pertaining to that group; since gangs are one of the greatest menaces in public school education today, it's time for adults to be creative in figuring out how to combat them

+ eliminate the time wasted every day in deciding what to wear that's "really cool"

+ strike a blow against narcissism

+ discourage overspending on clothes and accessories, since you don't have to follow fashion; the child's in fashion just by putting on school attire

+ make the learning atmosphere more serious and dignified, less distracting

+ enable the students to be proud of their school, because they stand out in public and are identifiable as representatives of that institution

+ discourage rowdy, loud behavior in public because they are identifiable

+ minimize the differences among students, so that the handsome ones are less noticeably handsome and the ones with figure problems are less conspicuous; point out to your children that kids usually look very attractive in uniforms

If Your Child Is Undersized or Oversized

Another appearance problem some young people suffer from, whether true or not, is the conviction that they are ugly, or at least not as attractive as their peers. For parents and caring adults around them, it is vital to make these young people feel they are *not* unattractive, and to do everything in your power to build their self-esteem.

A young person, particularly a boy, may be very upset if he is small or not robust. Every four years we go through two weeks obsessed with watching on TV the beautifully developed, no-body-fat, perfect specimens of athletes at the Olympics. The rest of the time America seems to be obsessed with perfect bodies, too, if attendance at gyms, bodybuilding classes, and the adoration of bodies in the magazines or on television is any proof.

A young person who, because of genes, accident, illness, or for whatever reason, does not have a beautiful, strong body and never will, should be taught the *theory of compensation* all through his or her life.

To a young man, you'd say, "You don't have to look like a Schwarzenegger to be a success in business or with the opposite sex. You can fully compensate with your brain, charm, and sense of humor. They are much more important than a perfect body."

To a young woman, you'd say, "You don't have to have big boobs and perfect curves. You can fully compensate with that superb personality of yours, that enchanting sense of humor, that sharp intelligence!" If a child asks you how those attributes can compensate for an unexciting body, you can answer that personality, sense of humor, and intelligence all age well, do not get fat, and do not lose muscle tone with passing time!

To this day, I am always fascinated by people who are less than beautiful—or even disabled in wheelchairs—or somehow different from the supposed norm of the day, but who compensate for this fact many times over. They truly know the meaning of charm, which means they *give,* rather than *just take.*

Sometimes it helps to explain that others, particularly older people, can see beyond the temporary mass of freckles or bad complexion to the good looks that are there and will bloom someday. (Just look at the high school yearbook photos of your favorite movie stars and see what they looked like at seventeen and eighteen!) Adults come in all sizes and styles, many more than the narrow stereotypes young people may measure themselves against today. Moreover, remember the Ugly Duckling legend—many a gawky teenager turns into a grown-up with killer good looks. If an adult keeps saying to an appearance-conscious child, "Someday you'll be spectacular-looking, I can tell," that child might well summon some of the patience he is going to need to get through adolescence.

I have often thought of how artfully my own parents handled me, six-foot-one by the age of thirteen, in an era when there were no girls we knew that tall that young, and few boys either.

They kept after me, again and again, reminding me how delighted I should be that I was tall, how I should walk straight, stand tall, never slouch, walk like a queen. . . . At times I felt more like a spotted giraffe than a royal, but my kind parents kept bucking me up, telling me how wonderful-looking I was. I finally believed them and stood up tall, even though every mixed-gender social event was horrible for an overly tall girl—and we had such events all the time in those days. Just horrible. (Comments from the heart.)

Most children need every ounce of praise anyone can mete out to them in life. It's hard to grow up at best, but really lucky kids have parents like I had and, yes, brothers like I had.

The Tragic Epidemic of Eating Disorders

School authorities have noted a worrisome, marked increase in the number of young girls (boys, too) with eating disorders, sometimes starting as early as the fifth grade. Parents, grandparents, and anyone who is around need to help in this emergency and to check the passion many girls have for being thin. It's not just a kindness, it's imperative to stop young girls (children, really) from becoming obsessed with the Barbie-doll image, or images of the emaciated-looking actresses and super-models on television, in movies, and magazines.

Sometimes a mom is no help, but is, instead, an unconscious enabler of her daughter's troubles. Many moms complain about every ounce they gain, they go on crash diets, start and stop new exercise programs, and discuss whether "something is fattening" at every meal. Daughters absorb this kind of conversation like little sponges. Just as evil is a mom's complaint about her daughter's "puppy fat" as she feeds her another brownie for dessert.

If moms were really smart, they would be dismissing any talk of figures, size of "boobs," waist measurements, and the like. They would be pooh-poohing this kind of conversational subject. "Hey, doesn't anyone at this table have anything more interesting to talk about than *that*?" If more parents spent more time downgrading the discussion of people's physiques, there would be less obsession with them, and children would learn to eat healthy, nutritional food—and run it off in sports and exercise—rather than spending sleepless nights worrying about their percentage of body fat, full bust development, or penis size.

Decreasing a Child's Tendency to Envy

Wouldn't it be a great new world if the third millennium saw a decrease in materialism—and therefore a decrease in envy? If that were to happen, then those who have much would stop boasting in front of those who have little. In the best of all worlds, it would be considered very unseemly to boast at all about material things.

Many of us have heard our children's friends talking about their new acquisitions and symbols of wealth, including witnessing a little kid boasting about the designer labels in all his clothes, a boy telling his classmates about the top speed of his dad's new racing car, or a girl gossiping about "the family's really rich friends in the Hamptons, where we have a house in the summer."

Materialism and the worship of money are nipped in the bud by smart parents or caregivers every time the subject surfaces.

"Gee, Mom, that looks expensive. How much was it?"

"Ask me any question but that. Ask me how I like it, tell me how pretty *you* think it is, ask me about the style of the coat, and I'll give you any information you wish—but not the price. That's *not* what it's about."

"This is my new suit, Aunt Beth. It's a designer suit. I waited for the sales, and I got it for a huge markdown at five hundred dollars."

"How can you possibly afford a five-hundred-dollar suit? You're in high school, for heaven's sake."

"But I need to make a big impression at my part-time job, and this is one way I can do it. And I'll pay on the installment plan. I want to be able to tell everyone I'm wearing So-and-so's suit!"

Aunt Beth can quickly get to work on her niece. A teenager of modest means can't afford a suit like that, even with the money earned at her after-school job. She would make a bad impression, not a good one, by boasting that she owned a designer suit. (As my old boss Ambassador Clare Luce used to say, "Wear it, but don't talk about it.") Also, Aunt Beth's niece needs a good lesson in economics—about what a person can afford commensurate with his income and future earnings possibilities.

I saw a smartly dressed woman in the Barneys store in New York one Saturday, nipping in the bud her granddaughter's purchase of costly sunglasses—"the coolest ones I've ever seen, Nana."

"But that's not only silly, it's unwise, Martha," the older woman said.

"Why?"

"Because you have perfectly beautiful eyes, they light up your face like stars, and when you cover them with dark glasses you look like everyone else."

The girl flushed, obviously pleased by the compliment, and said, "Well . . . I guess I really don't need them."

Her grandmother laughed. "No, you don't; they're outrageously expensive and my advice is to learn how to aim your eyes—not dark lenses—at your targets."

"You just wanted to save money, Nana."

"I just wanted to teach you that money isn't that important, Martha."

When children talk in materialistic terms, an adult can stop it right away. "We don't talk about how much things cost in our house." "Don't talk about how much his father makes. A person isn't judged by that kind of description. When you describe a person by how much he or she is worth, you're not describing that person at all."

Ambassador Clare Boothe Luce had a pet peeve: people who talked constantly about money and how much things cost. "A person who has absolutely nothing else in his brain but a sad, empty space talks about money. It's a sign of classic stupidity."

"Mrs. Luce," I said, "that's a strong statement. Do I, for example, talk too much about how much things cost?"

"Why do you think I just said what I said?" she replied.

Sometimes I felt I had more than one mother raising me. It made me think that instead of resenting Ambassador Luce's "getting on my case all the time," I should have been grateful for it. I am and I was. I tell young people today to be glad instead of resentful when someone is interested enough in them to help shape up their behavior when it's needed.

Your Child in Sports and at Play

A child's concern for others is certainly visible (or invisible, as the case may be) in sports, both as player and spectator. Safety and good manners overlap. The same principles apply to each: Be aware of your surroundings, and be considerate of the people in those surroundings.

If you closely observe your son or daughter when they're playing games or sports, it will serve to remind you to be a good sport yourself when your children are closely observing *you*!

TEACH YOUR YOUNG CHILD, PARTICULARLY WHEN IT'S PLAY-DATE TIME

1. *Be a good sport.* No one likes to be around a child who can't lose a game without arguing, sulking, claiming his opponent cheated, complaining that the sun was in his eyes or that his ankle hurts or that the wind was helping his opponent and hurting him.

2. *Share game and play equipment.* Tell him, "If you let your friends play with them, they will want to come to your house to play, and they will want you to come to their house to play."

3. *If he "accidentally" hits or hurts a playmate,* he should immediately find an adult to check the damage, then comfort his injured friend, show how genuinely sorry he is about what happened and that he didn't mean any harm. Put this idea into your child's head before the play date begins, so that if such an incident occurs, he will remember the ways to comfort a distressed child. He might soon begin to believe that they were his own ideas.

4. *Show your young child how to be a good citizen at the beach,* which means:

   + He doesn't make a lot of noise around people who are trying to relax.

   + He never kicks sand into people's faces, but walks with care around them.

   + He follows the lifeguard's rules quickly and without questioning them.

   + He carries his food and drink remnants carefully to the trash bins.

✦ He lets a little tot wander over to play with one of his beach toys (provided there is a caregiver watching the tot).

TEACH YOUR MATURING CHILD TO FOLLOW THESE RULES:

1. *Remember that safety, good manners, and kindness go hand in hand in sports.* Watch what you're doing at all times. Be aware not only of your own actions, but of everyone else's at that moment. For example:

   ✦ Treat the older people playing nearby with respect and patience (they might not move fast enough for you).

   ✦ Help small children nearby to stay safe.

   ✦ Look out for people who might be in your path when you're skiing downhill.

   ✦ When you're on that surfboard, watch out for someone in the water you might hit.

   ✦ Check around yourself constantly when you're in the water, so that you don't run into another swimmer (or get yourself hit by an oncoming boat, water-skier, Jet-Skier, surfer, etc.).

   ✦ Keep reminding yourself that others nearby may not know even the most basic safety rules, so be super-cautious and wary. It's the same whether you're on the water, in the snow, on the beach, Rollerblading, or riding your bike.

2. *Don't show off.* It's better to talk modestly about your prowess than to boast about how good you are at a sport—only to be no good at all. If you say beforehand that you're not very good, and then you perform well, everyone will sit up and take notice. That's the way to draw admirers rather than detractors.

3. *If you want other children to let you play with them or be on their team, play it very cool.* How often have you heard yourself and your friends using that famous phrase, "Let me play? Let me play, *please?*" These are desperately important words when you want to join someone else who's having fun in a game or in a sport. But you'd be wise not to be obvious or overly aggressive in try-

ing to play with others. I remember when we were growing up, my older brother Mac, whether he was playing baseball, field hockey, ice hockey, or tennis doubles, always had to cope with his younger brother Bob trying to horn in to join the "big guys." Mac would say repeatedly to his pest of a younger brother, "If you stop whining, we'll let you play with us—a little, that is, not all the time, I said 'a little,' and only when I say so." These privileges granted by Big Brother were the fulfillment of little Bobby's dream. If you yourself are an older sibling, being kind to your younger ones and letting them play will build character and compassion in you.

4. *Know all the rules of the games and the sports you play*—and stick to them. (Adult guidance here is essential.) Have someone obtain the printed rules for playing, scoring, and penalties for fouls. For your own protection make sure you understand them and memorize them. (I remember in my own childhood, certain bullies, always male, of course, would make up the rules as they went along and would say, "The rules on that *are*—" thus giving themselves the point each time.)

5. *Be a hero.* If the referee was terrible, if you've been wronged, if there was truly a bad call made against you, if a ball was out in your opinion when it was called in, make your opinion known. If the referee's decision stays against you, accept it, don't contest it. If you continue with a heated denial of the referee's or a teammate's call, you'll just hold up the game, and your peers won't forget about it for a long, long time. A final acceptance of an unfair decision against you means that the play can continue. Your teammates and opponents will admire you for your good sportsmanship, and you can feel really proud of yourself.

6. *Watch your language during a game.* Even young children these days can be foul-mouthed playing or watching games; they think cussing is very grown-up and sophisticated. "Really good guys," males and females, do not pollute the landscape with ugly language.

7. *Never complain about your own playing*—or anyone else's, but particularly a partner's or a teammate's.

8. *Never hold up the game with unnecessary interruptions,* such as stopping for a soda or taking time out to socialize with friends when the others are anxious to continue playing and to finish the game.

9. *During the game, mind your manners:*

   ✦ Keep your voice down, even silent, when necessary, such as when out hunting and fishing with others, or playing tennis, or in any game requiring concentration from you or the people playing next to you.

   ✦ Always bring your own balls, appropriate shoes, and equipment. Don't be a sponger. Don't delay the game by having to find equipment for yourself.

   ✦ Don't yell out approval of something you just did and don't get mad at yourself for doing something dumb. (That means you don't swing your bat, mitt, or racket or act up in any way.)

   ✦ Always be supportive of and complimentary to your partner, even if he or she is a terrible player. Even if it's true, it's really bad sportsmanship to blame losing on your partner. It usually evens out at the end of the year—you'll have had as many good partners as bad.

10. *There is special end-of-the-game etiquette:*

    ✦ Congratulate everyone for playing well.

    ✦ Thank them for letting you be part of the action.

    ✦ Even if you didn't, make them think you had a wonderful time.

11. *Leave the area where you have played in as good or better condition than when you found it.* In other words, put everything away where it belongs. You've stretched the tennis net tight (ready for the next players) and picked up all the stray balls; you've replaced and smoothed the divots on the greens; the basketballs, soccer balls, ice pucks, and hockey sticks have all been put away in their storage area, and all litter has been removed from the grounds.

✦ If you're old enough to go on supervised camping trips, you've brought your own garbage bags, so that when you leave, the outdoors looks as fresh and pristine as it did when you arrived.

✦ If you've been on a beach picnic, you've thrown water on the coals and thoroughly wet them down, before finally covering them with sand.

✦ A child should be taught at an early age that it's mean and unsportsmanlike to boo the players, no matter how poorly they may be doing. It's also mean to cheer loudly and applaud after a player has made a terrible error. If a child acts that way at a pro sports game, you can rest assured he's acting the same way at games in his school, which is the best ticket I know of to unpopularity.

Your Swimming Pool Manners

Teach your child that if you are lucky enough to be invited to a friend's pool—or to join a group for a party in a public or club pool—your behavior is even more on display than your bathing suit! For example:

A *private pool*

Don't invite yourself to a friend's pool, tantalizing as it may seem. Don't even hint at being invited. People who own pools are besieged by would-be guests, from tots to senior citizens. There may be many reasons why parents discourage their children's friends from coming to their pool. (I can think of fifteen or twenty offhand—drowning accidents, for one.) If you are one of the lucky young persons to be invited, make a very big effort to be a considerate, safety-conscious guest. (You will probably be invited back if you make a great impression with your pool manners.)

If *you don't know how to swim*

✔ Inform your pool hosts of this fact, and when you're in the vicinity of the pool, never remove whatever kind of flotation device you've been given. Never go into the pool without an adult's watchful eye on you, and stay in the shallow end of the pool; do not venture forth to the deep end even if you feel secure in the water and it all looks so effortless.

Check out your swimming pool manners with a parent before going to swim

- ✔ Always take a shower before using the pool—removing dirt, sweat, and sunburn preparations that your friend's parents obviously don't want added to their water—and be prepared by bringing your own suit, towels, cap, suntan lotion, sunglasses, life jacket, flippers, etc.

- ✔ Never tease anyone about how he or she looks in a swimsuit (too fat, too thin, too flat-chested, too busty). These remarks hurt like wasp stings and are the height of unkindness.

- ✔ No splashing your friends or anyone else. Not even the family dog. It is a most irritating habit some children relate to athletic ability. They could not be more wrong.

- ✔ Keep the noise level down. That means no screaming, fighting, or general boisterousness.

- ✔ Never go into your friend's house and sit on the good furniture in your wet bathing suit. (Don't even sit on the *bad* furniture in a wet suit.) And don't track sand into anyone's house.

- ✔ Have it understood between your parents and your friend's parents how and when you're going home after the swim. It's not your host's responsibility. Have your mother arrange the transportation and your lunch, and remember, don't stay at your friend's pool for longer than two or three hours. It's much better to be asked back again because of your considerate manners.

- ✔ Naturally, of course, you pick up all the litter around the pool—yours and anyone else's—and stow it away in a trash bin. I remember one little girl who came to a friend's pool one time and was never allowed back. She had managed to leave her soda cans lying around the pool landscape, and had distributed almost a full box of popcorn all over the wet tiled terrace surrounding the pool. She also jumped up and down on the popcorn, so that it filled in the cracks between the tiles, making walking barefoot painful for everyone.

THE POLITE SPECTATOR OF GAMES

A kind child knows not to upset the adults around him during a game or match, or to make any distracting noises. People come to watch, not to hear children yelling or commenting on the athletes' performances. Parents can easily control this behavior by laying down a rule: If the child does not remain quiet, or upsets the players, or throws objects onto the playing field, permission to attend these events will be withdrawn.

A Seat on the Bus and Other Public Transportation

"Quaint," "old-fashioned," and "irrelevant" are terms used today to describe the delightful custom that used to be taught to most children: *getting up to give one's seat on public transportation to someone who needs it more than the child.* (This means just about everyone.) A child would be immediately whispered to by his or her parent when a woman of any age beyond twenty-five boarded the trolley, bus, or subway car. Elderly gentlemen and pregnant women were also in the category of those who qualified for the "Jump up, give up your seat immediately!" category.

My grandmother told me it was important to understand what other people near to me were feeling, and that I should react to those feelings. She never did explain when it would turn around so that other people would react to how *I was feeling.* Such selfish thoughts were dealt with by my grandmother with total disdain. I remembered being truly exhausted, eyes stinging, joints throbbing, after one stressful twelve-hour day at Burlington Industries corporate headquarters in New York. Heading home, I boarded a crowded Madison Avenue bus. A sprite of a child saw me and jumped up to give me her seat. She also deterred a man who tried to take it before I could get there. I was all of thirty-two years old! I loved it. I'll never forget it. It was the only time it has happened to me (including both times later when I was pregnant). To the child I must have looked like the wreck of the *Titanic*, as seen from the ocean floor. I blew her a kiss to accompany my smile of gratitude. (When I was a child, I had given up my seat hundreds of times, but by the time I reached college, I had to stop because I was being met by the reactions of furious women who felt they were too young to have such solicitousness turned in their direction.)

Teach your child this obvious kindness.

Teach Your Child Respectful Behavior in a House of Worship

If it is in your family tradition to attend religious services, the way to teach a child to be respectful in a house of worship is to start taking him there when he is young. Show him how to be quiet, to listen intently, to sing when the others sing, to pray when the others pray, and to display respectful body language, i.e., sitting and standing erect, not sprawling in the pew, taking up two places instead of one, bouncing one crossed leg on top of the other in a nervous rhythm, or slumping down in a bored manner.

Teach him to address the pastor or religious leader by his or her title and last name. Teach him to dress in his best clothes, and not to appear at services during the summer in jeans, cutoffs, and torn T-shirt. Teach a girl that shorts and bare midriffs show no reverence.

Don't take a child to a religious service if he is too young to stay quiet. All during the service I attended last Christmas Day a five-year-old loudly sang "Jingle Bells," and his parents seemed proud of his performance!

It does not matter whether you go to your own house of worship faithfully every week, or if you expose your child to a series of religions, so that he or she may select a preference. What does matter is that if you believe in a certain religious faith, encourage the child to get into the habit of going to services.

A child should be given a cursory explanation of religions other than his own. When a child is in a house of worship other than his own, his simple questions should be answered. Detailed information does not have to be given, but basic answers are expected. As a result, an educated child will not make fun of the clergy, but rather give them respect. A Hasidic Jew in his black suit, wide-brimmed hat, and beard; a Russian Orthodox monk in his long black cassock and tall silo-shaped hat; an Anglican priest with a purple shirt and reversed stiff white collar; a Catholic nun in her black habit and head covering—they each deserve a minimum amount of explanation to an inquisitive child.

If your child realizes where he is, he will be silent and attentive. When he grows into adulthood, he will always maintain that dignified presence in a house of worship. There is nothing more attractive than that, and besides, he learned it from you.

Your Child at Movies, Concerts, and Theatrical Performances

A large number of children, old enough to go to the movies with their friends, learn at an early age that their peers think it's cool to act up during a film and make nuisances of themselves.

A FEW MOVIE MANNERS TO TEACH YOUR CHILDREN

+ *Once the lights go down and the screen is lit, it's the signal to keep quiet*—not just lower your voices, but keep totally quiet. (That means no bubble-gum popping, no popcorn-crunching, no rattling candy and gum wrappers.)

+ *Think of the other people present.* It should be your mantra in a public place. Whisper it to yourself when others around you are acting up, horsing around, and laughing raucously.

+ *Don't drape your legs over the seats in front of you,* even if the seats are invitingly empty. What you are saying to the world is, "I don't care about anyone else in this place, just me."

+ *Obey the food rules of the establishment.* If food and beverages are not to be brought into the theater, don't do it! The house has those rules for good reasons. Remind yourself you'll bring a plague of rats and mice to the movie house if you eat when you're not supposed to. If food is allowed, pick up your soda cans, popcorn bags, etc., that you stowed beneath your seat, and deposit them in the trash cans in the lobby on your way out.

+ *Always stand up when someone crosses over you to his seat.* People trip, fall, sprain ankles, and generally become clumsy, conspicuous, and embarrassed when you don't stand up to give them enough room to get by.

At Concerts and Performances Such as Theater and Dance

Our rock and heavy metal groups enjoy audience participation, which includes having their clothes torn off them by fans, while members of the audience enjoy being thrown around in the air by the many hands of the crowd held up high. ("Moshing" may be a sign of great exuberance, but it is also dangerous!)

Someone, however, should point out to our children that there's a difference between attending a play, ballet, or philharmonic concert and attending a rock concert. The ear plays an important role in the performing arts. There must be quiet in the house, so that the harmonious mix of notes, tempo, acoustical variations, tone, and diction can all work together in a performance onstage to bring great beauty to the ears and eyes of the audience.

Before your child goes to a theatrical performance, explain the story in the play, so he won't be struggling with the content and can enjoy the rendition of it. Before he goes to a ballet, explain about toe shoes and ballet slippers, and how it takes many years of practice and a total discipline of the body to enable a dancer to perform like that. Tell him the story of the ballet he will see, so he'll understand the action onstage.

Before he goes to a concert, explain how all of the instruments work together to produce an exquisite sound. Teach him to watch the conductor's arms and his baton and to follow the rapt attention the musicians give their director. Teach him to listen—and ask him afterward what emotions he felt the music was portraying.

And, of course, respect for the artists means that a child thinks hard before taking out gum or candy and rattling its wrapping; in fact, he should think so hard about it that he puts it away during the performance and opens the package during intermission.

Your Child Driving a Car

When a child goes through driver training school and practices with you, you'll find yourself in one of the most powerful laboratories of good and bad manners in existence. Point out to your fifteen- or sixteen-year-old the safety infractions and rudenesses people seem to commit all the time, but which you do not expect to see him committing *ever,* such as:

+ treating the fasten-your-seat-belt rule as a joke, instead of a law

+ filling the car with kids over the limit allowable by law

+ refusing to give way and allow anyone in ahead of you

+ ignoring stop signs if it looks like there are no other cars around

+ following the car ahead too closely

+ ignoring the rule that says give precedence at an intersection to drivers proceeding alternately through, each in a proper turn

+ thinking it's smart while driving to be concentrating on one's cellular phone conversation, putting everyone else at risk

✦ grabbing a parking space from someone who has been patiently waiting for it, either ahead of or behind you

✦ neglecting to signal, so that those around you don't know when you're going to make a turn

✦ changing lanes without signaling

✦ honking incessantly, thereby upsetting the nerves of everyone within hearing distance (an upset driver becomes an extremely *bad* driver)

✦ blocking the intersection by going through a yellow light on a traffic-clogged street and being stuck there, with the result that the cars that have the green light are unable to proceed

✦ parking in a handicapped parking spot when you are able-bodied

✦ not slowing down and waiting for pedestrians to cross, and either almost hitting them or scaring them to death

✦ driving fast by the side of the curb on a rainy, muddy day, so that pedestrians in the vicinity are thoroughly splashed

✦ driving noisily—i.e., without your muffler, or with the volume of your radio or cassette player turned to its ultimate high

✦ driving "smart-assed" (apologies; there's no polite synonym), with the left leg hanging out the window, or standing up through the skylight, or in general drawing attention to yourself, thinking you're really cool, when in fact you're just being a twerp

These are only *some* of the crimes committed against the laws of safe driving, but they're also a show of bad, selfish manners. Teach your child to keep repeating to himself, "I'm going to be a considerate driver this trip, I'm going to be a considerate driver." It's a speech your child can never make to himself too many times when he's at the wheel. A car, after all, can be a lethal weapon.

He'd better make that promise to himself with his seat-belt fastened, too!

The First Driving Lesson of All

The most important thing you can teach your child when he or she is about to handle a vehicle of any kind (snowmobile, golf cart, motorbike, whatever) is *never drive it if you've been drinking*. This means even if you've "just had a couple of beers." Someone else should drive at this point who has not had just that "couple of beers." Parents almost always financially aid their children when they obtain their first motorbike or car, and they therefore have the right to exact some proper behavior.

A high school freshman challenged me on this point.

"Just why do you include cutting out even one beer as part of manners anyway? It has nothing to do with anything." His tone was sarcastic, to say the least.

"Because it's bad manners," I answered, "to kill a person."

Kids and Pets

Many people consider their pets to be truly part of their families. Therefore, I have included animals in this book. (I think they belong!)

Children are always begging their parents for pets, but they just as often become easily bored by them. No one should be allowed an animal or bird until he or she is able to accept responsibility for the creature's care—not just pet it on occasion when there's nothing else to do.

The introduction of a pet into the family is a major event, requiring the active participation of every member, including making the following important decisions:

+ What kind of animal will it be?

+ If it's a dog, will it be pedigreed from a kennel or a mixed breed from an animal shelter?

+ Which child will have the major responsibility as to feeding it, getting it exercised, and seeing that it remains healthy?

+ If all the children are to share in its care, who will make the schedule of the separate and joint duties to be fulfilled?

All of these points can be decided in a family powwow before the arrival of the pet, as well as the extent of each child's share in the responsibility for the pet. These details should be recorded on the computer or on paper. Johnny, as the oldest child, may insist, for example, that the golden Lab sleep in his room at night, but Lucy may want the dog in her room, too. When Johnny hears that having the dog sleep in his room means he must also walk the dog every morning and every night before he goes to bed, he may change his mind and let Lucy have the honor. The family powwow should bring all the points of the care of the pet to the forefront, so that there are no surprises later for the child who desperately wanted that responsibility in his or her life.

Many adults today mistreat pets, and it obviously stems from their childhood habits when their parents didn't realize—or didn't care—that they were mistreating animals. A pet is like a younger sibling to some younger children—an object to tease and torment. To allow an animal to suffer pain for a child's diversion is one of the sickest activities that go on today—right into adulthood, when grown-ups attend cockfights and pit bull fights. (A cobra-and-mongoose fight to the death in India is not such a kind and pretty happening either.)

When a pet becomes part of the family, a child should learn first to play gently with it. Show the child how to hold it and stroke its fur with a calm, light touch. Explain that a dog, for example, likes having his fur stroked in the direction in which the hair grows, never the opposite. A very young child should be watched at all times when with an animal, to ensure he does not mistreat it or provoke it to react from pain, which could hurt the child. Never let a child pull on an animal's ears or tail or stick his fingers in the eyes. Keep reminding him, if he's handling an animal roughly, that this is the way to hurt his pet, not love it.

In teaching a child to have responsibility for an animal or bird, make sure he keeps fresh water available at all times and gives it food at a regular time each day. A pet likes its privacy when it is eating. A child should learn to leave his pet alone when it's the dinner hour.

Dogs require regular exercise and walking, even when their masters may not feel like getting dressed for the elements outside. Litter boxes for cats require regular, careful cleaning. Many birds need to exercise outside their cages for a short period daily. The rug may need vacuuming because of scattered birdseed. The only pets that perhaps don't need regular attention are the little creatures who live in a glassed-in ant farm.

Grooming is essential in the proper care of a pet. A dog, for example, should be combed or brushed regularly and its sleeping area kept clean. It needs to be bathed, sometimes with medicinal shampoo. Except for a few exceptions, most animals are not happy unless they are clean. (After their baths, our dogs are so pleased with themselves that they put on a supercharged gymkhana demonstration around our apartment for a full hour.)

As a responsible owner, your child should keep a calendar of when his pet needs to visit the vet for shots, and he should remind you when to make the appointment. He should also go with you so that when he is older, he can do this by himself.

One of his very first responsibilities as a pet owner is to keep doors and gates closed so that the animals can't get out and get hurt. A puppy, like a baby, must come to learn what "No" means, and must follow certain rules before he is allowed as a reward to sleep in his master's bedroom.

Common sense should tell your child that a pet must never be left outside in severe weather—cold or hot. *He should never be left in a closed car in warm weather.* Teach him patience when the pet is undergoing training. The animal needs time to learn, so your child should never show anger at it or think it will understand what it has done wrong if the "mistake" was not made this very minute at this very place.

Teach your child always to speak quietly to it, unless giving a command. Animals, particularly horses, hate the sound of loud, excited voices. Teach him also that not everyone shares his enthusiastic love of his pet. Visitors to the house may be allergic to animals or afraid of them or just wary—in which case, a child should put his pet away in a closed room (along with water, food, and toys) during that visit.

My friend Sally Young, of Dallas, gave me much of this advice. Her house is always teeming with children and animals. She told me that children and animals share a common bond: They are happiest when they know what is expected of them and if they have been taught patiently how to do what is expected. That makes a happy child, a happy dog, and a happy household.

When Your Child Visits

Instill in your child the feeling that he or she is very privileged to be asked to visit another young person's house to play or have a meal or spend the night or even to spend a vacation week away at another's home. Prepare him, advise him, let him know what to expect and what is expected of him, too.

Teenagers sometimes give manners a low priority. It is particularly important that you impress on them that they represent your whole family when they are someone's guest, and that they also represent everything you have taught them about manners and kindness since they were little.

My own children took umbrage at this thought, since their mother writes books on manners. They did not want people to expect them to be any different from their friends in manners (they weren't!). After I gave our son a good-bye pep talk before he left for a long weekend visit with friends, Malcolm at age twelve said to me, "Hey, Mom, that's heavy. Do you think they'll [his hosts] expect me to be *perfect?* I'm not, you know!" There was a look of defiance in his eyes, but I assured him that everyone who knew him was aware of the fact that he was not perfect, so that was one worry he didn't have to retain. "Malcolm," I said, "all I'm asking is that you think a little bit about your behavior, and do things like eat your salad with your fork instead of your fingers, okay?"

ADVICE TO YOUR CHILD ON SLEEPING OVER

A gentle reminder of how he or she should behave is a very good gift for your child, including the following manners tidbits:

+ *The hellos and good-byes are important.* Always find the parent or child-care giver the minute you arrive at your destination, and also the minute before you leave, to say:

  ✔ "Hello, I'm so excited to be here."

✔ "Good-bye; gee but I had a great time, thank you!"

✦ *There are three parts of the house* that are of great importance in being considered a well-mannered guest:

✔ *Your room:* Keep it straight, picked up, and make your bed (even if it's your friend's room and he or she is very messy). Put all your gear in the closet or in your suitcase, out of sight. Before you leave, ask if you can change the bed. If your friend's mom says don't bother, at least pull the spread or comforter up over the bed, to make it look neat.

✔ *The bathroom:* Clean off the basin, hang up your wet towels and facecloths, put the tub mat where it belongs, and mop up the floor if you've showered and splattered water. Clean out the soap dish, too. On leaving, take your used towels, mats, and washcloths to the washing machine and offer to wash, dry, and fold them.

✔ *The kitchen:* Always discard your beverage bottles and cans in the proper container. Keep the sink clean; put all the dishes, glasses, and flatware into the dishwasher; and clean off the tabletops. Take out the garbage, if it's needed.

✦ *Volunteer your help to the parent of your host friends,* whether it entails running an errand, walking the dog, watching over your friend's baby sister for an hour, watering the lawn, raking leaves, shoveling snow, whatever.

✦ *Be a smiling guest.* In other words, be agreeable to anything your friend and his or her parents suggest. Be enthusiastic, whether the plans entail going to a movie, visiting a museum, roasting hot dogs on the grill, playing softball, or—something that reminds me of my own youth—making fudge.

After you've given all of the sage advice listed above to your child, he or she might say, "Just why is all this so important, Mom?" and you might then answer, "Because if you show some concern, you'll be invited back again and again."

Then, if your child asks in a tired voice, "All right, Mom, is that all?" you might answer, "No. I forgot to mention the thank-you note you need to write to Jimmy's mother the day after you return."

"Geeee, Mom!"

Your Child in a Restaurant

It's hard to tell your child and his or her noisy friends to "cool it" in a restaurant or fast-food place—particularly when they make you aware that the children at all the surrounding tables are making more noise than they are.

Make the point again that those other children are not *your* children, that each family has its own standards of conduct, and that your standards are pretty high, for good reason. "You happened to have been born to your father and me—not those parents over there—so you're expected to behave the way we want you to, not the way they're letting their kids carry on."

When your progeny question just why having some good-natured fun is so terrible, ask them to listen to an interesting story you have to tell them. Lower your voice when you do, and with the racket coming from the nearby tables, they won't be able to hear you.

"All right," you point out to them, "you can't understand me because of their noise. No one else can understand what anyone's saying either. Noise is nerve-racking and can ruin one's appetite or enjoyment of their food. Do you think those kids have the right to do that to all of us?"

BRIEFING BEFORE GOING TO A RESTAURANT

An intelligent, kind parent gives his or her children a thorough briefing before they go to a restaurant (or to someone's house, for that matter) for a meal. You might say to your brood and any of their friends who happen to be going along with you to the restaurant: "You're going to be out in public in a good restaurant, which is different from being in a fast-food place. This is an exciting excursion and a very grown-up thing to do. We want to be proud of you."

+ *I want you to be nicely dressed.* Mom and Dad will be, too.

+ *Once you're seated, I want you to remain in your seats,* instead of running around, bumping into waiters, irritating the other diners, and drawing attention to yourselves.

    (I remember once when I was with my brothers and parents having lunch at the Plaza Hotel in New York. I sat like a perfect lady without leaving my chair, and a couple came by our table later and complimented my parents on my behavior. They pointedly avoided making any reference to my brothers, who had, as usual, been pretty obnoxious, with my father sternly calling them back to the table more than once. They were not permitted to have dessert as a result, and my brothers, of course, soon thereafter gained their revenge against my "Pollyanna Perfect Behavior" by somehow surreptitiously stealing most of my dessert.)

+ *Don't dawdle over the menu or your decisions.* Study it carefully, ask any questions immediately, and once you've decided, stick to it. Too many children send their food back to the kitchen, "because I didn't think that was the thing I ordered." It makes life really difficult for the waiters and the kitchen staff when children constantly change their minds about their orders— and when their parents allow them to.

+ *Every time you give an order to the waiter, say "please,"* and every time he or she brings you something, say "thank you."

+ *Don't take forever eating.* You may be starry-eyed at all the excitement around you, the interesting people, and the details of the beautiful interior of the restaurant. Just looking at the exotic dishes being served around you may hold you enthralled, but remember, a child doesn't have the right to be such a slowpoke in eating that he makes the entire table stay put for two or three hours.

+ *If you don't like something that has been served to you, keep it a big secret.* In other words, don't comment. If you do like something that's been served to you, say so. If you tell your waiter to tell the chef you especially liked something, it will be reported to the kitchen and make the chef a very happy person.

+ *Try to eat as neatly as possible.* Mistakes are made and spills happen to everyone, but if you pay attention to how you're handling your knife and fork and glass, you'll have a minimum of mess as a result. Make good use of your napkin, because if you keep wiping the food off your mouth, it won't get all over your milk or water glass and look gross. Younger children can get help from an adult with cutting something or dipping something in a sauce, or whatever. If you don't know how to eat something, ask an adult who is with you.

✦ *Going to a special place means you make a special effort to behave.*

✦ *When you get up at the end of the meal,* put your napkin neatly on top of the table (for the first and the last time), look the waiter right in the eye, and say, "Thank you very much." Before leaving the table, push your chair back into the table. If there is someone who gets your coat for you from a cloakroom, say thank you again.

    You probably don't know how much a smile and a warm "Thank you" from a child means to a grown-up. Trust me—it means a lot.

What Are "Kind" Table Manners?

If your daughter asks you how table manners can be related to kindness, point out that she berates her baby sister for being "disgusting" when she drips her pureed food down her chin and onto her high chair. Remind her that she teased one of her friends for being "gross" when she allowed the chocolate ice cream to slip from the cone down onto the dining room carpet. In short, sloppy table manners can be very unattractive and unappetizing for anyone nearby who is forced to witness them. A person who doesn't know how to eat his food commits an unkind act against the people who have to share the table with him. Sloppy table manners also make a lot more work for whoever has to clean up after the messy eater—yet another unkindness!

When a child doesn't improve his eating habits effectively beyond the age of five, it's not his fault. There probably was no adult around with sufficient patience and determination to work with him. It's tragic that so many prepare their children with the most expensive computer training techniques and quality educations, but don't give a thought to how those children stack up in *human* behavior.

An older child who eats with the manners of an orangutan is in societal trouble. People don't want to be present when he's at the feeding trough. The effect is one of revulsion when the rim of his water glass is observed to be greased with food remnants (because he didn't use his napkin first) and the table mat around him dotted with messes and spills (globs of catsup and chocolate cake, like a Jackson Pollock painting). It's unkind to force others to look at the stains made by the wet bottom of his mug adorning the tabletop, and the medley of peas, carrots, and potato bits blooming like wildflowers in the carpet beneath him. It's bad manners to arouse slight feelings of nausea in others because of anyone's habits at table— unless it's a child who has not yet successfully graduated from the terrible twos.

To be messy is bad manners; to be messy is to be unkind to others who must behold it; therefore, there is an alliance between uncaring manners and unkindness. If you have invited guests to an expensive restaurant for dinner, you don't want the view of slobs eating their meals at the next table to ruin the atmosphere in the restaurant. And if you run a company, you don't want your executives eating like slobs when they dine with clients or associates. (Many major corporations today give their entering management trainees a quick course in table manners for just that reason.)

THE WELL-MANNERED YOUNG PERSON AT TABLE

✦ *Always comes to the table the moment the meal is announced.* No one has to keep trying to find him or urge him to put down whatever he's doing, wash his hands, and "come when called." It's rude to the cook to come late to the table, because it means the food is not presented at the optimal moment. It's also rude to the host and to everyone else at that table, because of their busy schedules.

✦ *Waits until the adults are seated* before taking his place (the exception is when the only adult present is a busy parent who is dashing back and forth, cooking and serving).

✦ *Begins eating only when his host or another adult tells him to.*

✦ *Uses his napkin adroitly* (i.e., unfolds it immediately, places it on the lap and keeps it there, doesn't squish it into the size of a soft-ball, doesn't plop it on top of the table during a meal, but uses it whenever it is needed). "Chauncey, use your napkin!" are words that an adult should never have to utter. Chauncey should know that when his mouth is full of unswallowed hamburger and he has cherry-ade drooling down his chin, he needs his napkin badly. If he asks "Why?" just answer, "Because otherwise no one else at the table will be able to continue eating."

✦ *Passes the food first to any adults present* before taking his own portion.

✦ *Doesn't "pig out,"* but takes modest portions (one piece of chicken, for example, or one lamb chop) and knows he can help himself the second time around if there is enough. A glance around the table to see how many people must be served, then a glance at the serving platter to see how much food is on it, will give him a good idea on how to proceed. If there are five more people at the table to be served after him and there are twelve more little lamb chops, he should con-clude that he may serve himself two lamb chops.

✦ *Takes a small portion of food on his fork or spoon, chews it thoroughly,* and swallows it without benefit of any sip of liquid.

✦ *Knows it's incredibly unkind to take the biggest piece of dessert,* or to steal the cake frosting from the plate of a younger sibling who has been waiting to eat it at the very last exquisite moment. (I speak from the heart on this matter, since from the time the Baldrige kids were young, my older brothers spent their lives trying to steal my saved-up dessert toppings from me.)

✦ *Does not complain about the food or utter expressions such as "That's yucky. I could never eat that."* It's definitely unkind to give an inferiority complex to the cook, whether the latter is your child's friend's parent or the chef of a restaurant. A good guest learns to eat around what he doesn't like, without draw-ing attention to omitted items.

+ *Politely asks to have his meat or fowl cut up for him,* if he can't do it himself.

+ *Doesn't pour a veritable flood of meat sauce over everything.*

+ *Doesn't crumble his bread or rolls all over the table,* as though he were scattering birdseed in the park, but rather tears off a small piece of bread or roll, butters that piece, eats it, and continues to do the same until all of it is gone. Neither does he use his rolls as missiles to be thrown in jest or anger at siblings and friends across the table.

+ *Sits up straight at the table,* and either rests his wrists on the table when not eating, or keeps his hands quietly in his lap. No fidgeting, drumming fingers, or banging the flatware for this polite young person.

+ *Is mouse-quiet in eating his soup.* No slurping allowed—except in the Far East. He tips the soup plate away from him. After spooning up anything in the bowl, cup, or soup plate (like bits of pasta, shredded carrot, or croutons), he may pick up a *cup* and drink the rest of the liquid. He always leaves his soup spoon on the saucer or plate beneath—never sticking up in the cup or bowl.

+ *Uses his utensils, not his fingers, to eat his food* (with the obvious exception of burgers, hot dogs, nachos, tortillas, pizzas, chips, and the like).

+ *Uses a knife and fork instead of his fingers for finger food*—for anything incredibly messy, such as overly greasy french fries, an overcatsuped hamburger, a mustard-sodden hot dog, or pieces of chicken swimming in sauce.

  (I have seen children perform wondrously dexterous feats in getting food into their mouths, more or less successfully. Our son managed to eat an enormous platter of spaghetti alla carbonara entirely with his fingers at a friend's house. It was simply too tiresome to trap the long slippery strands on a fork. I was sitting in another room when it happened, but received compliments from those who witnessed his dexterity. He got no spaghetti on his little navy blazer, but a lot on his necktie, and, of course, a good bit on the floor.)

✦ *Uses a small piece of bread or roll to help get something difficult to eat into his mouth.* If he has imprisoned a few peas on his fork, for example, he can use the bread as a support to the forkful, to escort it safely into the mouth.

✦ *Rests his fork and knife (or fork and spoon) side by side, in a vertical position, on the outside right-hand rim of his plate when he has finished eating a course.* His fork is on the inside; the sharp edge of the knife blade faces the center of the plate. When his knife and fork are in this position, anyone serving the meal will know he has finished and his plate may be removed. If his utensils are crossed at the top middle of the plate, fork on left, knife on right, it's a signal his utensils are in the "rest" position, and that he wishes to continue eating.

✦ *Conversationally, he:*

  ✔ keeps his voice down at table

  ✔ always answers questions cheerfully and launches new topics if things are slow conversationally, and if he has something interesting or amusing to say; if he's at a total loss for anything to say, he can't lose by complimenting the cook. "Mrs. Jenkins, these cheese tortelloni are really good!"

  ✔ never interrupts others who are speaking, but listens respectfully to the adults and tries to make a comment if he can; it shows he's listening, a most flattering way to treat a person who loves to talk and impress others

  ✔ never criticizes what he's eating or talks in a gross way (Example of grossness, overheard coming from an eleven-year-old: "This stuff looks like a pile of mashed cockroaches.")

✦ *Always asks his hosts if he can help serve the food,* take out the empty plates and glasses, help load the dishwasher, and feed the dog. He may be turned down on all counts, for the sake of preserving the table accoutrements, but it's nice of a child to ask.

✦ *Remembers to insert in his mealtime conversation* the three most important, witty, impressive phrases ever used by a child: *"Please," "May I," and "Thank you."*

✦ *Does not leave an adult's table early because he's "bored,"* but rather suffers through a long, tedious meal without grimaces and tortured expressions. He should even be praised for having done so, as part of the necessary lesson to be learned in life that at times one has to "tough it out." Of course, the adults at the table should remember kindness and manners, too. If the older-generation guests are lingering over a long conversation after everyone has finished eating, the children should be excused from the table and urged to go play or do their homework or, more realistically, to start the cleanup in the kitchen.

✦ *Always thanks his host(s) for the meal* before leaving to go home, whether the menu consisted of sandwiches, hamburgers, spareribs, ravioli, peanut butter sandwiches, filet mignon, smoked salmon, or chili. A child should get in the habit of saying thank you to his mother or father, too, or whoever feeds him *each night*. ("Thanks, Mom, for the good dinner.") Any food-preparer (including one who just opens cans) deserves gratitude, and a simple "Gee, thanks, Grandma, that was delicious!" should come easily from a child's mouth. If you keep reminding a child, it will come easily. Even if the sitter stuck a frozen meal in the microwave, she (or he) deserves a thank-you at the end, too.

WHEN THERE ARE GUESTS FOR A MEAL

An entire symphony of manners comes into play at a meal with adult guests present:

✦ The conductor is a parent; the symphony hall is the table.

✦ The children follow the conductor's lead and signals in playing the music of good manners.

✦ Conversation flows around the table with rhythm and orderliness, like a symphonic piece played in an orderly tempo.

✦ The musicians follow the conductor and play their compositions accurately, without mistakes, in the same way that the meal is consumed.

+ The guests (the orchestra) thank the conductor at the end, and leave the stage in perfect order—their chairs pushed in to the table and all litter removed by the children of the family and brought out to the kitchen. The well-deserved applause continues for a great performance.

The essential point to be made in any discussion of children's table manners is that before any real training and the formation of good habits takes place, *adults must sit down at a table and eat with the children.* Children learn by watching, by trying to copy, and being corrected when they do it wrong. They also deserve to be praised when they do it right. A child:

+ Watches his elders and cuts the meat off the chicken leg until he realizes it is all right to pick it up and finish it off, holding it in his fingers.

+ Ladles the soup away from him, after a gentle signal from his mother, who shows him just how to do it after catching his eye and saying in a low voice, "Spoon away, but less slurping and more sipping, okay, Alex?"

+ Starts to put the whole puffy popover in her mouth, until Grandma laughs, ever so softly, and says, "Phoebe, try pulling some of the popover away in your fingers, like a quarter of it, then butter that piece, and then you can pop it in your mouth."

+ Gets into trouble with a tough piece of steak gristle caught in his mouth. His father sees his dilemma and whispers, "Jamie, push the gristle forward with your tongue onto your fork, just like I'm doing with this piece of meat, then lower your fork down to your plate and quietly unload the gristle there. No one will notice."

+ Uses a piece of bread or roll as a quiet kind of "pusher" to help her get through a meal that is complicated to eat.

When Grandpa or Aunt Catherine are dinner guests or when the Jenkinses (friends of the child's parents) have come for a meal, there is a cross-generational flow of conversation and good manners ("Always pass the rolls to Grandpa first, Johnny"). How can children be expected to understand deference, including passing food first to guests and one's elders, and how can children practice not interrupting adult conversation at the meal, if there is never anyone at the dinner table except themselves?

Even if you have imported the world's most expensive Swiss governess or English nanny, children are best trained around the dinner table by their own parents and relatives. What they learn in a house where there are reasonable rules but also praise, good humor, and warmth is what turns them into polite, giving, attractive adults. It doesn't matter if the dinner table is a prized mahogany Chinese Chippendale antique treasure or a beat-up, Formica-topped dinette table that came from the Sears catalog in the 1970s. It's just as important that children share this experience with caring adults and parents.

They might even carry the traditions their parents have instilled forward into the next century. They might be the only ones left who do.

Thoughtful Guests and Hosts at Birthday Bashes

Giving or attending a birthday party provides the perfect training ground for children to begin to learn the people-to-people behavior they will need as they grow up. Birthday parties teach a child social skills, such as diplomacy in receiving and giving presents, sportsmanship in games, table manners at the birthday feast, skills in saying thank you to the birthday child and the parents alike, and many other basics of behavior, most of them involving kindness.

At times, birthdays can be disastrously disappointing, such as my own first big birthday luncheon for grade school friends, which I planned and agonized over for six months. (It had to be canceled two hours before party time because of a violent snowstorm.) Mother tried again the next year. My invitation list had now grown to thirty guests, with twenty-eight acceptances. Mother made her famous creamed chicken with peas, my pink cake had a ballet dancer with a pink tutu pirouetting on top, and the card tables were covered in pink crepe paper with tiny bouquets of pink garnet roses in the center. (In my opinion, Marie Antoinette could not have ordered a better bash at Versailles.)

I never saw my guests that Saturday either, although everyone reported they enjoyed themselves tremendously. I was upstairs in bed with a 103° temperature from tonsillitis. The kind way to treat a child after one of these disasters is to comfort him by predicting, "Just think, because of what happened this year, next year's birthday is going to be a hundred times better! You're going to have a fabulous party next year." (I'm still waiting for *that* birthday celebration!)

It's curious how, many decades later, my memories of failed family birthdays are vivid and affectionate. There was the huge birthday cake, for example, that I nervously made at age eleven for my father. It landed on the kitchen floor when I tried to bear it triumphantly from the kitchen into the dining room. My brothers had teased me about my culinary shortcomings from the first shake of the flour sifter. What had been, at least to me, a beautifully decorated chocolate confection was now a shapeless mound of collapsed frosting and particles of cake beneath. I watched through my tears as Brother Mac tasted it by scooping a huge portion from the floor and stuffing it into his mouth. I expected a glowing tribute to my cake, but he only said that "Tish's having dropped this cake on the floor was the biggest honor she could have paid it."

An Invitation List that Excludes as Well as Includes

All birthdays involve a certain amount of concern, beginning with the invitation list. Who to invite? Who to exclude? And why? As an adult, it hurts to be excluded from a party to which most of your friends or colleagues are invited. Think, then, how it must hurt a child to be left off someone's list, particularly when everyone else in the class has been invited. This sometimes happens when one child in the class is of another color, nationality, or religion, or is physically challenged or simply unattractive. It's human nature to want to have "pretty people" around you, but a child should learn at an early age that a person's looks are external and unimportant in comparison to his personality, and that making another child happy by inviting him when he's usually excluded is one of the most important aspects of growing into a good person.

If parents are snobs, their children will most likely grow up to mirror their attitudes. Take Amanda's mother, for example:

"Mr. Jenkins has a really important job at the bank, and they have a very elaborate house, Amanda. Don't you want to ask her to your party? You might be asked back." (Poor Amanda will probably grow up to become more of a social climber than her mother, and have the same kind of false values.)

Another parent, who is not a snob, would react totally differently to a child's guest list.

"Mom," Nancy might say one day to her mother, "the reason I'm not having Mabel to my party is that her brother's in jail. Everyone at school is talking about it."

"How awful for her parents, and how sad for her," her mother replies. "But what does that have to do with your party?"

"The kids are saying I shouldn't invite a jailbird's sister to my house."

"That's cruel of them! Your friends are wrong, Nancy, for two reasons. First, Mabel is not in jail. She has nothing to do with her older brother's mistakes. She is herself, your classmate, and a very decent girl. Second, Mabel and her family must be terribly sad to have Johnny in prison. Your party invitation would cheer her up. And if she comes, she'll have a good time. No one need mention that she has a brother in prison. You could see to that by telling the other guests beforehand not to talk about it."

"What if one of my friends does talk about it anyway?"

"If it's a simple question such as, 'When will your brother be home?' let Mabel answer it. If it's a nasty question like, 'What was it again that your brother did to get sent to jail?' as the host, you should step in and change the subject. Take charge. Say something like, 'Hey, we've got lots of other things to talk about. Who here likes the Litterbusters' new album as much as I do?' Then you play the new album, and that remark will be forgotten."

The Present Your Child Brings to the Party

Opening birthday presents at the party can be a lot of fun, but if there are many guests, it can be chaotic. The scene soon becomes a cloudlike profusion of wrapping paper, lost gift enclosures, and general confusion. Also, a young birthday child often has difficulty hiding how he feels about a gift, and his lack of enthusiasm can hurt the donor's feelings. It's far better for the birthday honoree to open all the presents later, with his or her parents and siblings present, while a careful list is made of who sent what, for the sake of making the writing of thank-you notes easier. In case of this "opening the presents later" custom, have a huge empty box (gaily decorated, of course) inside the hallway, where guests can deposit their gifts.

Plan well ahead for the presents your children bring to their birthday parties, because you can purchase items in advance on sale and make good choices. Last-minute purchases are not all that successful. You can never find what you want and the prices may be high. Until the child is about eight, his parent usually chooses the gift he gives to birthday hosts. Then the child himself takes over and makes the choice. You can teach your child that a good present is well thought out, even researched. Teach him to get his own creative juices flowing.

"Didn't you tell me Tony has a lot of maps on the wall of his bedroom?"

"Yes, he collects old ones."

"Why don't you make a list of the maps on his wall without his noticing, and perhaps you can buy him one he doesn't have in that shop on Main Street that sells old maps. They're reasonable, and he would probably really like that. It shows thought."

Of course, you want your child to bring a gift that will send the birthday host into whoops of delight. Your parental ego, after all, is at stake, but no matter how hard you try to be the perfect gift selector, it's human to err. I remember when a friend told how she had bought the wrong present for her eighth-grader, Denise, to bring to a friend's birthday party. When she asked her daughter how the birthday girl had liked the expensive gift, Denise replied, "It was really bad. She just looked at the box when she opened it and said, 'Oh, I already have one like this.' And then she threw it into a corner of the room without even saying thanks or anything."

"And then?" My friend wanted to hear more, feeling resentment over the rudeness that had been shown to her daughter.

"When I was saying good-bye at the end of the party," Denise related mournfully, "she told me I was to take the chemistry set back to the store and exchange it for something she didn't already have, and bring it over to her house. She sort of like ordered me around."

Denise's mother was aghast at the birthday girl's behavior, but in the spirit of teaching her child not to retain resentment, she made little of it. "Let's go down Saturday to get it exchanged, find something else for her, drop it off at her house, and get the thing over with. It's not important, so let's forget it." Silently, she was thanking God that her Denise was not like the birthday hostess—no way.

DON'T OVERSPEND ON GIFTS

What about the cost of presents? Families having a hard time financially shouldn't even think of buying expensive gifts for their children's friends. Teach your child never to be ashamed if his or her gift for another child is not an expensive one.

Your daughter might lament one day, "But I'm only giving Jennifer a jar of bubble bath and Joan is giving her a new Barbie doll with a complete skiing wardrobe, goggles, and skis, too."

"I'm sure Jennifer will love her bubble bath, and I'm also sure that she doesn't base her friendships on the price of the presents given her."

"She will too. Joan will be her best friend from now on."

"I'm sure Jennifer's close friends are her best friends, and a doll isn't going to change that. She's a better person than that."

"What if she isn't a better person? What if she really thinks my present isn't good enough?"

"If she feels that way, I think you deserve another friend, but I'm positive she doesn't feel that way. Jennifer loves you for who you are and for the fun you have together. That has nothing to do with the cost of gifts."

The great redeeming factor about children's disappointments is that they are quickly forgotten.

ACCEPTING OR DECLINING PARTY INVITATIONS

An example of the logic and efficiency of the rules of manners is the very cornerstone of entertaining: the RSVP in invitations. If a young guest does not accept or regret an invitation to a birthday party, the birthday child's mother won't know how much food and beverages to provide, how to set the table, how many table favors to purchase, or how big a cake to buy. She won't be able to organize the table with the place cards children love so much, so that each child can find his own place at the table and the basket of candy or whatever table favor is set out for each guest. Frankly, there would be chaos (or at least, much more than usual at birthday parties!) if guests didn't bother to respond to the invitation. Manners are supposed to make things work well and increase the enjoyment of the occasion.

BIRTHDAY THANK-YOUS

A child should learn at an early age how to thank not just the birthday child for his or her party but also the parents or other adults in attendance. The thanks should be offered twice: on-the-spot verbally, and by written note afterward. When told he is to thank his friend's mother at the conclusion of the festivities, your son Michael might ask, even in a bit of panic, "But what do I say?"

"You'd say something as easy as 'I had a very nice time. Thank you, Mrs. Swift, for letting me come to Ruthie's party.' Then you'd go over to Ruthie and say, 'I had a lot of fun, thank you.' If you win a prize, you would mention that, too. 'Thank you for my prize.'"

If your child had an awful time at a birthday party, would you be teaching him to lie? No. You are teaching him diplomacy.

"Hank, there *must* be something about the party you liked."

"I liked Toto, their dog."

"Anything else?"

"The birthday cake tasted good."

"Anything else?"

"No," in a firm voice.

"Well, when you said good-bye you could have mentioned how much you liked Toto and the birthday cake. You wouldn't have had to add that otherwise you didn't like the party. Just mention nice things, not bad. Then you're not telling a lie."

"Why do I have to say nice things?"

"For a very simple reason: because it's kind. We do things like this to make people feel good. You're being kind when you make someone feel good."

"Will he make me feel good when he comes to my party?"

"I hope so. But whether he does or not, I want you to be known to your friends as the kind of person people like to be around. That's the best thing anyone could say about you."

"I'd rather have people say I'm good at baseball."

Kids at Work: A Laboratory for Adult Life

I remember hearing a CEO address the new hires in his corporation. "If your attitude is good, you'll do well and please us all," he said. "But if you have a poor attitude, you'll do a lousy job and may not be around here very long. The way you feel about working here is very important to me. If you want to work hard and do well, I'll like you. Take that advice, for starters."

High school students' summer and weekend jobs have become more important in today's economy than they ever have been. There is so much extra money needed: to help out at home or for school activities, and certainly for leisure activities as well—clothes, sports, dating, and "the support and loving care of one's wheels"— as well as saving for college. It is every parent's obligation to brief their child who's taking a job, no matter how menial or poorly paid, on how to conduct him or herself at work. Whatever a young person learns at age fourteen on the job will help him or her at age thirty-four just as well.

I once attended part of a training seminar given to high school students who were summer hires of a fast-food chain. *The major thrust of what the executive said was pertinent to any kind of job:*

✦ *Responsibility:* Never lose sight of it. You are responsible for a specific number of tasks. They're *yours, not someone else's.*

✦ *Reliability:* We're *counting* on you. To have people relying on you should make you feel good—and proud. Punctuality is not just important, it's mandatory, and without a good reason, there is no excuse for being a no-show.

✦ *Kindness:* This is something we want you to show to your fellow workers and customers alike. Look at every person who walks in this door as your customer, whether you're waiting on him or not. Don't bring your complaints, antagonisms, and bad humor to work. Park them at home. If you're considerate, you'll make a difference in the whole atmosphere of this place.

✦ *Cleanliness:* We expect you to be meticulously well groomed. Hands and nails must always be clean, hair washed and neat, uniforms freshly laundered and spotless. No dirty sneakers at work—remember! Do you know how much better looking you are when you're well groomed?

✦ *Cheerfulness:* The customers who come in here often come to be cheered up as well as fed. Every employee of this company is supposed to be willing to make an effort to spread a little cheer around here, so that people leave this place with a smile on their faces.

✦ *Respect:* This is to be shown to everyone, whether they deserve it or not. In other words, no talking back to or sassing your customers. If someone doesn't merit your respect, pretend that they do. You'll have to do a lot of "pretending" as you go through life, so you might as well start practicing it now.

The executive concluded his briefing with a promise of a reward: "If you live up to this code of conduct, you'll receive a bonus at the end of the summer, and you'll be assured of a job here next summer, probably a better one than you have right now."

Leaving the bonus aside, this kind of advice could be applied to almost any part-time or summer job, except perhaps to the kind of job my two older brothers had one summer in Omaha. They were grave diggers at Forest Lawn Cemetery, which they felt would develop strength and muscles for football. My father told them they were darned lucky to have a triple purpose in working a hard job. And what was that? they asked.

"First, you're making some money," he replied. "Second, you're building body strength and muscle. Third, you're enabling the dead to be buried." He was a great parent/job motivator, but what he didn't know was that there developed a fourth reason to work hard on the job. The girls from Central High used to come out and watch them shovel and bring them cold sodas, much to their pleasure, but also extreme embarrassment.

BECOMING A SITTER, NANNY, AU PAIR, AND MOTHER'S HELPER

For boys and girls, but particularly for girls, child care is something often learned at home with siblings. For many, child care is going to be an important part of their adult lives, so it might as well be learned early. A child who learns to have a professional attitude about his or her job, in or out of the house, does it well and enjoys it more.

A *sitter* takes care of children for a certain number of hours or days at a time. A *nanny* lives in or else works full-time at the employer's house every day and lives elsewhere. An *au pair,* from another country, lives with a family, helping with the children and housework during a year's visit to the United States as a "student." A *mother's helper* works by the hour, staying with the children and helping the mom with whatever needs doing, but she is usually too young to be left solely in charge of the children.

A KIND, WELL-MANNERED CHILD-CARE GIVER

- ✦ She is punctual and totally reliable. She arrives exactly when she said she would, if not before.

- ✦ She does not leave extra work for mom and dad behind her but takes care of her own and the children's dishes and is fastidious in cleaning up. A very competent sitter can cook the children's meals, but a parent should care more about having a loving, kind person with her kids than a good cook.

+ Instead of just watching TV all the time, she actually plays with the child, developing his or her manipulative and creative skills. She can enrich his life and open new doors by teaching him games and working with him on exciting, fresh projects. She *reads* to the children.

+ She has a sense of appropriateness, so she does not dress in clothes that are too sexy when she is on the job. She knows not to ask a friend—male or female—to join her while she's working (unless, of course, her employer explicitly tells her to).

+ She knows not to touch alcohol, tobacco, or any other drug on the job. (A young friend of mine had to fire her sitter because of an addiction to chewing tobacco, but this is a rare problem—at least I hope it is.)

+ She is completely professional about her responsibilities and:

  ✔ knows exactly what medicine is to be administered and when

  ✔ carries out the parents' instructions as to the children's food, play, bath, and bedtime schedule and follows the desired routine exactly

  ✔ knows how to get the fire department and emergency rescue (911)

  ✔ knows which neighbor to go to for help, if an emergency requires it

+ She is honest and would never think of telling a lie so that she can get off work to go to a party or on a date. Her own parents have instilled in her the fact that when she takes care of children on a regular basis, even if it's once every Sunday, they are hers during those specified hours. Her parent has told her how much an influence for good she can have on any child, how a child can flourish under her guidance just with quality storytelling and role playing. She has been told how a child's imagination can be sent soaring by the child-care giver, and how important that is when the working mother is too exhausted and overscheduled to be able to worry about things like soaring imaginations. In other words, the children should prefer playing with her than watching TV or a video.

✦ She shows by her own example what thoughtfulness is. She inspires the children to make cards and gifts for their parents and siblings' special celebrations. She remembers the children's special celebrations, too, with little gifts or poems.

✦ She is sensitive to the fact that one thing that absolutely "kills" a working mother is to hear her young child calling the caregiver "Mommy." It's natural for a toddler and even an older child to call the one they see the most "Mommy," but it is the sitter's responsibility to say firmly each time, "No, my name is Maria. I'm not your mommy. Your mommy is coming home tonight straight after your supper." The sitter would be wise to keep talking about mommy all the time, to firmly plant the absent person in the child's mind.

THE KIND, WELL-MANNERED CHILD-CARE EMPLOYER

✦ Is an expert list-maker who explains and writes job instructions so clearly that the sitter will know exactly how to reach the parent at any time, and how to feed the baby, as well as at what times.

✦ Makes the rules of the house patently clear: no smoking, no booze, no boyfriends, etc.

✦ Leaves sandwiches and tasty snacks for the sitter—plus sodas in the fridge.

✦ Pays her immediately when the job is finished—or when payday comes—and never says, "I'll settle with you next time." (The caregiver may need that money *today*.)

✦ Pays her for her hour or two of travel time if she comes from a long distance. Pays her fifteen cents a mile, or something appropriate, for the use of her car in getting to work. (Too expensive, you say? Is a wonderful, reliable person worth the fifteen cents a mile to come to you?)

✦ Leaves the sitter good magazines and books to read when the children are asleep if she has to stay long hours at night.

+ Checks out the state of the sitter's car if she is going to be driving the children and checks to make sure she has the proper insurance to cover them.

+ Arranges for the caregiver to learn CPR and the Heimlich maneuver. One never knows!

Environmental Awareness

Everyone has his or her priorities for a child's good behavior "out in public." Environmental awareness ranks number one with many people who see the earth, skies, and seas all deteriorating at a fast clip, thanks to mindless abuse. "When you hurt the environment," you explain to a child, "you're hurting yourself, because you're destroying the world you live in. You're being unkind to all of the children of the future." It's environmentally selfish, you explain, when you:

✔ drop food containers in the street

✔ throw things from the car

✔ leave a mess on a table in the school cafeteria

✔ leave soda cans, plastic bags, newspapers, or other trash anywhere but in a trash bin (if there is no receptacle in the vicinity, trash can be stowed in pockets or bookbags and brought home for disposal)

✔ injure trees and shrubs meant for everyone's enjoyment

✔ run, ride bikes, or skate through people's property, injuring their plantings

✔ deface public or private property, such as park benches, bus shelters, etc.

✔ don't bother to clean up outdoors after your pets

✔ don't leave an outdoor campsite in cleaner, better shape than when you found it

✔ ski, snowmobile, or ride horses over other people's property without permission, hurting the land

- ✔ don't rigorously obey the rules in the wilderness, many of which are made to prevent destructive fires

- ✔ ignore the fishing and hunting laws in regard to the season for hunting, the size of the catch, etc.

The Beauty Destroyers in Particular

People who destroy the beauty of our environment are not only sick in their minds but in their hearts. They are trying to rob the world of the things in it that bring delight to all the senses. There are the smart-aleck kids, for example, who lack self-esteem and spray-paint graffiti on fences and buildings to feel big and powerful because their signatures have been left on public property. Teach your own children early, when you are together and come upon examples of graffiti, that these are acts of cowardice, the opposite of heroism and daring. These are acts of bullies, who only work under the safety net of secrecy and darkness. A child who hears parents reacting strongly about graffiti grows up not to do it.

The same thing can be said for parents who stop their own children and their friends from tramping through someone's pachysandra and from picking flowers in public or private gardens.

The Noisemakers

Our world is such a stressed-out one that any loud noise robs us of a sense of peace and security. City inhabitants become fearful as we hear noises and try to sort out their meaning. Was that a shot I just heard? Was that the sound of a car running over a pedestrian? Is that the sound of a dog attacking someone? Is that the sound of a cannon blast or just a terrible explosion?

Whether a child makes noise himself, with friends, or with the help of a CD player or TV, it can seriously disturb other people. Post an enlarged photograph of the interior of a human ear receiving sound signals and put a warning sign next to it, perhaps that of the proverbial skull and bones, to remind him of how, in keeping the sound turned up high on his music player, he is:

+ risking permanent eardrum injury

+ aggravating the neighbors and ruining the family's relationships with them

+ rendering terribly nervous all the occupants of his home,
including the family dog and cat

+ ruining the concentration of everyone around, including anyone who's trying to write or think or work with figures as well
as whoever's in the kitchen cooking the delicious-smelling
meal he will soon be consuming

A child must learn, as we say in the vernacular, "when and how to
pipe down." The glorious natural ebullience of children who are
playing together, and later, in adolescence, who are listening to
loud music together or revving up their mufflerless cars or bikes
together, is their hymn to noise. They must learn to temper it, even
if it's an expression of the joy of youth.

It is more effective, in restraining him, not to use cusswords or to
shout commands such as "Shut up!" and worse. Go to your child in
the house or in the yard or wherever, and say quietly and privately,
almost as though you were telling him a secret, something like,
"You guys have really got to lower it. It's upsetting people. It's getting them angry at all of us, because you're not acting your age. I
know you're too smart to want to continue acting like that."

If your child complains, "But why do I have to care about what
other people think? What does that matter?" tell him you'll explain
later. And don't forget to do just that.

Teaching Your Child to Volunteer

Help your child to understand how important it is now, and always
will be, for him to be a community contributor to a cause that's
important to him—whether it's work in kind or a small part of his
allowance, or a small percentage from a part-time job. It might be
his church or temple, the Humane Society, the Salvation Army, college, local, or national institutions, or an area of the arts.

His contribution might be given to help send the school band to

Washington to march in the inaugural parade. It might be a donation to the citywide drive for victims of floods or storms.

When a child reports that an important upcoming fund drive at school will take place for a worthy cause, help him realize that it's not just the parents' responsibility to contribute to the drive, but that it's also his. Make some helpful suggestions. Could your child possibly donate a percentage of the profits from his or her baby-sitting, dog-walking, garden-watering, lawn-mowing, or household chores? Could he or she give up some presents received at a holiday or his next birthday?

MAKE IT A FAMILY PROJECT

A child learns about giving from the heart if the decisions are made from within the family circle. When a child listens to older relatives discussing annual donations to be made or service to be given to a good cause and the child is allowed to participate in the discussion and to express an opinion, the whole arena of giving becomes something he feels is of major importance to him. The art of lending a helping hand gracefully (i.e., quietly, willingly, modestly) becomes an integral part of growing up to be a responsible adult who really cares about his fellow men and women.

Our country has never been more in need of assistance as our population grows, health care costs rise, and government support programs diminish. Everyone knows that. Let's get kids volunteering at an early age. They might be interested in pursuing a cause, such as:

- ✔ adopting a homeless shelter
- ✔ cleaning a city park
- ✔ tutoring a learning-disabled student
- ✔ reading to the blind
- ✔ political activity with a group of the young person's choice
- ✔ watering the trees planted on choked city sidewalks
- ✔ visiting and getting food to the elderly

✔ docent work in a museum

✔ assisting in a free day-care center

✔ volunteer work in hospitals

If you know young people who could help in some way, including raising money or stuffing envelopes for political campaigns or
fund-raising drives, get them motivated, inspired, and attached to a
cause.

If you give money or volunteer time to a local hospital, show the
buildings to your children and explain how the hospital needs
money to buy new equipment and to fund research that helps keep
people alive. If you are active in behalf of a museum, take them
there on a visit and show how your efforts help keep the place
going. If you volunteer at a local drug rehabilitation center, take
your children there someday, and let them see the kind of work
being done. This is how a child learns how to "think outside and
beyond," to a world that needs his or her help.

When children help feed the elderly on Thanksgiving, collect
gifts for the homeless at holiday time (some purchased from their
own allowances and savings), it is an unforgettably moving experience. Just ask them what it feels like! Don't act as though it's a big
deal and overpraise them for helping. Act as though it's expected
of them as members of your family.

Latchkey Kids: An Early Solution to Keeping Teens Out of Trouble

Maybe it's time to stop wringing our hands about how easy it is for
teenagers to get into trouble after school and to start doing something
about it. It's a known fact that some high school students who come
home to an empty house, and are therefore "out and about" with their
friends, may use that free time to jump-start their addictions.

Most of us have heard the public service commercials on network television, when an announcer's voice comes on in the
evening and says, "It's ten o'clock. Do you know where your children are?" *It's unfortunate there isn't an announcer's voice in the after-*

noon piped into offices and businesses throughout the land, asking, "It's four o'clock. Do you know where your children are?"

Perhaps it's time for some real hard-edged creativity in this regard. It's time to try out ideas to combat this situation, starting small, but building bigger later. Remember the old trial-and-error spirit by which we used to launch targeted programs to solve specific problems? How about trying out a flexible afternoon "Leadership Program" for seven or eight kids in high school—a diverse group from the point of view of race, sex, nationality, economic status.

Let's inform our children (not ask them if they'd like to join, but inform them) that there will be a challenging after-school program for them, their own custom-tailored "Leadership Program," which would be volunteer-run, with enough elasticity in it to allow the athletes to go to practice and still participate, and to allow kids with after-school jobs to benefit from them, too.

PURPOSE OF THE
"WILL YOU COME TALK TO OUR KIDS?" PROGRAM

This would be an all-volunteer program organized in every interested neighborhood by the parents of teenagers who worry about what their kids are up to every day after school. The leader (surrogate parent) hosting the group would not discuss with the students the risks and dangers of their teen years. Rather, he or she would discuss how these kids would be getting a jump on their peers by spending time in this leadership program.

One of the stated goals of these sessions is to help the students get into the right colleges or trade schools for them (materials from different institutions would be discussed and promotional materials would be shown—videocassettes, slides, etc.). The group leader would motivate the kids to work harder in order to get into the institution of their choice once they know what they'd like to aim for.

This would be a volunteer effort for kids who would otherwise be home alone in that neighborhood after school. The emphasis would be on success, not failure. It would involve:

+ a group of about seven or eight kids per unit

+ a meeting that lasts about one and a half hours

+ a home or an apartment in which these sessions can be held weekday afternoons

+ some group leader (a parent or relative in the neighborhood) who cares enough to donate time and leadership skills to manage this activity

+ a frequent guest (a friend or associate of the parents of the kids) who will speak informally on his or her field, and answer questions. Each speaker would be told, "If you're greeted with apathy and indifference, it's your job to wake 'em up and change that situation!"

+ enough money donated by an individual or by the parents to provide a nutritious snack and a beverage (this will help keep up attendance)

TYPES OF VISITING GUESTS OR SPEAKERS

+ a college freshman, who describes his trials and tribulations his first year and how he plans to do better next year

+ a college senior, who discusses what he is facing in the career market upon graduation, what he wishes he'd done differently, what his hopes and aspirations are, what he thanks the institution for giving to him, etc.

+ an alumnus volunteer, who would describe the scholarship programs offered by his alma mater, how students apply, what kind of job they might have to get to handle the financial load, what student loans are available

+ a high school athletic coach, who would answer questions about sports, fitness, and training; he would discuss teammanship, leadership, and the character of a great athlete

+ a music educator, who would talk about what it takes to love an instrument enough to learn how to play it, what groups perform locally, and how a student could aspire to be invited to play an instrument with that group

✦ the parents of the kids in the group could send someone from their office or shop or business to talk about careers and what they should be doing to prepare for those that interest them—if they aspire to them, what classes they should be taking, what books they should be reading, etc.

✦ someone from the film industry, who could talk to them about what goes on in the world of film production, set design, promotion, etc. (the students will all have seen the movie to be able to intelligently discuss the film)

✦ a speaker from the public library, who could talk on library science and what's available in the newly electronic world of information services

✦ a nearby farmer, who could talk about his crops, soil conservation, government subsidies, etc.

✦ someone who's qualified could talk about teen manners, or lack thereof, how to behave at the movies, when driving, etc.

These afternoon sessions could start the young people stretching their minds, thinking about planning their futures, and keep them, at least momentarily, out of trouble.

If parents got together and talked about what they might do for their kids to keep them from hanging out with the wrong people, solutions would be found. Again, how will you ever know what will work until *you* try it?

Communications

A Child Learns Kind Communication

A young child often needs help from someone older in communicating a kind thought. It's difficult not to appear affected or sickly
sweet when carrying out an act of kindness that some peers might
ridicule. A child needs an assist on *how* to do it, the content of it,
and the timing of it, particularly if there's an urgency to do it "*now,*
not tomorrow, but now." To delay a communication of kindness is
to forget it, or to spoil its effectiveness because of the time lag.

In the sections that follow we will cover many of the ways a child
can be helped to communicate kindly with others.

The Kindness of a Telephone Call

The business world today is riddled with complaints about young
people's telephone manners. Clients and customers are often
offended by the way they're handled on the telephone, and it
affects the company's bottom line. If people handling the phones
had been taught early on to have good telephone manners, the
business community would be much pleasanter today. (So would
our social lives!) It's easy to use the telephone, but the ease does
not justify sloppiness, forgetfulness, and downright rudeness.

SOME RULES TO TEACH THE YOUNG

+ *He or she has a responsibility, when answering the family phone, to
make your family sound well mannered and kind.* Therefore, the
child should think about the way he talks into the receiver.

Instead of just saying "Yeah?" or "Huh?" when answering, he should learn to speak up, enunciate his words, and speak in a cheery tone—so that the other person will be glad to hear that voice and be in communication with that person.

✦ His or her parents should state what to say when answering— something appropriate for your household, perhaps saying, "The Doe Residence." That's a formal way of answering, but when it's said in a child's voice, it's very appealing. Of course, you may not wish your child identifying the house, for security reasons, in which case he would just say "Hello," or "Good morning," or "Good afternoon," or "Good evening."

✦ Teach your child your own telephone security rules, such as, "Never say that Mom and Dad aren't home. If a person you don't know asks for us, just say we can't come to the phone right now, but we'll call back."

✦ It's pretty safe if your child answers the telephone by stating your telephone number. When a child gives this information in a cheery voice, he doesn't have to say anything else until the other person speaks.

✦ Of course, if it's a relative or friend who has called, that person will recognize your child's voice and say hello to her. The caller would probably say something like, "How are you, Dorothy?" to which your daughter would probably answer, "Fine, thank you. And how are you?" If the caller is a stranger, Dorothy would say, "Who's speaking, please?" The child should not give his or her name if a stranger asks for it. Teach her instead to repeat her question, "With whom do you wish to speak?"

✦ Practice telephone answering with your child. Role play and pretend you're a friend one time and a stranger the next. Practice with your child the art of taking down the caller's name—at least the telephone number—accurately.

✦ Teach your child to return his telephone calls the day he gets a message, but not to call people at home after eight in the evening.

✦ At special times of the year, you might teach a child to answer with a seasonal message: "Merry Christmas! With whom would you like to speak?" or "Hello, Happy Fourth of July." People are astounded and pleased to hear a pleasant message on a home telephone.

✦ Keep a notepad and a working pen or pencil at every telephone extension, and keep on replacing them. (The "Message Monster" has a constant habit of making them mysteriously disappear.)

✦ Write down some sample telephone messages for your child to follow, so that he will know what you expect in a message (full name, date, time of call, telephone number, area code, extension, and a simple reason for the call).

✦ Teach your child to make "friendship calls" to relatives or friends when they are sick or sad or have injured themselves or have had something bad happen in their lives.

✦ It's kind if your child calls his friends who are going away on an extended trip, to say good-bye, have a good time.

✦ It's utterly beguiling when a child calls a family member to say thank you, I love you, I hope you feel better, or we'll miss you when you're away. It takes an adult to remind the child to do it. It takes an adult to monitor the situation, perhaps to place the call, perhaps even to write down a few phrases to prompt the child. A grandmother will feel like doing handsprings if a young child calls and says, "I hope you and Grandpa have a good vacation at the seashore. I called to say good-bye."

✦ Teach a child to react if he's given, and asked to relay, a message of calamitous news. For example, when he hears something like this:

> *This is Mr. So-and-so. I'm sorry, I won't be able to call back. Just tell your father that my wife has died. I wanted him to get the message, that's all, and I can't stay on the line.*

He might be able to react automatically (if a parent has taught him this beforehand). Instead of saying nothing, the child might respond to the sad news with: "Oh, I'm so sorry! So sorry!"

It means a great deal to the person on the other end when a child shows true compassion. The adult automatically feels comforted. A child's words make, after all, the most soothing medicine in the world.

Children often have a hard time voicing their feelings (not to mention the many adults with the same problem). If you overhear a child accepting a friend's or relative's bad news with a cursory "That's too bad," quickly give that child some suggestions for what he *could have said* that would have helped the sad person much more. A child hears, for example, that Mrs. McQuaid's husband just died. It would be very sympathetic if he would say, "Gee, Mrs. McQuaid, I'm sorry." It would have been much stronger and more helpful if he had thought a minute about what the loss of her husband was really going to mean to her, and if he had said, "Gee, Mrs. McQuaid, I'm sorry. It must be very lonely for you in that house now. I hope it'll get all better soon for you. I know how much you must miss him."

When a child reflects—and then speaks from his heart—the person to whom he is speaking is deeply moved, and comforted, too. When a parent talks over with a child how powerful words can be in comforting another person, the child almost always "gets it," and if the words don't come out today or tomorrow, they'll come out another day in that child's life, in time to make another person feel better. Once learned, it's a lesson that remains.

The Electronically Entranced Child: The New Era of Communications

Today, so much is changing so fast that many of us, rather than appear irrelevant or behind the times, are desperately trying to "go with the flow." That doesn't mean, however, that we should let some of our kind customs and traditions disappear without a complaint (correction—without a *fight!*). We are all well aware that children today are attached to their computers at the hip. They're on-line, enamored of surfing the Net, exchanging e-mail messages and chats with strangers all over the world, and finding information on more subjects than their parents wanted them to know. Rather than getting out on the field with their softballs or lacrosse sticks, they're sitting, pressing bars and keys and wielding joysticks to make their electronic gadgets function. It's going to be more and more difficult to bring them into the warm world of human communication (not to mention outdoor exercise), as they spend more time with electronic devices rather than with humans. Young people are leaving the skills of good conversation and good letter-writing unpracticed and unlearned, lying damp and cold in the foggy mists of their parents' memories. Some are having a tough time when it comes to corresponding with a friend or relative, or someone of whom they want to ask a favor. Some can't sell themselves on paper to a potential employer from whom they wish a summer job or a permanent career.

Yet many of us still cling to the touch, texture, and symbolism of a fine piece of stationery for sending important messages to people— messages that come from the heart are looked upon as being rare and unusual, messages that are reread by the recipient and passed around. Therefore, regardless of what is happening in cyberspace, our children should be taught to write really important communications on human and personal matters on stationery. (It's a proven fact that children write more careful letters when they compose them on good stationery!) So it's up to the parent (more than the teacher) to make sure that a child is growing up literate, able to write good letters and use proper sentences in conversation. *However,* if children will author communications *only* via e-mail from their computers or via their parents' fax machines, it's better to have the messages sent than not at all. Let's take what we can get.

LET'S IMPROVE E-MAIL ETIQUETTE AND PROTOCOL

If you can't lure your child away from his cybertravels on the Web, at least teach him and her the proper form of a letter to send by e-mail. Most of what is being tapped out by young fingers in communications classes is formless, shapeless, and far less understandable than it should be. Ease of sending a message does not excuse sloppiness. In the interest of saving our English language, teach your child these basics:

+ *How to set up a letter.* For example, the date goes at the top right and the person's title, name, and address go from two to four spaces down on the far left. Give your child a book that spells it out plainly for him. A book will also teach him:

+ *How to write and punctuate a salutation.*

+ *How to make margins on a computer, as well as paragraphs,* and how to organize the major points to be made in that letter.

+ *How to close the letter with something personal* and gracious, so that the recipient of the letter is left smiling after reading it. (This gift doesn't come from a book. It's a talent that comes from the heart.)

+ *How always to sign his letters.* An unsigned letter is like a piece of laundry that isn't dry—it's cold, intimidating, and unfinished.

A LITTLE POLICE WORK ON YOUR CHILD'S COMPUTER

Give your child some friendly, relaxed supervision of his or her use of the Internet, to determine what kind of programs are being used. Make certain your child isn't being influenced by the "super-cyber jocks in school" who are experts at finding the pornographic offerings, and whose messages are peppered with foul language and rude, slamming criticisms. Guide your child by respectfully asking if he wants your help in editing his letters and messages, for proper usage of the English language, particularly spelling and punctuation. Keep praising him and delighting in his advances on the computer. If you make him realize how proud you are of his skills, he will be more open and cooperative.

Children today are simply not being taught well enough how to express themselves in decent English. *Make your children the exception.* In other words, teach them to help save our beautiful language by using it, not abusing it!

The Kindness of Letters from Young People

Parents who suggest, motivate, inspire, and supervise their sons and daughters in writing letters are heroes for three reasons:

+ They are teaching their children human communication—an antidote to all the impersonal electronic gadgets with which we presently communicate.

+ They are teaching their children not only manners but compassion.

+ In getting children to express themselves in writing, parents are engaging in an important cross-generational creative exercise. In the process the adults, of course, become much better letter-writers themselves!

LETTERS OF THANKS

A thank-you is probably the first letter a child writes, with the help of his parents or some other adult. My mother used to reminisce about a letter I wrote to her mother, my grandmother, to thank her for the present she gave me for my fifth birthday. It was a little black patent-leather handbag with a brass button closing. A red-and-white polka-dot handkerchief peeked out of the corner of the top of the bag. I remember it vividly. My mother said my letter to Nana covered the following points:

✔ I loved it, because it was like Shirley Temple's (the child movie star I worshiped).

✔ I took it to school proudly; it was stolen in the bathroom.

✔ I prayed to the Virgin Mary to "get the kid" who stole it.

✔ The handbag mysteriously turned up in the art classroom the next day, which proves that it pays to pray to the Virgin Mary.

I'll never forget a thank-you note I received when I was about ten. My group of Camp Fire Girls in Omaha, Nebraska, had begun a volunteer Saturday "cheer up" program for children in the hospital. I had learned from our Camp Fire instructors how to work simple puppets and was using them in the children's ward one day. I came across a girl who was about two years older than I, in bed with a severe orthopedic problem. I was told she would never walk, which made me very sad, so to cheer and divert her I put my three puppets on her bed and showed her how to work the strings. She studied them and immediately began to make up a conversation, using three distinctly different voices for the puppets. She worked the strings over the side of the bed while the puppets danced on the floor. She definitely had a gift for acting and mimicry and instead of my entertaining the children in the ward that day, she did the job for all of us. Three months later I received a letter from her, in which she thanked me for starting her on puppets. They had made a big difference in her life. People were now sending her gifts of puppets, and now she could hardly wait to wake in the morning, because there was so much to do in perfecting her skills in working them and creating puppet plays for the other children to enjoy.

If you keep after the children over whom you have influence, your own children or someone else's, and if you cajole, threaten, encourage, bribe, inspire, push and pull a child to get that letter written, in time the child will eventually start to write the thank-yous himself or herself without being told to do so. There will no longer be any need for someone to remind the child, "Have you written So-and-so to say thank you?"

"Have you written Aunt Mabel for her birthday present yet?"

"Have you written to thank Uncle Jacob and Aunt Sarah for their bar mitzvah check?"

"Have you written your grandmother to thank her for your Christmas bicycle?"

"Have you written Amy's mother and father a thank-you note for that nice weekend at the lake?"

"Have you written notes to your classmates yet, thanking them for those nice birthday gifts?"

"Have you written the Lawrences for their eighth-grade graduation present?"

If the answers to all of the above are negative, it's time for an adult to get cracking. Of course, it would help if that adult were a proficient thank-you letter-writer himself or herself, to set a fine example to follow.

I remember watching a mother help her seven-year-old son write a thank-you letter to a schoolmate. It was really she who phrased it for him, but she made him part of the process. She bought some juvenile stationery featuring his favorite video cartoon figures. Since her son had been remiss in saying his thanks, she told him, "The absolute final deadline is tonight." She made the little document sound urgent and important to everyone. The TV was turned off, she sat by his side at the dining room table, and she said, "This is now a priority in your life." ("Priority" needed a little explaining.) After the draft was written, she went over it with him and he corrected it, so that the final version would be accurate and neat. She praised him lavishly and they mailed the letter together. That child will probably grow up writing many thank-you letters.

If your child is in high school, he may very well refuse to let you read his thank-you letters before they are mailed, but just make sure they go out.

If your teenage daughter thought her aunt's Christmas present was a nothing and did not require an acknowledgment, you should persuade her otherwise. Explain that she can always find something affirmative to say in a letter, to which she may reply, "What can I say that's affirmative about a pair of gross kids' bedroom slippers with bunny heads on them?"

Tell her she can always find *something* to praise about the slippers. Without lying, she can write her aunt that the slippers were "very cute" (because when she gives them away to a younger child who would really appreciate them, they *will* look very cute). She can describe in her letter how "nice and warm they are," which they are, even if she will not be wearing them. Then she can round out the letter with some newsy remarks about how great the family Christmas was.

TEACHING A CHILD TO WRITE

There are various persuasions to use in teaching a child to write letters, the most important of which is to *write good letters yourself.* Read snatches to your children of letters you've written and received that are interesting or amusing. Read aloud a letter you wrote your brother, for example, who lives in another country, giving him a detailed description of your family holiday dinner. You tell him, of course, how much he was missed. Then you ask your children if you should have included this and that bit of news. Involve them in the content of the letter.

Even three-year-olds should be taught to write letters. Well, not actually write them, but be involved in the process while an adult sits down to be their scribe. The adult explains why the letter is necessary and what should be said in it, and even says the words aloud as they are written. The child begins to understand right then and there that people deserve to be thanked for various reasons, and that one way of doing so is to write the words on a piece of paper and send it through the mail. A letter, unlike the printed words seen on the screen of a computer e-mail communication, is something to handle and keep.

Children are thrilled by letters and cards addressed to them. I have seen them take letters they have received to bed, like favorite toys. Human communication at any age is a special thing!

THE WRITING CORNER FOR A CHILD

A good way to make writing thank-you notes less of a chore for a child and more of an occasion in his or her life is to set up a small writing corner in your home. Such a "special place" can easily become a family tradition for children. Place a child's table and chair in this corner, add a small vase of flowers, a box of juvenile stationery, some bright-colored pens, a roll of stamps (that the child helped select), a favorite drink, and a plate of cookies (to be consumed only when the job is finished).

Give the child a clearly printed list of all the names and addresses of the people who need to be thanked for holiday or birthday presents. If his writing is not good enough, you might preaddress the envelopes yourself. When he is able to write the letters himself, give him some prototype paragraphs to help him compose his letter. (Example: "We had a great Fourth of July with all the family here for a picnic, a softball game, and home movies. I got into a poison ivy patch, but had a good time anyway. Your present helped me get well again, so I really appreciated it. . . .")

During the child's supervised writing session (the only way you're going to get the task accomplished, believe me), turn off all distracting devices, including the computer, radio, video games, and television. Put the dog out of the room. Set a clock near your child so he can time his project. If he needs your help and encouragement, stay nearby, but if he's old enough to write reasonably well, leave him in silence. When all the letters are finished, show him how to properly fold the pieces of stationery, insert them in the envelopes, and seal and stamp them.

As a final step, accompany him to the nearest mailbox so that he will deposit his letters with pride and know they're en route—to give pleasure to those who will be receiving them.

OTHER KINDS OF LETTERS CHILDREN WRITE

Letters of Condolence

I have seen many unforgettable written communications children have sent other children. They have an impact that reaches far beyond the person who opens the envelope. One letter of condolence written truly from the heart was composed by an eleven-year-old girl with a mild case of dyslexia. She wrote to her best friend, the daughter of a lawyer friend of mine, on the occasion of the lawyer's wife's death. Not only did he borrow that letter from his daughter to show to his family and all the neighbors, but he sent copies to all of his friends, and showed it to all of his close business associates. He gave it to me to read at the beginning of a seminar in New York. The young girl had written to his daughter:

Dear Maureen,
I'm very sorry to hear that your Mom dyed yesterday. I know she ment lots to you, and you meant lots to her. You're rite,

she was a very spesial Mom. She was so nice to us kids, even
when we ate her kake when she said not to. No one made
choclat kake like her. You must be fealing sad. Some day
you'll see her again in heven. She must have lots of friends up
there. (I hope she won't have to make too many kakes.)
When can you come over to play? I bot a new game, really
neet. Come over this wekend. I dont want you and your Dad
to fel sad.

A fourteen-year-old wrote a truly touching letter of condolence
to her high school teacher, who commented that it comforted her
more than any other communication she and her husband
received when their baby was stillborn. The letter-writer was obviously someone who felt emotions deeply and could express them
with ease. Her mother gave her some points to cover in the letter,
but the girl covered those points in her own way:

Dear Mrs. Jacobs,
We're all really sorry to hear you lost your baby. After such a
long time of anticipation you and your husband must feel
awful. Our whole class knows how much the baby meant to
you and Mr. Jacobs, and we were as excited as you about it.
That baby was going to be our class mascot. We were fighting
over who would babysit for you on weekends.
    You must tell us the name you had picked out for him,
because we'd like to remember him next year on his birthday.
To us he's a person.
    Hurry up and get well, and come back to school. (The
substitute teacher is nice, but we're not learning anything.)
We'll cheer you up—and we'll even study harder. Won't that
please you?

A Letter of Congratulations

The following letter was sent by a twelve-year-old to a summer
camper:

Dear Anne,
Your mom told my mom that you were chosen Camper of the
Year at Camp Arcadia. Mom says it's a big deal, so I guess we

should all be proud of you. When you get home from camp, I'll still be able to beat you at tennis, but until then, guess I'll have to say you're probably the best athlete in our school. Hurry home. There's nothing to do around here.

A Letter of Encouragement

This letter was sent by an amazing fifteen-year-old to his best friend Jim at boarding school. He did it on his own, after hearing from his friend's father that Jim was deeply depressed and about to be kicked out of school for bad grades. The boy's letter shows a basic wisdom and an ability to express emotions that few adults ever achieve.

> Dear Jim,
> Your Mom said you were going to have to leave your boarding school because of grades. I just wanted to tell you it will be good to have you home again.
> We've sure missed you. If it makes you feel any better, my grades suck this semester, too, but you'll get back up to speed here pretty fast and make us all look dumb and unsophisticated. Maybe we can both make a New Year's resolution to work harder so we don't have our parents heavy-bugging us all the time.
> One reason you'll be glad to be back in our school again is that there are three really cool new women in class. So far they don't know I exist, but maybe you and I can work on this together and change things.
> I just hope that snotty school made you a better basketball player than when you left. (Is it really true they've got *three* courts there?) If you've gotten too big for your jockey shorts at that place, the guys will be ready and happy to take you down a peg, so get your butt on home, man. I never thought I'd say it, but we miss your ugly face.

OPTIONS FOR SAYING THANK YOU

If you're enthusiastic about saying thank you for a book, gift, compliment, gesture, dinner party, whatever, you will infect the children around you with that same enthusiasm and warmth of feeling. The explosion of your energy when you say, "Well, let's get right away to that thank-you note to Rod!" will be transmitted to the child.

The options for thanking a person are many:

✔ Thank the person on the spot.

✔ Telephone your thank-you.

✔ Write a letter.

✔ Send a studio card.

✔ Fax a message.

✔ Put your thank-you into an e-mail communication.

✔ Dispatch it by letter in a courier package.

✔ FedEx it or send it by Post Office Express Mail.

✔ Messenger it, perhaps with an accompanying gift.

✔ Hire a small plane with a streamer flying behind it.

✔ Use a carrier pigeon.

A letter is perhaps the best solution on this list, because it is inexpensive, warm, private, and shows that the sender made a thoughtful effort to get in touch. Hopefully, it is written on nice stationery. If a child sees you writing a thank-you note to the people who took you to dinner in a restaurant the night before, he is going to realize that this is what is expected of a person after he has been taken out to dinner. Read snatches of your note to him as you write it. Involve him, so he learns the mechanics of this graceful art of manners.

"All right, Ricky, let's see, should I say how delicious the dinner was?"

Ricky will probably say that's a good idea. He will want to know what you ate, so tell him what everyone had, and write a complimentary mention of it. "Bob really loved the curried scallops, and I thought the grilled salmon was the best thing I've had in a long time." If your son Ricky remarks that the food sounds "really yucky," remind him that his taste buds will change as he grows older.

Walk him with you through the steps of your grown-up thank-you note, so he will catch the logic of saying how much "we enjoyed seeing you two again, after such a long time" and "how delightful it was to get all the family news." Mention something else that was pleasant about the restaurant—the wines, the flowers, the music, whatever, and then sign your name, let him look at it, then seal, stamp, and send it on its way. Remind him that a standard thank-you note takes five minutes out of a person's life to write and mail.

Rites of Passage: Customs and Rituals

Our lives are usually hallmarked by a predictable pathway of growth and maturation, with special ceremonies marking the attainment of each succeeding stage of life. Sometimes these rites of passage are enshrouded in religious ritual, like a christening, confirmation, bar mitzvah, or wedding; sometimes they are based on lighthearted, amusing customs, like birthdays, sweet sixteens, and graduation parties.

Just as prejudice begins at home, so does tolerance. Understanding does not entail embracing another's religion or traditions, just respecting them, and the way a child hears his parents referring to other people's customs establishes his own respect or disrespect for them.

Teach your child to rejoice in the celebration of the rites of passage in his own and his friends' lives.

"Look, Ezra, this christening you'll be attending may not be the way we do things when a baby is born, but the service is very special to the Gallaghers, and very beautiful. You're lucky to have been invited. So observe carefully, be respectful, ask questions about the ritual, if you wish, and enjoy it.

A BABY IS BORN

The first rituals, of course, concern the first rite of passage: the birth of a child. Catholics and Protestants baptize their newborns, usually in a church, usually from six weeks to a year in age. A celebratory reception for invited families and friends often follows, with perhaps a light lunch and often champagne for toasting the baby. Presents are often brought for the newborn, and a truly perceptive guest brings a small gift for the baby's sibling whose nose may be out of joint because of the super-attention being given to the newborn. If one of your children has a "best friend" who is in such a nose-out-of-joint situation, it would be really nice of your child to bring his or her friend a small gift, as a way of congratulating him "for having a new sister (or brother) whom you have to help bring up."

Jewish girls are "named in the synagogue" on the first Sabbath within thirty days after their birth, and there is often a reception following the service. Jewish boys are circumcised eight days after birth (a *brith milah* in Hebrew), usually at home, with a meal following to celebrate the event. The customs in every church, synagogue, temple, and mosque are beautiful, and if you and your child are invited but are not of that religion, be sure to have the rituals properly explained beforehand. If your children will accompany you, particularly to one of the later rites of passage, such as a bar mitzvah for a thirteen-year-old boy or the bat mitzvah for a girl, prepare them for what they will see. They will most likely enjoy watching the rituals unfold, and will be moved by them. Experiences like these help children grow into aware and sophisticated adults.

It doesn't matter *how* you react when a baby is born. The important thing to remember is *to react:*

✦ Certainly a *telephone call or an electronic message of congratulations* from your family, which includes your children, to the baby's family won't take much of your time.

✦ You might send some congratulatory flowers from your family to the parents' home (have each member of your family, including children, sign the card).

✦ You might send a *present* to the baby—something practical, like a sweater, receiving blanket, feeding tray, or something lavish, like a sterling silver engraved mug, silver baby flatware set (consisting of a baby fork and feeding spoon), or a hundred-dollar deposit in the baby's first savings account in a bank. (In order to open this account, the baby must already have his or her social security number.)

✦ You can always help out the family with well-appreciated *gifts of food,* such as baked goodies or frozen casseroles. You might offer to run errands for the new mother (such as grocery shopping), because she is inevitably tired and has too much to do. You can take the baby's siblings out for a Saturday or Sunday treat (the movies, ice-skating, a ball game, or their favorite fast-food emporium). Children who see their parents acting in this kind manner about a birth in another family grow up to do the same.

+ Fathers are often overlooked at a time like this. You might give a *small gift to the new father,* a tongue-in-cheek admission that he did, after all, have *something* to do with the birth. When our first child was born, actor Vincent Price sent my husband, not me, a present "to mark this great event."

To ignore such an important milestone in your friend's or a relative's life by not communicating when a baby is born is a mistake, because the parents of the baby consider the arrival of their child a matter of earthshaking importance. I heard a mother and her ten-year-old son discussing this one day.

"Mom, why are you bringing that package over to the Finnertys?"

"A gift for their new baby, of course."

"But they have had other babies. Do you have to give them a present every time? Isn't one present enough?"

"If there are more babies yet to come, I'll still bring each one a gift. You know, a baby doesn't know about its presents. It's really to congratulate the parents. Since each new baby is a different human being, each deserves a special welcome."

The First Rite of Passage: Birth

+ Explain the excitement of birth to your child in terms of that baby's family, and how enthusiasm for a new human life has been a basis of society all over the world. Describe how the mother and father prepare for nine months before the birth, and how a tiny, breathing, pink-faced "thing" one day comes into that family and changes it forever. (If you're not ready to explain the physiological aspects of birth, you don't have to; just dwell on the wonder of it with your child.)

✦ Even if you have called the parents or written to congratulate them, involve your child in this rite of passage if he or she knows the baby's parents. In other words, teach your child his responsibility as a "friend" of the new baby's family to make note of it himself. For example:

> ✦ Your child might scrawl a few words on a birth celebration card.

> ✦ If your child is a poet, perhaps he or she will be inspired to write a few lines of poetry.

> ✦ If your child is an artist, he or she could draw a picture of what the infant looks like—or will look like someday.

My favorite memory of a child's gift was when a four-year-old arrived at the door of a house in our neighborhood that already housed three young children as well as the baby. The little girl, dressed in her party dress, carried four colorful balloons on long satin ribbons. Once inside the house and well rehearsed by her mother, she solemnly handed one to each of the three siblings and said, "This is for you, to congratulate you on your baby sister." Then she handed the fourth balloon to the mother. "This is for the baby, to tie on her crib. It's to say welcome from us."

Whether the idea of the balloons was the little girl's or her mother's didn't matter. It was an instantaneous act of kindness.

✦ Children do come up with their own great ideas without a parent's help. One ten-year-old went to see a neighbor's baby with her camera, and without anyone knowing, managed to get a couple of excellent flash photographs of the family dog gazing lovingly at the baby.

One second-grader who had just learned how to knit on big wooden needles was very excited about the birth of her little cousin. I saw her the day after the event, and there she was, surrounded by yarn, busily working her needles. When I told her she was doing beautiful work and asked her who it was for, she replied with immeasurable pride, "I'm making a blanket for my aunt Jean's baby."

"That's such a kind thing to do," I said.

She turned to me and surprisingly asked, "Why?"

I thought fast and found an answer. "Because when it's cold, the blanket will keep the baby warm."

+ If you have a religious faith, contact the family of the new baby with a note saying that you have said prayers of thanks for the baby's birth and that you have prayed for the mother's quick recovery from the birth and for the baby's continued good health. (Hopefully, you have said the prayers you take credit for!)

+ It always greatly pleases a parent when a child asks after the new baby. Teach your child to mention the baby whenever he happens to see the mother or father. All he has to do is ask, "How's Matthew?" Not much memory work needed there.

+ Teach your child to be ready with a compliment to relay to members of the family when viewing the baby. For example, you can tell her, "If the baby's mother or father answers the door, you can say 'I brought some flowers to say hello to your baby.' Then it's nice to add, 'We're glad she's been born.'"

When you rehearse children on kind little things to say to people about happy news in their lives, the children rarely say what you've practiced them to say. They might come out with a part of it, or maybe something totally different (and much better, because it comes from their hearts). Whatever words come out of their mouths, it's a good thing. They're learning how to react to—and not just observe—the world around them in a positive way.

Your Child and a Wedding

Weddings for the most part are really very joyous. Everyone has memories of fainting brides, a shrieking mother of the bride, wedding cakes going to the wrong place (the best story I remember was the cake that was mistakenly delivered and consumed by corporate male executives at a golf picnic), and the big-name band for the reception being stranded by a flood on the Missouri River. (The father of the bride played the piano at that reception—"Let there be music.")

Along with such sagas of wedding stress, every year in every country there is an inevitable mountain-sized collection of beautiful, blissful stories of weddings that were perfect. Very often one of the reasons the wedding was such a success was the presence of small children who were flower girls, ring-bearers, train-bearers, and junior brides-maids, not to mention all the children who were properly invited to the wedding (*please*, parents, don't bring an uninvited child with you), who are appropriately dressed and trained by their parents or grandparents to behave like little angels (most of the time, that is).

Our four-year-old grandson Luke Smyth, a nervous wreck from the excitement of his job as ring-bearer (the ring was to have been sewn on top of the pillow), came bounding up the aisle last year at a beautiful church in Virginia Beach where our daughter-in-law, Carey Shoemaker, married our fortunate son, Malcolm Hollen-steiner. Wise heads decided to give the ring to the best man and to give Luke an unadorned lace pillow to carry ceremoniously to the altar. He had practiced mightily, but it was all too much. He marched up the aisle carrying the pillow under his arm as though it were a football, but he never made it to the altar. He slipped into the front-row pew on the right with me, went to sleep, and snored loudly during the recitation of the religious vows. The sound rever-berated through the church, but a four-year-old in gray shorts with a double-breasted navy blazer, gray knee socks, white shirt, and necktie is forgiven. Particularly when he's wearing the same bou-tonniere as the groomsmen and ushers. Carey's niece, all of eigh-teen months old and dressed like an angel from heaven in white organdy, tripped up the aisle in her tiny white tights and Mary Janes, holding her father's hand, smiling and greeting people, right and left, as though she were a politician working the crowds. She had heard that Luke was to be part of the wedding ceremony, and she was not to be denied. By the time she's grown, she'll prob-ably be a minister and will be marrying couples. These two children almost stole the scene from the bride and groom, but every bride knows that's the danger, and most brides don't mind.

What Do You Tell a Child
Who's Been Invited to a Wedding?

+ You explain what the beauty and symbolism of the wedding mean: the joining together of two people. You explain the religious significance, going back to ancient times. Many children at a time like this ask their mother or father, "Well, then, if it's so special and symbolic, why did you two get divorced?" Tell your child that what happened to your marriage was a sad development that need not happen to him or her. End of conversation.

+ If your child is participating in a wedding, several rehearsals at home are needed ahead of time. Have the child practice in the dress or suit to be worn. If she is to scatter rose petals up the aisle, give her a basketful of leaves and let her practice in your hallway or out on the walkway in front of your house. Junior bridesmaids should carefully practice their role of marching two by two in cadence to the music, or carrying the bride's train and arranging it decoratively on the altar steps during the ceremony.

+ A child who is standing up for a parent as a witness at a second or third marriage ceremony should understand the solemnity of his or her duties, and carefully remember the cues he's been given for his part in the ceremony. Explain to him that no matter how informal the ceremony, his role is important, and the proper execution of it will make the wedding a much greater success for everyone involved.

+ If your child has been invited to a family wedding, he or she should be properly dressed.

    + For a little girl this means something like a party dress, dressy shoes (like patent-leather flats), and white tights.

    + For a boy this means shorts or trousers, a shirt, and a jacket or a dressy sweater (like a V-necked solid color model). (*No* baseball caps!)

    + No jeans, sneakers, or sockless feet.

    + No slacks or shorts on a little girl.

The proper dress rules given above apply to a formal wedding. If the wedding is a very informal, outdoor one, such as a ceremony held on a mountaintop, aboard a sailboat, or while skiing down a mountain, the apparel of the wedding party and guests is equally informal.

+ Don't put makeup on a little girl who's in the wedding. Lipstick, eyeliner, nail polish all look cheap and unsuitable on a child.

+ Invited children should be strictly controlled by their parents in their seats in the church and should never be loose, running up and down the aisle. If they can't adhere to such rules, there is an excellent alternative: Leave them at home. If a sitter can't be found, in deference to the wedding, the entire family should stay home. Some thoughtful parents attend the wedding in halves, so there's always someone home with the child. The mother, for example, attends the ceremony and a part of the reception, then returns home so dad can take in the rest of the reception.

TEENAGERS' DRESS FOR THE WEDDING

Corporate executives are always talking these days about the need for a dress code for their employees. But there's also a great need for a dress code in young people's lives, too.

A child should be properly dressed* when attending any rite-of-passage ceremony, such as Cousin Sue's wedding, or any adult event, such as his parents' fifteenth wedding anniversary, or Thanksgiving lunch at Uncle Harry's and Aunt Martha's. Children need to feel the sense of dignity that should accompany such events, and dressing appropriately is one of the most important acts of propriety. A properly dressed child is saying to the guest of honor, without using words:

+ I love you enough to dress up for you.

+ I understand that this is not just any day—this is a very special day.

+ I am nicely dressed so as not to draw negative attention to myself or detract from the dignity of the occasion.

---

* "Properly dressed" means that *a young man* would wear dress slacks, a white shirt, a tie and a coat, and leather oxfords or anything but sneakers. *A young woman* would wear a suit, dress, or blouse and skirt, with hose and dressy shoes (flats or low-heeled pumps).

AT THE RECEPTION

+ Teach your child to go through the receiving line with you (your child can always play before and after but should be with you when you approach the bride and groom).

     All the child needs to learn to say is: "You are a very handsome groom," "You are a very pretty bride," or "I really liked your wedding." To the parents of the bride and groom the child might be able to say: "It was a beautiful wedding. You must be so happy for them." To a bridesmaid, the child might say: "You are very pretty, and I like your dress. . . . I love those flowers in your bouquet." (I learned some sentences like these from my parents when I was four and went to my first wedding; I've been using the exact same sentences ever since. In spite of the apparent triteness, it's much better than total silence, when neither child nor bridesmaid knows what to say.)

     One of the best greetings I ever heard was made by a four-year-old in a receiving line. Upon seeing the groom up close, she cried out, "You're Ken! You're Ken!" Then she hugged him in delight, leaving him totally perplexed. The bride was laughing so hard she could barely get out the words, "She has a Barbie and Ken doll set, and she even has their wedding garb."

     Hopefully, your child has gone through the receiving line with nonsticky fingers—with all the vestiges of soda and hors d'oeuvres off the hands. (It helps if a parent gives a quick wipe to messy fingers before the child goes through the line.)

+ Explain to your child in advance that dancing at the reception is a universal tradition, so a big person might ask him or her to dance, and that it's a lot of fun. (Maybe that big person will be you.)

+ Have someone already lined up to take your child home early and sit with him (or her) when the child gets tired and cranky. No one appreciates children running around exhausted and having temper tantrums in the middle of a happy, noisy wedding reception. Smart brides (who can afford it) hire a sitter or two, complete with toys, to take care of all the small children in a hopefully soundproofed private room near the reception area.

+ A child who has attended a wedding should write a nice thank-you note to the mother of the bride. If the child was a member of the wedding party, he or she should write a beautiful note to the bridal couple. If your child can't write well as yet, be his substitute scribe.

+ If your child was a participant at the wedding, he or she will receive a gift from the bridal couple to mark the occasion. The child should send his own gift to the couple, too. It would please them very much to receive a modest token from the child, however young he or she may be.

NOTE: If your child was in the wedding and is featured in many delightful photos, remember the bride's family is paying—usually a great deal—for a professionally photographed wedding. The prints are expensive, so order away, but insist on paying *for all of your order*—except for the print of the entire wedding party group you will surely receive, compliments of the bride and groom.

Celebrating Others' Traditions

If we do a good job of instilling in children the sense of awe, reverence, and understanding of customs and religious traditions, they will be quiet and respectful in other people's houses of worship, such as when they accompany parents to weddings, funerals, or other ceremonies.

A child should be given a cursory explanation of religions other than his own. When a child is in a different house of worship, his simple questions should be answered. Detailed information does not have to be given, but basic answers are expected.

I remember hearing a Chinese Buddhist uncle answer his college student nephew's questions on why he was being forced to learn about the major Western and Middle Eastern religions.

"Why is it of interest to me and you as well that I should learn all about that, too, Uncle? I have so much other work to do already. I live in America now and don't wish to live anywhere else. Why are you pressing all this information on me about other religions in other lands?"

"Because I want you to live by my four codes of conduct."

His nephew asked politely with a touch of boredom in his voice, "And they are, Uncle?"

"The first is to 'Hold another's beliefs with respect.'

"Then 'Understand what others' beliefs are, so that you can speak with the tongue of intelligence.'

"The third is 'Defend a person's right to his beliefs when others mock him.'

"And last, 'Weep for him if he loses them, for he will never find comfort again.'"

+ *At Easter,* explain to a young person who is curious about it that Easter is considered one of the Christian world's greatest religious feasts, that it is a celebration of the resurrection of Christ after His crucifixion.

+ In the Catholic Church, first communion is an exciting, solemn rite for a six- or seven-year-old. Confirmation is also important for children in the Protestant, Jewish, and Catholic faiths. A lunch for family and close friends usually follows the religious service, and presents are given to the children who have assumed the first step of adulthood.

+ If you are in a city with a large number of Muslims, explain to your children that *during the month of Ramadan, in the ninth month of their calendar, the Muslims pray and observe a strict fast.* Your child might be invited to a feast in the home of a Pakistani classmate, for example, at which *Id-ul-fidtar* is celebrated (the end of Ramadan). Make certain your child goes prepared with a gift for the family (candy perhaps), and that he listen with respect while prayers are being said. Ask him to come home able to describe the setting of the table, the food and drink, and the clothes worn by the host family and guests. If a child concentrates, it is amazing how apt a reporter he or she can be after returning from a very special experience.

+ *During the Jewish festival of Hanukkah* in December, close to Christmas, we all see menorahs (nine-branched candelabra). To a curious child, explain the significance in the Jewish faith of lighting a new candle of the menorah during the eight days commemorating a historic military victory in the Holy Land. If your child is invited to a Jewish friend's house for a *Passover dinner*, inquire about the traditions beforehand, including the fact that even the smallest child present plays a role in the meal's rituals. (There are excellent books on the subject.) Usually the most important event in a Jewish boy's life (at age thirteen) is when he is bar mitzvahed (girls have a bat mitzvah). This bar mitzvah rite of passage occurs only after much Hebrew study. The child is the star of the ceremony, and if you and your children are fortunate enough to witness such an event, be sure to congratulate him and his parents on his performance as he is accepted into the adult congregation of his temple.

✦ *When you and your children have been invited to something totally unknown to you, like a Greek Orthodox wedding*, with its rich rituals of prayers, chants, processions, and crowns held over the couple's heads, ask a Greek friend to explain it beforehand to your children. Do some research yourself, so that all of you can properly appreciate the pageantry that will unfold during the formal church ceremony.

✦ *Your child might be invited by someone of an Asian culture, a Korean classmate, for example, to a family New Year's Day celebration* (a date fixed according to the lunar calendar, changing every year). Your child will probably be expected to arrive at ten in the morning, and be picked up at noon. Explain that upon arriving at his classmate's home, he should immediately find his host's parents and introduce himself. "How do you do, my name is Michael Jones. Happy New Year to you." He will undoubtedly be served a delicious brunch, with rice cake soup as a first course. He will be given a spoon instead of chopsticks to cope with his food, and if he doesn't like the inevitably served tea, he shouldn't say so. He can just avoid it without commenting. The most important thing for him to remember as a guest is not to roughhouse or be noisy on this dignified occasion.

In our diversified society a young person should realize that someone else's rites of passage and religious customs closely parallel his own. A child's sensitivity to cross-cultural differences doesn't need to be forced. It can grow quite naturally in a child's mind. It's like being a spectator at a play. Some children are enthralled by what takes place on stage. They usually have been given a hint of what to expect and have been instructed to enjoy the magic unfolding before them.

Honoring Others' Holiday Gift Traditions

Each country has its holiday time of exchanging gifts, and many of the customs revolve around children. (One exception: the Japanese December ritual of businesspeople's gifts, called *Oseibo*.) Jewish children often receive a gift for each of the eight days of *Hanukkah,* the "Festival of Lights." African-American children often receive gifts during the six days of the *Kwanzaa* cultural festival, celebrating the African harvest, which occurs close to Christmas.

It's a gift of kindness for adults to teach children to give their friends or others warm greetings and/or gifts on these special occasions, to say "Happy Hanukkah," for example, to a Jewish friend or "Happy Kwanzaa" to an African-American classmate. It's a considerate way for one child to acknowledge and pay honor to another's important cultural and religious traditions.

Your Child Makes His or Her Own Holiday Gift List

You can teach a child to be giving by involving him in composing a list of people who should receive some kind of gift from him for whatever holidays your family or his friends like to celebrate. Some parents mistakenly feel that since they automatically take care of all the family gifts for relatives and close friends, the children do not have to be involved.

It's important that they do become involved, because their gifts mean so much to the recipients, and if they grow up accustomed to being gift-givers, they will spread a lot of cheer and become more appreciative themselves of the efforts of others. (They now know how much thinking, planning, wrapping, mailing logistics, and general effort has gone into those presents.) Possible kinds of candidates for your child's list:

Mommy. Daddy. Brothers and sisters. The habitual sitter. Grandparents. Aunts and uncles. The cleaning lady. The pastor of your church or the Sunday school teacher. The pediatrician and nurse (if your child has been in their care a great deal this past year). The teacher(s). The music or dance teacher. The team coach. The special education teacher. (Don't forget the family pets.) And friends!

I know one child who annually gives a prettily wrapped Christmas tree ornament she selects to each of her special "friends" outside the family, and another who wraps up a gingerbread man for each of his friends. Another buys inexpensive little Asian baskets each year, decorates them, and fills them with candies like M&M's and multicolored sour balls. Even the most blasé adult is touched when presented with a gift made for him by a child.

Holiday Gift Observances with a Personal Touch

Schools do a good job in helping students make holiday presents for their parents and siblings. Parents might suggest that their children enlarge the scope of the gifts they make to include some of their good friends. And also some good causes, such as foster homes, shelters, etc.

For example, you might suggest to your artistic niece what a fantastic gift she could make for everyone in the family if she did a special little drawing for each of them. "If you start now, you could easily have them finished by the holidays."

When the child asks why would they want her drawings, her aunt could point out that it would please everyone who loves her, because it would be an "original work of art," and something "really from her."

Her aunt might further enhance the gifts by promising to provide some inexpensive cardboard frames for the drawings. "You can sign your name as the artist and date each one, just like a real artist."

For children who can't draw or paint, there are other options.

For example, a child might be:

+ *A good baker,* who can produce a package of goodies for each relative and friend.

+ *A talented musician,* who can perform or compose: An aspiring high school rock musician might make a cassette of his own music, using ordinary taping equipment. At the beginning of the tape he could announce his own name, the name of his composition, and the names of any fellow musicians who might be recording with him. At the end he would sign off with a hearty "Merry Christmas" or "Happy Hanukkah" or "Happy New Year."

+ *An accomplished poet,* who can compose anything from an amusing six-line limerick to a short poem celebrating the holidays: People love receiving a gift of poetry. Have your child sign his or her name and date on the poem and gift-wrap it, even if it's written on a piece of bond paper. (If an older sibling has desktop publishing capabilities on his or her computer, the poem could be illustrated with holiday motifs, to great effect.)

+ *A builder or sculptor,* who constructs something that shows the child's talent with blocks, balsa wood, clay, or some other material: He or she might make a portrait sculpture, building, house, bridge, or any kind of fabrication or rendering. The accompanying gift card would prove the pride of authorship: "I made this just for you, Dad." (That gift just might reside forever on top of his father's desk.) The "object" a child makes can be used as a paperweight or an ornament to hang on a doorknob, a Christmas tree, or a bedpost. One year I kept our eight-year-old daughter's Christmas gift for more than a year in our bedroom. It was a plaster cast of a large blue foot with bright red toenails. It looked as though it had been hacked off some monster's leg, but we loved it, because our daughter had made it.

Children can use their imaginations to make their own gifts, provided an adult has taught them beforehand that the holidays are meant *to bring pleasure to someone else.* (How far would you say we have distanced ourselves from that original meaning?)

The Final Rite of Passage: Your Child Faces Death and Mourning

A proper observance of grief at a time of mourning can help a child gain a perspective on life. It can strengthen him *inside*. He suddenly realizes it's all right to feel things deeply, even if he doesn't understand what has happened. I remember so well young Caroline Kennedy and John at the time of their father's assassination—with what must have seemed like hundreds of shadowy, silent figures milling around them. Their home—the White House—was draped in black, their father was lying still in a flag-draped box in the East Room, with four military guards standing at attention around the catafalque. The children were shepherded about, mostly out of sight, by their sad-faced mother and grandmother. They were quiet, uncomprehending of why everyone was so sad, but sensing nonetheless the grief that permeated the White House walls. A little boy or girl does not have to be a Kennedy child in the White House to feel the same inexplicable sadness. It is a feeling shared by any happy young person whose life is changed forever by the death of a loved one.

The acknowledgment of this final rite of passage in a person's life teaches a child that kindness is the most important component of survival. Everyone around him is supportive and kind to his parents or other relatives. He can become part of that circle of comfort himself. He realizes that the people who are hugging him wordlessly and squeezing his hand are trying to make him feel better, but he concludes his presence is probably making them feel better.

When a death occurs in the family of a friend of your child's, try to help him or her express feelings to the friend. There may be no words that he can summon, so, if he is four years old, give him some simple phrases he can say to his friend or the friend's surviving parent:

"My mommy and daddy and I are very sorry that your mommy has died."

If you and your child's friend's family are religious, it's very easy, because you can give spiritual comfort, even on a child's level:

"I'm very sorry, Maria, that your mommy has died, but she's up in heaven and will be looking down on you."

"Your daddy was so nice, Dick, and he doesn't have to suffer anymore, now that he's up in heaven with the angels," and so on.

Every child is born with some basic seeds of sympathy, but they need nurturing and careful cultivation for them to grow into full-blown sympathy.

"Why is it so bad that Jimmy's brother died, Daddy?"

"Because, for one thing, he won't see him again in this life. He'll miss his brother terribly. Tell Jimmy you're terribly sad for him. Tell him that after the funeral, in time, you guys will do some really fun things together."

When someone like a grandfather dies, a child can console the widow. Some short visits to the grieving woman can be the best possible therapy:

"Hi, Gramma! How are you doing today? That's good. I brought you a flower from your yard."

The older the child, the more capable he should be of writing condolence letters. It's important that he go on the record with a note to convey his sorrow over his friend's loss, right away, but he might also:

✦ Try to see his friend at his home, and understand if it will take a few days before he can do so, because of the funeral arrangements and confusion in the house. Even if he is not admitted to the house, he can have someone who answers the door convey to his friend that he came by "to cheer him up a little bit." Just knowing he did that *will* cheer up his friend, who is probably lost in a sea of grown-ups in the house.

✦ Other options:

   ✔ Have him bring his friend a little present, like a new video game—or some food for the house, on his parents' behalf.

   ✔ Arrange to have his friend come over to be with him the first weekend he is able to—for a sleepover, a Saturday game of ball in the park, an ice-hockey game, renting an exciting movie and making popcorn, and the like. Keep the child busy, not just at first, but keep on remembering him—on his birthdays, special holidays, etc.

✔ Teach your own child that there will be times when his friend will want to talk about his mom, and other times not. He should follow his friend's lead on this, because the desire to talk about the death will probably be unpredictable.

✔ Have your child offer to "hang out" with him any time, anyplace, when he's feeling blue.

It's difficult for a new widow or widower to part with the child for sleepovers soon after the death of her or his spouse, but it's good for the child to realize that there is a normal life out there for him again. I remember a friend of ours who had just lost his wife and who came over to our apartment at three in the morning, in his pajamas, to pick up his daughter, because he was too lonely at home without her. His daughter, all of six, was very touched by that and made a heartbreaking statement as she left us to go home: "You see, I have to take care of my daddy now. It's very important."

A compassionate family or single parent wisely looks at someone else's tragedy in a holistic sense—giving comfort to everyone, not just one member of the family.

PART III

When Kindness Matters Most

THE FAMILY BREAKS UP,

REGROUPS, AND

MOVES AHEAD

What a glorious picture on the family Christmas card: the hand-some, beaming parents; their attractive children holding their favorite stuffed toys—or perhaps one of them has an arm around the family Lab, who's wearing a Santa hat. They look healthy, happy, optimistic, bouncy, like an ad for a breakfast cereal or per-haps even like a frame from the old *Brady Bunch* TV show.

Along comes the next Christmas, and, curiously, there is no card from that family. The mantelpiece looks forlorn without it. It was always the biggest and brightest family photograph card. Fate threw a rock at the image of that perfect, smiling group of people and shattered it. Perhaps fate arrived as a parent who died. Perhaps fate came in the guise of discord and divorce. In whatever form it came, that family unit was blown apart. The comfort and security of "the way things used to be" are no more.

The battle now is but beginning for the survivors, and if ever a sum-moning of kindness was needed, it is now. Kindness for the ones who are left behind after a death seems obvious, but our society is not that automatic in its reactions today. Kindness often doesn't last too long after the funeral. We are a busy culture, and we excuse our lapses in good resolves by reciting the many demands on our own time. An extra measure of kindness for a mother left alone seems a given, but we forget so quickly. And a lack of kindness for a man or woman who has been deserted by a spouse for another person is devastating to the loser! Momentarily we feel great compassion for this person, but with passing time, compassion often turns into impatience.

As a widow friend of mine phrased it, "My friends' patience with me didn't last long. Pretty quickly, their slow, comforting refrain changed to an exasperated 'Get on with your life, girl!' So you know what? I got on with my life! Best thing that ever happened to me."

You can't put a bandage on the hurt caused by the breakup of a family, but at least when friends offer their help, one little drop of kindness can help soothe serious pain. *And the kindness of those left—* the children to a parent, a parent to the children—*becomes the most vital factor in their mutual recovery from the crisis.*

Someone's Gone . . .

Wow! Changes, drama, tragedy, rage, loss of equilibrium, confusion, fear of the future—children who have lost a parent through death or divorce feel those emotions passing right through their parents' bodies into their own, engulfing them.

It's suddenly so hard to fathom what's happening in the house. Where has their familiar routine gone, why is the cast of characters that's always there suddenly changing? They may now often feel as though they're riding on a whirligig, being tossed around at high speed, beyond their control, against their will. They need someone to get them off that whirligig, hold them and tell them that they're grounded, safe—and that the dizziness will go away. They may *look* quiet and sober, but they may be in deep trouble.

A parent in a child's life has gone away, and with it perhaps the security of living in the same home, going to the same school, belonging to the same teams and groups, taking the same lessons in music or ice hockey or whatever they love to do. The parent who is still with them may no longer be with them all that much. If their mother has to take a more demanding job in order to earn extra income, or go to school in order to get that better job, if she is now outside the home as much as inside it, their world will be vastly different.

When a parent leaves the house, because of death or divorce, a child usually doesn't care about the *reason* for the departure. The child cares about the *fact* that someone is now gone from the house who used to be there, who used to be part of his life, and who left without his understanding why. "Daddy's gone," or "Mommy's gone," spoken by a child, is a heartbreaking phrase.

There's anger. Children suffer from anger at all ages when a father leaves (and when a mother leaves, too, of course). When a parent dies or leaves a spouse, the child says to himself:

"Why *me?* What have I done to make my mother [or father] die [or leave]? Why didn't it happen to Anne and Lizzie, my best friends in school? Did I deserve this to happen? Am I being punished for having been bad? Am I the reason he [or she] is no longer here?"

When a parent dies, or moves out and leaves children behind in a divorce, the child may feel guilty, then depressed, then angry at the parent who left and thereby changed his life so suddenly and so traumatically—or even, in the case of a divorce, angry at the parent left behind to care for him, whom he may unfairly blame for the split. In his small world, he's "the only one" who's ever had anything so bad happen to him.

Of course, this loss *does* happen to other kids in the class, but at the moment, a child's concentration on the self is too strong to be comforted by having it pointed out that others have experienced it, too.

Everyone calls up the widow—or the divorcing woman whose husband has left her for someone else—to commiserate. "You're going to get through this, Betty, we're all here for you." There are always so many people around consoling the adults that the kids sometimes get lost in the shuffle.

How about making some calls to the children in that household? They're suffering, too. A call from a friend of his parents to twelve-year-old Anthony could help him immeasurably with his anger and his grief. "Hey, Anthony, you're a strong guy, and we all know you're going to help your mom, because she needs you so much now. You're the man of the house and you can do it. You've got the ability, and you'll keep your cool and help everyone, and things will go just fine. Remember to call me when things get too tough, or when you could use a little advice—*do you promise?*"

When an adult makes a call like that or comes to pay a visit to a child at a vulnerable moment in his life, the child usually never forgets it. The comforting words become written in stone in his mind, and the child, when he himself is an adult, may very possibly be motivated to help out another young person in distress.

After a death or divorce, the widow or former wife needs *more* than emotional support. This is no time for sitting on hands—or wringing them either, for that matter. The spouse left alone has many things with which to cope, plans to make, a set of lives to reorganize, and a multitude of matters to learn about that she probably never thought she'd have to face. She needs emotional bolstering, but she needs good professional advice almost more.

A Woman Who Is Newly Alone Would Be Wise to

+ *Put her child (children) as her first priority in her heart and her mind.* This will help in her own healing, because when something like this happens, the first, usual reaction is to concentrate on her own overwhelming problems. It's natural for a woman in these circumstances to feel sorry for herself. But if she feels too sorry for herself, she won't have anything left to give others, including her children. When she redirects this focus, and forces herself to think about something other than her own dilemma, it will give great comfort to her child. She is proving her love and devotion for him, and he knows that even with his father gone, he's not alone. Her actions directed toward her child will serve as a great healing therapy for her, too.

+ *Get her finances in order, after learning what they are.* Her *first* order of importance is to get professional help in order to understand exactly what her assets are and how to manage her estate, no matter how small.

    "When Dad's gone" she is going to find that financing the lifestyle she and her children previously enjoyed may well be impossible. She may have to sell the house or apartment. Whatever it takes, she should act upon the advice of the best possible lawyer and accountants she can find. Then comes a strict budget, which probably will entail a major decrease in her standard of living. (After decades observing women who have had to go to work for the first time or who have seen their standard of living change after the loss of a husband, I must conclude that American women are wonderfully strong, resilient, and tough when they have to be.)

+ *Make sure that her child's education is taken care of* before any other expenses are assumed.

✦ *Mobilize her family and friends to help her dispel her children's anger or depression over the loss of their father through death or divorce.* She sees to it that there are adult male figures in the house as often as possible. Even a very young child benefits from "seeing male mentors around the house," as one young divorcee with two boys expressed it. She was an inspiration in the way she maneuvered her brothers, cousins, and her sons' paternal grandfather to be around as much as possible. She would buy three tickets to a professional soccer match (the sport her sons most loved), then invite her brother over "for a heart-to-heart brother-sister talk" for lunch on a Saturday. After serving him a good meal she would suddenly have "other plans," put the three tickets into her brother's hand, and ask him to take the two boys to the soccer match. It gave her some free time to do chores, but she primarily wanted her brother to take the boys alone because "they needed to spend some time at a sporting event in the company of a surrogate dad. They needed good masculine bonding, and in my brother, they got the best kind there is." Eventually, her brother got the idea and began planning such expeditions with the boys on his own.

She was a kind mom to realize her sons needed some "between us men" time, but her brother was kind to give up time with his own family and spend it with his sister's children instead.

GIRLS NEED FATHERS, TOO

When a woman raises a daughter after the death or divorce of her husband, her growing daughter usually misses her father with a kind of desperation. "Mom" is such a center, "forever there" kind of influence in her life. A daughter tends to idealize the one she saw much less of: her father. She tends to remember him as someone who let her be more free, who was fun, and who wasn't the major dispenser of discipline in the house, because her mother was. When her dad is completely removed from her life, along with feeling grief, she often feels she has lost a strong, effective friend—someone who can influence her mother on her behalf, someone who is on *her* side, not her mother's.

It's a kind mom who realizes this and who tries hard to be sympathetic to the emotional loss of the man in the house in her daughter's eyes, as well as her son's. It's a wise mom who gets her children out of the house and into the action—where there are other families with fathers present—such as sports activities on weekends, popular movies ("Genny, are you and Eric taking your kids to see that new film at the Cineplex this weekend? Would you mind if I brought the kids and joined you?"), civic events ("Mac, be a good brother, will you, and allow my kids to come with your family to the fireworks?"), and the like. In other words, if your family and friends don't remember how much your child or children need some "family" time, give them a gentle nudge every so often.

SOME HELPFUL TIPS FOR WIDOWS AND DIVORCEES

+ *Always pay for yourself and your children when it's a question of tickets and meals* in shared activities with other families. People's kindness will be stretched too far if you don't pay your share of the costs.

+ Remember, too, Mom, in your rightful desire to have a man around the house for your kids, don't put up with something inferior. Your children are much too smart to be able to accept and enjoy your having a man around all the time who is patently not up to your standards. It just doesn't work.

+ Plan your vacations to go where other families congregate— places where people fish, sail, and the like. If you can afford it, try taking the kids to a ski resort over the winter break, even if you don't ski yourself. With a few lessons, little ones can become very proficient at the sport. In a family resort you'll meet other families whose kind fathers and mothers, knowing you are alone, or don't ski, will see to it that your kids get down the mountain along with their children.

+ Above all, never get depressed about doing the job of child-raising alone. Think of the hundreds and thousands of suddenly single men and women who have brought up successful, wonderful people. Those children will say, yes, they missed not having two parents, but they will also say, "Look, I'm me. I got along very well with just one parent. I think I turned out pretty darned good—and other people say that, too!"

The Kids Learn How to Talk About What's Happened

The family has been hit with terrible news. A parent has died—the worst news of all. Or there is going to be a divorce—the second worst kind of news. Someone has to prepare the children in the family on how to handle this subject out in public—at school, at church, at sports. The children must be warned that for a while, mercifully just for a while, they will be objects of curiosity and conjecture, and that there might be unwelcome, impertinent questions asked of them, or tasteless comments made to them. People simply don't know how to handle grief. Most can handle the pain of a burn, but not the pain of an intense emotional loss.

WHEN A PARENT HAS DIED

When this happens, the school should be notified at once, and, even though the student might be absent for a few days—mourning his or her parent at home with family members and friends—the child's teacher should also inform the class right away of the news. No one wants a situation where, when the child returns to classes, he is asked, "Hey, Martie, where ya been?"

"Home."

"Why?"

"My mom died."

The teacher might say, in preparing her class to be kind and welcoming to their peer on her return to school, "It's fine to come up to Dottie separately, quietly, and tell her you're really sorry about her mom. Don't make a big issue of it. Just give her a hug; you don't have to say a lot of things. If you're a good friend, take her hand and squeeze it. Words may be hard to come by. If you're just a classmate, not a close friend, privately welcome her back to class: 'We're glad you're back.' She will feel your sympathy and support in the expression on your face. Don't bring up the sad news every time you see her. Make your sympathy statement once and then spend the rest of your time devising ways to cheer her up and make her feel better."

It's a kindness to a child to prepare him for all the types of questions he will be facing—rude, blunt, and insensitive though they may be. No one wants to offend or hurt someone who has suffered a loss, but children are born curious. It's one of their charms. A child may offend simply because he doesn't know what else to do or say. (I'm a perfect example of an overly emotional person who always handles consoling someone badly; the nuns at Duchesne Convent became so accustomed to my dramatic gestures and stricken, tearstained face—even for a schoolmate I hardly knew who had lost a member of the family—that they politely restrained me from going near any grieving student until some time had passed.)

If a child to whom you are close has suffered a great loss in his or her life, warn him that his classmates are going to feel terribly awkward at first when they're with him. Even some teachers will feel uncomfortable with their own emotions, so a young student—the one who lost someone in his family—can be heroically kind by making everyone around him feel better. When he first appears in the classroom, if there's a long, agonizing silence greeting him, he might say something like, "I feel very bad that my dad has gone from us. It's very hard. My mom and I still feel he is with us, though." If you have to rehearse this kind of scenario with a child to whom you are close before he or she returns to school—after the funeral services—don't be ashamed of it. Every young person, even a senior in high school, at a time like this needs every bit of help he can get.

Children need the kind of simple words you can supply to know what to say to their classmates, family, friends, including the school bus driver and the pizza delivery person. Teach the children you are close to some phrases that they feel comfortable with, and, believe me, they will use the ideas in their own lingo and be grateful to you for having taught them how to do it.

Children of a Widowed Parent

A child whose parent has died clearly has some different needs from a child whose parents are divorcing. Primarily, the surviving parent, relatives, and friends need to be sensitive to the child's need to memorialize and remain true to the thoughts about the departed parent.

Helpful kindnesses might include:

+ encouraging the child to talk about the deceased parent and to share his or her special memories

+ placing a child's favorite photo (or photos) in a frame in his bedroom

+ observing the memory of the late parent with love and respect on that parent's *birthday*; it usually is a happier occasion to celebrate the departed parent's entry into life itself on a birthday than it is to observe the anniversary of the death

+ joining the child in a visit to the burial plot of the parent, if the child wishes to do so, once or twice a year, to leave flowers and, if the child is so disposed, to say a silent prayer together

Always invite the deceased's *own* parents (the child's grandparents) to join in this special celebration

In the beginning of a remarriage after the death of a parent, a bereaved child should always be encouraged to talk freely about memories of his departed parent within his new family (talking it out is necessary for a child to heal).

Children of Divorce

Wouldn't it be a marvelous utopia if there were no divorces because parents stayed happily married forever? Wouldn't it be great if children never heard adults fighting; if one spouse never moved out on the other in an enormous huff; if there were no slammed doors, raised voices saying nasty things never before uttered, exasperated banging of pots and pans in the kitchen, and fast escapes with screeching car tires in the driveway? Wouldn't it be wonderful if there were no long periods of silence and bitter sulking competitions between two parents? Wouldn't it be nice for the children if there were no openly aired battles on the subject of alimony and child support? Wouldn't it be pleasant never to hear vocalized disagreements such as, "I'll keep this house" . . . "Over my dead body will you ever get this house."

Life isn't fair when children are the center of this disruption.

PARENTS FACE UP TO THEIR CHILDREN AT THE TIME OF DIVORCE

✦ *Parents have a real job to do in calming down and explaining their split* in a sensitive manner to their children, making certain the young ones do not feel responsible in any way for the divorce or for any of the unpleasantness leading up to it. They must be made to understand that this change in the family is of the parents' making, *not the children's.* Both parents should make an effort to sit down at a quiet time at home and tell their children together, using a tone of dignity and reassurance, "We are going to see to it that your lives will change as little as possible." (Even though things will be very different, it's important to explain what "divorce" means and make them as comfortable as possible with it.)

✦ *The children will want to know who is going to live where, with whom.* "Where will you be living, Dad? Can I go over to your house at night when you come home? Can I bring Shep [the dog]?"

If the father will be living in another part of the country, the reassurances must be even quicker and stronger. "But how often will I see you? When? Will you come next week? How long will you stay? When you come, will you stay with us? Why not?" and on and on.

Kids are smart. You can't buy their peace of mind. They want proof of when and how often they'll be seeing the parent who is leaving them. They want the details—and concrete promises. How withering it is to their emotions when those promises aren't kept!

✦ *When the children, greatly troubled by the divorce,* ask if their parents ever loved one another, the answer should be, "Yes, of course. We're not in love now, but we *respect* one another, and have a really big, important interest in common: you children. *You* are much more important than our love for one another ever was. Even if we will no longer be living together, you belong to both of us, and each of us will *always* love you just as much as when we were together."

✦ It's terrible when a parent takes a child aside during this traumatic period to seek solace from the child by blaming the other spouse, as in this scenario:

"I want you to know that your mother and I are getting this divorce because she doesn't love me, she's nasty to me, and I can't take it any longer. This divorce is her fault, not mine."

It's horrible, however true it may be, when a mother takes her child aside after the father moves out and blames him completely: "He's leaving me flat—for a cheap woman he thinks he's fallen in love with. He's deserting you, his child, just as much as he's deserting me."

✦ It's only kindness to make the children understand that formerly their parents *did* have great times together, and that once upon a time they were in love. Children need to know that, so that their views of marriage won't be any more warped than necessary. It's very sad for a child to think there was always hate in the household, that the angry accusations they've heard behind closed doors were always present.

✦ It's a kindness to speak optimistically of the future. It will cheer up the children. "Your mother and I will work to be happy in our own new lives and so will you be in yours. We'll make sure that whether you're with me or your mother, you'll be safe and having a good time. You're our number-one priority, don't ever forget that."

And you, parents, remember you said those words to your children. These are sacred promises—promises made to children, even at a time of divorce, are among the most sacred of all.

The child may be in a class where, by eighth grade, nearly every student has parents who are or have been separated or divorced. Someone who loves this child should come and help arbitrate what is going to be done with him during the divorce proceedings. In the flurry of lawyers and telephone calls, who will be looking after the child? A friend of both parents, someone who is rational and trustworthy in the child's eyes, should take him as a house guest. They can have long chats, because normally no one else around is being rational or cool-headed. Regardless of his age, the child needs reassurance that this is not the end of the world. He should not be ashamed of it, nor should he lie about what has happened in the family. He should be matter-of-fact about it and give just the very basic information to people. "My parents are separating [divorcing]. I'm going to be living with my mother now, and spending weekends with my dad."

Taking Sides—or Not

+ A divorcing or divorced couple's friends should resist gossiping about and criticizing the new spouse to the other spouse's face or behind his back. Friendship entails acceptance of the new arrangement and the promise not to make comparisons such as "Jim's new wife has no taste at all; their apartment is so tacky!"

+ Divorced spouses should not criticize one another to mutual friends either. As a sensible divorced friend of mine once remarked, "I'm already unhappy, and when my only conversations with friends consist of bitching about my ex, no one is exactly craving my company. I've discovered no one's interested in my whinings. Marital discord doesn't make your friends sympathetic, only nervous and finally bored."

+ In a divorce, one spouse is usually more harshly treated than the other. Regardless of your feelings of liking one more than the other, kindness decrees that you quietly support the one who is left humiliated and deserted and that you refuse to listen to the departed spouse's accusations or criticisms against his or her ex.

+ Children, of course, don't like to take sides in their parents' fights. And they should never be forced to. They are not pawns, only victims in this situation. When the parent of a child tries to involve him against the other parent, it is not only unkind, it is morally reprehensible.

✦ The bickering, disclosures of hatred between the parents, threats of revenge, and disruption of the household absolutely pulverize the emotions of the kids in that house. Therefore, a continuous exercise in self-control by the adults is called for—for the sake of the children. This is the true measure of a man's (or woman's) character. Good or bad, character hangs out on the clothesline at a time like this, for everyone to see.

DON'T CRITICIZE YOUR EX-SPOUSE IN FRONT OF YOUR CHILDREN

If you are divorcing and consider your ex-spouse to be an evil witch or a nasty manipulator, remember that your children don't deserve the discomfort of having those opinions expressed. One woman I know makes all her friends think she's a martyred saint, because she vows she "never ever says bad things *to them* about their father." What she does instead is berate him constantly to all her friends on the telephone, making certain the children are nearby, so they can accidentally overhear the acrimonious accusations.

✦ A divorced man I know went around the house muttering diatribes under his breath against his former wife whenever his daughter appeared for a weekend visit. He "had to let it out," he explained, but he honestly thought she couldn't hear his mutterings, since he talked a lot to himself anyway. His daughter was able to decipher every word, and the hatred in her father's heart for her mother cut deep and hard inside her. Adults become so obsessed with their own feelings, they are sometimes oblivious to what is going on in the minds of the young and innocent.

When the Children's Father Is a No-Show at Joint Custody Time

There probably isn't any disagreement over the fact that a divorced father (or mother, for that matter) who shares joint custody and who reneges on the weekend or vacation visits with the children is a wretched human being. The child's disappointment over this abandoning behavior can be monumental. "Daddy didn't come for me? It's Saturday morning, isn't it?"

The young one thinks he's at fault, not the parent. A divorced mother should do her best not to criticize her ex-husband in front of the children when this happens; in fact, she should try all the harder to keep them loving and respecting their father. To me, any woman who manages to do this is a shining heroine. One such mother I know successfully explains her ex-husband's despicable behavior to her kids as the result of "his hurting about something. Something isn't going well in his life, he's low and depressed over it, and he doesn't want to bring that gloom into your lives. So, kids, come on, try to understand why he lets you down. He can't help it. Forgive him, have patience, and he'll feel better very soon and want to see you."

In the meantime, of course, this woman is fighting with every weapon in her arsenal—legal, psychological, and getting mutual friends to assist—to make this man assume his moral obligations to his children. The fact that he is still revered by his kids is a testimonial to the strength of his children's mother. There are great people in this world!

After the split, the parent remaining behind must:

+ *Attack head-on her child's anger at the other parent's departure* by assigning the blame *to no one* for the marriage breakup. A mother must communicate to her child that she does not blame herself or her ex-husband (at least in front of her child), and she does not allow the child even a moment of guilt for having been responsible for the divorce.

"Jen, it's not your fault there isn't the money to send you to camp this year!"

"Yes, it is, Mom, because if I had been nicer to Dad when you and he were fighting, he wouldn't have left us. I should have stuck up for him and not said he was so mean. Then he wouldn't have married that other person and he wouldn't have had to take our money for her and her little boy."

"Dad and my battles had nothing whatsoever to do with you. You are not responsible for his departure from this house, and I won't let you think that way. Your father's having a tough time financially, so he's not keeping anything from us. When we can afford it, you'll go back to camp. In the meantime, let's make the best of today. There are a lot of wonderful things to do this summer right here in town!"

+ If your college roommate, after giving birth to four children and being a loyal mother and corporate wife, sees her husband leave her for a twenty-two-year-old with a seventeen-inch waist and an implanted thirty-eight-inch chest, it might be very difficult to remain impartial and equally sympathetic to both husband and wife. Stay in a neutral place.

Don't make cutting comments to those children either when referring to their dad's new wife-to-be, entrancing though the thought may be. The new spouse is also the new stepparent of your best friend's children and you don't want to be party to more ill will in that family.

One friend of mine would speedily deflect the topic of conversation when one of her good friends would lash out at her former husband, who had left her for a "younger, thinner, brighter woman." One day she confided, in a quick moment of self-pity, "If that woman had had a number of children like me, she wouldn't be so young, thin, and bright today either," but most of the time, she would interrupt whoever was making a crack against her errant husband, saying, "Look, don't. The kids will hear that. They love their father very much." She didn't defend her husband or say he was a great guy. She simply stated the fact that their "children still love him and he's not to be knocked."

+ On behalf of the children and as a good friend of one of the parents, you should work to calm things down, rather than cause further deterioration in the relationships. Help temper the justified anger of your friend—the deserted wife (or deserted husband, as the case may be). Help that person to move onward, always *ahead* in a positive, affirmative sense. That is real kindness and it is a kindness to the children, too, because it cheers up the one left behind. Tell her, "Now you can do everything you've been yearning to do. You won't have anyone holding you back. You have all that wonderful energy.

Use it to explore new projects, try new directions. Don't waste it feeling bitter. Get up and *GO*. I'll be there to help—and so will everyone else who loves and respects you."

The kindest act a friend can do for another woman (or man) who has been clobbered in a divorce is to reinforce with all your heart your conviction that he or she is a person of substance, attractive, with much to give to the world as well as to the children—and, someday, another spouse as well.

No matter what one parent feels toward the other, divorce is a time in which the factor of kindness toward the kids is almost as important as it is at a time of death. In a way, the dissolution of a marriage *is* a time of death for the children involved.

A good friend of a family that has been coping with divorce and remarriage can start talking to a child whom he's known for a long time by starting with, "Hey, Sally, how are things going? Is everything okay?"

If Sally looks all choked up at this question, the friend should press further. "Anything I can do? Anything you want to tell me?" Sometimes a child just needs an adult to talk to. Sometimes the adult will hear the child say something that needs to be brought to the attention of his or her parent. Words may tumble out of the child's mouth about a feeling of abandonment by a parent that needs to be communicated to that parent.

Kindness among all the players on the stage of a loss in the family can make life bearable, heal wounds, and even result in the formation of helpful new relationships.

The Single Father Who Cherishes His Role— Rather Than Complaining

A widower or divorcé who has custody of his children has a major opportunity to be not just a good parent but an outstanding one. One of the finest volunteers at an abused women's shelter is a young woman who was raised by her widower father. She spends her time "working on the heads" of the abused women who are repeaters and who seem to live only to go back for more of the same treatment. She tells them to wake up, that their men are not normal, that they do not have to accept this life of subjugation and violence. She tells them stories of her own gentle, caring parent's life, and it comforts them. Ginny keeps exhorting the women in the shelter, "Don't accept less. Get out and take care of yourself and your children before you settle for less. Do it alone, if you have to."

A single man is not "the norm" as a parent, so he is sometimes overscrutinized and unfairly criticized. If he works in a regular business, he has the added burden of not being around during the day—an important time for young children, who are attending their first schools and struggling through life with feelings of confusion. "Why am I the only one in this class who lives with a father, instead of a mother?"

The father, in this case, is charged with the responsibility of ensuring good, open communication with his child or children. He's "it." While it's more common for a woman to become the major nurturer of her children as they grow out of babyhood, a father who is the primary caregiver must look upon this period of intimacy as a goal for himself, too. There are daily family talks to have with the children, even when he's away on business—often on the telephone, sometimes via e-mail. Weekends should belong to his children, and if there's a girlfriend in the picture, ideally she is introduced to the family scene gradually and naturally, not abruptly. Demonstrations of affection between them should be muted, discussions of marriage kept silent in the beginning. It's wonderful when the children say to their father one day, "Gee, Dad, wouldn't it be great if you married Marianna?" Even if they tease their father, "Are you and Marianna going to get married, Dad?" it's a sign of acceptance. In the meantime, when he is very much a parent alone, it's his duty to:

+ make the children feel they are the most important thing in his whole life

+ make them realize that he is incredibly proud of them

+ make them aware he is following their progress in school, on

the playground, in ballet class, etc., every bit as closely as any
mother would

+ help them grow strong in character—at an early age—so that
they can resist drugs, alcohol, and tobacco at a time when
their peers consider those activities "the cool thing to do"

It certainly makes life easier if the single male parent has a sister,
cousin, aunt, or, best of all, the children's grandmother to act as a
surrogate mother to his children. Otherwise, he will just have to
learn how to teach his children manners (single fathers can do a
superb job of this, because they recognize the importance of manners out in the business world). A father alone may not be able to
sit with a sick child all day, so his only alternative is to be resource-
ful about arranging for good child care or temporary emergency
care of good quality. (One father I know takes a widow's two children with him and his children to his lake cottage every summer
for three weeks. They have become part of his family and close to
his children. In return for this she takes over when his children are
sick. Her number is on file at the school, so she is the one called if
one of his children becomes ill during the day.)

A father alone is a great mentor for his own sons, a role model with
the responsibility—as well as the possibilities—for turning those
boys into kind, caring men. He will have to show them how to be
considerate of the women in their lives. He should talk about that
subject when they reach their teens. When he hears them making
ribald, chauvinistic remarks, it's his cue to break in with, "I don't
want to hear you—EVER—talk like that." When they're watching a
TV sitcom and the husband in the sitcom unfairly ridicules his wife,
he should let his sons know what he feels about that. "I hope to
God that when you get married someday, you won't treat your wife
that way. No, it isn't funny. It's just gross. Guys, you ought to be able
to analyze what you see and hear in public for yourselves, and know
the difference between something that's funny and something
that's tasteless, mean, and degrading. Wise up!"

A young girl, by virtue of having been raised by her widowed or
divorced father, also has a special opportunity to have easy, caring
relationships with men and to love and respect them, thanks to her
single parent father's example. I will never forget the second toast

given by an attractive, successful young man on the occasion of his and his wife's tenth wedding anniversary, a dinner dance:

"I would like to raise a toast to my father-in-law," he said, with his arm around his wife's waist, "because he raised this wonderful, beautiful woman all alone, when her mother was gone. He is responsible for raising her to become the woman I always dreamed of spending my life with one day. He taught her how to love, how to respect, how to encourage, console, and assure everyone around her. All of these great qualities in my wife he taught her by his own example. So I salute you, father of my bride—and ask everyone else here to salute you, too. I thank you for the great job you did on this beautiful person standing by my side!"

When a Single Parent Starts Dating Again: Romance and Sex in Front of Children

Whether a child's parent disappears from his life because of death or through divorce, it's quite normal for that child to be jealous of anyone who may be trying to take the missing parent's place, particularly when the young one is present while the couple is engaged in the "lovey-dovey stuff," as one ten-year-old titled it. When a child catches sight of Mom being touched by another man or Dad kissing a woman other than Mom, you can almost see the hackles rise on that child.

One mother, after saying good-bye to her male visitor and asking her son what he thought of the show of affection the boy had accidentally witnessed, heard his entire one-syllable reaction, "UGH!" She had been hoping he would have reacted with pleasure that someone cared enough about her to kiss her good-bye affectionately. It was not to be. Her son, however, acted much more politely than another little boy who sicced his hostile dog on the man he found kissing his mother in the kitchen, or the nine-year-old girl who called 911 and reported an emergency in her house because "a man was killing her mother in the bedroom." (He was actually only kissing her, but it made for a great deal of excitement in the neighborhood!)

Whether it's a man paying attention to a child's mother or a woman acting romantically with the father, the child may unfairly resent that show of familiarity, which he considered the prerogative only of the parent who is no longer present. The parent should understand this and instruct his or her date to hold off on the "mushy, sexy stuff" until they have privacy, when young eyes and ears cannot witness their actions. Sex is confusing to children whose parents are courting, so they should be exposed to it as little as possible after their parents have divorced or after one has died. A child is quick to notice even a little kiss on the lips and to jump to conclusions about that gesture. The closer a child is to puberty and the more TV dramas he has witnessed, the more aware of and curious about his remaining parent's sex life he will be.

How different it was in my day. Kids were so innocent about sex. There was no TV to tell us how to start and what to do. My father told me with great amusement many years later that he had overheard me speak up in a group of girls who were having a Camp Fire Girls' meeting in our living room.

"Sex? I know what happens in sex," I boasted with considerable pride.

The other girls looked at me in awe. "*You do?* What happens?"

"Well, you see, it's like this. Remember how two Eskimos rub their noses together to show affection? Well, that's sex. That's it!" An expert had spoken.

In a single-parent household, when a person of the opposite sex becomes a fixture in the household, the parent should have a good conversation about it with the child. The child doesn't understand what is really going on. False ideas may have been festering in the recesses of his mind. This mother, for example, has a talk with her teenage daughter Elyse.

"Yes, I've become very fond of Guy, Elyse. I don't feel I have to hide that fact. You've got to know him pretty well, too, in the past months. I hope you agree he's a nice man, a real friend."

"Just why are you bringing him up, Mom?"

"Because I've grown very close to him. I'm more than just fond of him."

"How can you say that? He could never take Dad's place. He's not my father!"

At this point Elyse's mother explains that no one will ever take her father's place, that her father has a special section of her heart devoted to him alone. "Your father was unique, we both know that. Guy is different, but he's very helpful to me. I need someone like Guy to help me live my life better, to help me raise you, make the right decisions, and make sure that you're as happy and as protected as you can be."

"Will you be having sex with him?"

"Yes, we'll be married someday. Yes, we will be having sex."

"How can you let a man make love to you after Dad? How can you let him? It's disgusting!"

Keep on talking to her. Don't let anything interrupt this conversation. Even if she runs away to her room, chase her, find her, tell her it's important that she understand that this man is not taking her father's place. He's *taking another place in another compartment of her heart, her life.*

"You expect me, Mom, to treat him the same way as I did Dad?"

"I expect you to treat him with kindness for the simple reason that I have asked you to, that he helps me and makes me happy, and if you make him unhappy, you'll be hurting me terribly, that's all."

"Mom, I don't want you to have another man in this house. We've been doing fine, you and I. We don't need anyone else."

"I do take care of you, Elyse, and always will. But I need someone to take care of me, too."

Enumerate the many things Guy has done for you and your daughter, the way he has helped around the house, the kind things he has done for your friends, the fun you've had going to the movies together, and playing cards and surfing the Net together.

If your daughter suddenly asks if you two are going to be "slobbering all over each other all over the house, like they do in the movies," laugh and say *absolutely not.* And keep your promise. Keep your physical attraction for one another under constraints, away from her sight and ears. It will make your time together alone, in private, even more precious. In time, she will become accustomed to his presence and the gradual increase in his decision-making, his giving advice and support. When you are married your displays of affection will not hurt as much. In time he can show her fatherly affection that will be gratefully accepted. Until she is ready for that, he should be patient and wait for her trust. At a certain moment, she'll kiss him good-night on the cheek. At a certain moment, she'll welcome his arm around her and a hug when he returns from a trip. The key is to let the presence in the house of another person who is obviously beginning to take the place of the missing parent become a natural development.

If the child's parent does not marry the person who has moved into his or her life and their house, if the child's parent merely entertains a succession of lovers who are needed for sexual gratification, the child stands a good chance of "growing up thoroughly screwed up," to quote a friend who led a life just like that, and became "all screwed up, too," thanks to her mother. She finally escaped from the maternal influence by seeking comfort in drugs and alcohol—a sorry solution to her problems.

A child needs exposure to good role models in order to develop a sense of morality. Only his parents and the people who interact with them can provide the behavior to be emulated. For two decades now, we Americans have been bombarded with messages to keep ourselves *physically fit*. It would be a kindness, also a necessity, to give our children a little moral fitness training, too!

Kindness to Kids When a New Family Begins to Form

It's traumatic enough when children lose a parent to death or divorce, but there is usually a bank full of kindness, with deposits made by the people who care about them, for the children to draw upon at the time this loss occurs. People realize that there's suffering in that household. They want to help so they make themselves available. This isn't a time to be shy about offering—or accepting—help, it's a time to be aggressively forthright about it. When a new family forms, when parents remarry, and their new spouses' children come into the picture, there's often a serious need for many new deposits to be made by friends and relatives into that kindness bank. The parents are often absorbed by their own readjustment struggles, and the kids are usually undergoing a certain amount of depression over the newness of everything, and over the fact that any dreams they may have had about things returning "to normal," to the way it *used* to be, are now impossible. Friends and relatives should step forward to do what they can (and it can be a great deal!).

+ *Have some heart-to-heart conversations with each child of the person you're closest to.* Troubles will be voiced that need to be on the table and dealt with—things that seem very insignificant to the child's parent at that particular moment, in comparison to the other more serious problems with which he or she is coping. One seven-year-old I knew, Davie, was in a state of "the deep blues," as his busy mother referred to it. So I took him out for some buffalo wings, his latest food fad. He had a new stepbrother, but what upset him most, he confided, was that along with the stepbrother came an "awful dog," who took an instant dislike to his own miniature schnauzer, "Jebbie." His brother's much bigger dog tormented Jebbie, fought him, chased him, bit him, and drew blood on several occasions. Davie's stepbrother thought it was all very amusing. Things in the house were destroyed in the melee, and Davie's brother blamed it all on Davie and Jebbie. His mother, trying to keep her new husband and his child happy, sided with them. Davie was sinking deeper into gloom, because he felt everything had turned against him and "Mom doesn't have time for me when she comes home from work. She says she's going to be busy getting dinner on the table."

I called up the mother that night after the boys were in bed and said, "You owe me two pizzas and two apple juices, because that's what it took me to elicit some very important information from Davie."

I told her what Davie had told me, and she said she could—and would—rectify the situation quickly. Davie's mom had not realized how much the new dog had made her child's life miserable. "I had thought," she said, laughing, "that the adults were the ones who were supposed to need Prozac at a time like this. It never occurred to me that Jebbie would be the one who needed it most, with Davie a close second. Don't worry, no Prozac will be provided, but some more love, attention, and

support of Jebbie and his master will be immediately forthcoming."

✦ *To be a real friend of the kids in the newly forming family, remember:*

✔ Always have time to listen, leave the door open, and give the
young person your full attention whenever he or she asks—
or even if he or she doesn't ask but could be helped by you.

✔ Always keep their conversations with you in confidence,
unless it's a problem one of their parents *must* know about
and respond to—as when, for example, the child, your
friend, confesses to using drugs.

✔ Advise them to *have patience* in reaching a solution to their
problems. Remind them that what they consider today to be
of "major terribleness," as one of my godchildren calls it,
might not be so bad tomorrow. Therefore, they should
think before speaking or acting in reaction to their problem, and perhaps seek some counsel with you or another
close family friend.

✔ Build up their self-confidence. Each child might be blaming
himself for the death or divorce, or trouble with his or her
siblings and stepsiblings. A relative or friend can counter
this effectively, because he or she is not a parent, but a more
objective "outside source." A seriously depressed child
needs to see a therapist or counselor, of course. Tell the
child how proud you are of the way he handles himself in
school, of his rapport with his newly forming family. Congratulate him for being so kind to his biological mother or
father and stepparent, which bolsters the new family unit
and enables it to come into harmony and thrive. Bring out
his individual achievements, which may have been getting
lost in all the emotional turmoil another marriage brings.
"You know, Sam, we were all really proud of that article you
wrote for last week's *Central High Bugle.* You have a real jour-
nalistic talent. Ever thought of studying journalism in college?" In just such a conversation you can get a child
thinking about his future, and give him direction toward a
positive goal. It's something for him to think about at night

in bed, instead of just about sad things that have been going on in that house.

A friend is *invaluable* to a person who's been having a tough time, especially when that friend stops in the middle of his or her busy day and calls up the one who has been left behind. "Just thought I'd call to see if you guys would like to go to the miniature golf place tonight for a short while. I have a feeling the kids would enjoy it. You, too. How about it?"

When those kids who were taken to the miniature golf by their mom's friend are adults, maybe they will make some similar calls, offering help to lonely friends with children or just to lonely children by themselves. It's amazing what one telephone call or one e-mail message can do for the human spirit.

Before a Remarriage Takes Place: A Most Important Step

We all know that many remarriages fall on parlous times, but one excellent insurance to prevent this and get the new family off to a rock-solid start was described to me by a friend who was entering a remarriage and launched it successfully on this basis:

A dinner was held in a restaurant well away from any little ears that might be listening; the biological and about-to-be stepparents in the two families sat down together to break bread in a thoroughly civilized way. Their mission: to positively, affirmatively explain everything about themselves and their families that might help these newly forming families make a go of it and bring up the children successfully.

On the menu: an open discussion of their various children, who would be moving into new living arrangements and adjusting to new presences. Each parent explained each of the children truthfully. A divorced mother would have one perspective on her daughter, whereas her ex-husband would have quite another, and the ex-husband's new wife-to-be needed the information from both sides. The exchange of information was frank, with one goal in view: a *real* understanding of the children and their problems for all to see and process. Information tossed out on the table ranged from minor to very important problems concerning the six children of the two about-to-be-rearranged families, as seen in these examples of topics discussed:

+ Rick's obsession with his weight and the possibility he may be becoming anorexic.

+ Anne's totally unforgiving attitude toward her new step-mother, and what joint efforts might be undertaken by both families to make it less of a struggle for her.

+ John's trauma over not making the high school football team, when he thought he was a shoo-in.

+ Becky's resentment that the divorce means she won't be able to ride every weekend, for financial reasons.

+ Ginger's need to see a counselor, because the school has suggested it. This formerly all-A student did miserably on her college entrance exams.

+ The failure so far in curing Greg of his unbelievable sloppiness in his room or in any part of the house where he happens to be.

For the good of the child, it is very helpful if the biological parent does a thorough job of communicating each child's assets, failings, emotional history, talents, and potential—anything that might help the new spouse understand and be kinder to the child. Knowledge is a great bonder of people.

The communication should be two ways. Your new spouse also needs to be explained thoroughly to your children as much as they need to be explained to your new spouse. Explain to your children why you fell in love with this marvelous person and how happy he or she has made you. Talk about how your happiness will be spread around to everyone in the family. Extol your new spouse's achievements and fine spirit, *never* using the occasion, of course, to compare unfavorably or put down your ex-spouse to the children. And if your children don't want to hear about your new spouse, that's all right, too. *Just wait*—"cooling it," to use their language—until they want more information about this new person who has come into their lives.

The Stepfamily Becomes Successfully Organized: A Meeting of the Board

If both halves of the new couple bring children into their second marriage, it is urgent to set up some kind of continuing system for interfamily communication: a family forum where plans can be made and gripes can be aired calmly and without anger or high emotion. There are new and complex needs and feelings to be dealt with.

One solution that works for many families is to have regular family meetings, with everyone present. It can become a comforting tradition—democracy at work. It's a healthy way to make the family more cohesive, to vent complaints, to reach compromise between family members who have different viewpoints on important issues, and to make plans for the future. Plans can involve everything from heavy budget matters, to allocating TV time, chores, volunteer duties, or reaching agreements on family vacations and college plans. (In one family I know, the smallest child felt her cat's rights were being abrogated, and that was put on their meeting's agenda.)

Every member of the family should be present (even the baby, in her Portacrib). There must be a clear chain of command—the mom or dad (or even a grandparent, if it is a single-parent family living with grandparents) as "leader," or CEO. "Senior management" calls all the shots, but family board members should be ready, willing, and able to stand up for their individual rights. Someone must be a recording secretary, preferably taping the meeting and then getting help in transcribing as needed.

Calling the Meeting

It's best to hold such a board meeting every month or two, according to need. If you teach children this is how business works—in a democracy—they will have fun learning as the meeting progresses. Finding a time when all members can attend will be the toughest challenge of all. The corporate secretary (perhaps the oldest teenager in the family) notifies everyone by note a week in advance of the family board meeting of the date (when there isn't a sports event, practice, or rehearsal the children must attend—perhaps a Sunday evening?), the time (such as eight P.M.?), the place (such as the family room or kitchen?), and the agenda.

Some Rules Governing Procedure

Attendance is compulsory. No cutting out early or arriving late.

Attention to the proceedings is also compulsory. There will be no TVs watched, telephones answered, computer games played, magazines read, or tapes listened to while the meeting is in progress. It also means people listen to the speaker and don't interrupt whoever has the floor (the chairman decides who has the floor and when he or she has to stop to allow the meeting to move on). The chairman would be very wise to have special treats and refreshments on hand for meeting attendees.

An Agenda Is Followed

An agenda, containing input from each family member, is compiled—after individual consultations with participants—by the CEO and passed out a week or so before the meeting, so that everyone knows in advance what will be discussed. A sample agenda:

The budget

This part of the meeting concerns allowances, children's bills to be paid, and estimated projected costs of:

- ✔ a party at the house for friends
- ✔ clothes and shoes that parents will pay for

✔ frivolous clothes purchases to be paid for by the kids from allowances or after-school jobs, sports equipment that may have been paid for by parents or from allowances or after-school jobs, etc.

Particular complaints

✔ Dad complains about the mess in the garage, including exhortations to the worst family offender.

✔ Mom complains about the disgusting condition of the bathrooms of late and tells everyone to shape up.

✔ Jordie protests that David is always hitting him.

✔ David protests that Jordie is always hitting *him.*

✔ Mom says the neighbors complain about the boys' skateboarding.

Special requests

✔ Suzy, because of exams coming up, wants to change her daily chore for the next month, from setting the table for breakfast and dinner to weekly weeding and soaking the lawn and shrubs. Also on the agenda: the need to buy a new, more efficient garden hose.

✔ Joanie makes her bimonthly emotional plea for a dog.

✔ Donna asks urgently for quiet on the upstairs hall so she can study for exams.

✔ Sam begs for his own stereo system with earphones, so he won't keep getting jumped on for the loud music coming from his room.

✔ Mom demands that coats not be dropped on the hall floor; that the ice-maker be kept full, instead of left empty by the last person who uses it; and that bathtub rings be dealt with by each tub user—or else.

Accomplishments

This part of the meeting deals with the various members' accomplishments since the last meeting, if there have been any. It's important for senior management to assure that during a board meeting no one is permitted to belittle or disrespect anyone else for having opposing views. If there is violent disagreement on any one point (example: how late are the teen family members allowed to stay out on Saturdays?), the board should appoint a committee of at least three family members to investigate the viewpoints of the opposing sides and report back to senior management on what "other kids in our classes are allowed to do," so that a just decision can be reached.

I talked to an eleven-year-old whose parent and stepparent have run that family's successful lesson in democracy for five years.

"What did you learn about the corporate world in your meetings?" I asked him.

"Lots," he replied proudly. "I know all about how business works. There's a lot of arguing that goes on at a meeting, then Mom and Dad—excuse me, the CEO and the president—make all the decisions, and then try to persuade the board members that it was really they, not Mom and Dad, who decided it all."

The great thing about being able to vent one's complaints within the family in an open meeting is that an unfairness may be uncovered by the parents for the first time in this kind of situation. It may come out, for example, through the admissions of two of Jordie's siblings, that Jordie usually starts the fighting and biffs David more often than the reverse. It may come out through an older sister, when Joanie is momentarily out of the room, that she seems to be somewhat depressed lately, and maybe having a dog to love and take care of would cure her blues.

Certainly, each meeting provides the parents with the opportunity to put the record straight on how their orders "are being followed these days." The children can get a sense of their parents' priorities during the family conference. The family meeting often results in several wrongs being righted, and in spite of one young boy's observation of his parents making all the decisions and trying to make the children think the decisions are theirs, it's a great chance for children to learn their responsibilities and know what they're supposed to accomplish before the next meeting. In true corporate governance style, the CEO sets the date for the next meeting as the last bit of business on the agenda. When all members agree they understand what is expected of them before the next meeting, the CEO calls the meeting adjourned.

It can be very compelling when a child hears his stepfather say, "Let's get all our gripes out on the table at this meeting. You may think you're being treated unfairly, but I think I'm being treated unfairly, too. Let's talk it out, and perhaps resolve to be kinder to one another."

Some families will have success trying this idea, others won't. It's worth a try. The kids will enjoy the food and drink treats in any case, and maybe they will inch ahead in understanding how one learns to take orders in a democracy "for the common good." It's quite a victory when a child moves ahead from appreciating only those victories that concern him alone to the point where he starts sympathizing with others around him.

Settling into the New Family: Answering the Nitty-Gritty Questions

There are some lifestyle questions that a new stepparent would be wise to know how to answer, whether a stepchild comes to visit only on some weekends and vacations or to live permanently. It's upsetting to the child to have had one routine of meals, sleep, and play at home with one parent and quite another when he goes to visit or live in his other parent's house, where a new spouse rules the roost. The solution is good communication between the two households—even if it hurts.

I know one newly wed stepmother who sent her stepdaughter's mother a list of questions concerning the girl via e-mail, and received polite matter-of-fact answers immediately in return. Both women found it much easier to communicate by computer than face-to-face or by telephone. Less emotional for both.

Perhaps the first question to ask yourself is: *What will my stepchild call me?*

Some options:

+ If it's a baby or very young child whose mother died, you will be raising him or her. So "Mommy and Daddy" or "Mother and Father" is logical.

+ If the child's other biological parent is alive, you might try having the child address his own parent as Mother and Father and the stepparent as "Dad Joe" or "Mom Jane."

+ Sometimes it works when a child calls a stepparent by a pet nickname—"Ginger," "Racer," "Pug," etc.

+ Some parents have their stepchildren address them by their given names right from the start. (Personally, I don't like this trend, because I think when a young person calls a stepfather "Joe" or a stepmother "Barb" it shows a lack of respect and somehow makes discipline just a little bit harder.)

+ When a child stops referring to a stepparent in conversation or in introductions as "my stepmother" and begins to say "my mother," you know that this is a family where everyone has pulled together to make it work. When the "step" disappears from the daily vocabulary, the family circle has closed and the bond is firm.

Questions to Ask When a Young Child Enters a Newly Formed Family

+ Does he need help dressing himself? Laying out his clothes? Getting his schoolbag ready? Lunch box?

+ How much should I enter into his school life if he is to live or spend a lot of time with us? Should I join the PTA? Check his homework? Carpool with other parents?

+ Does he have any learning disabilities of which I must be aware, and is there anything I can do to help with this?

+ Should I visit his or her teachers right away or wait to be summoned for an interview?

+ Does he need help with his homework? How much—and what kind of—pressure should be brought to bear to get the homework done?

+ Will my dog or cat frighten or please him? Would having his own pet make him much happier?

+ What foods does he enjoy and what does he dislike? Is he allergic to anything?

+ Does he have any chronic health problems we should know about?

+ How much TV should he be allowed to watch and which programs—and when? Which ones are not allowed?

+ Do we eat together or do the children eat separately? Stepmothers complain across the board about this subject:

  ✔ Some women want the children to eat earlier so they can have some precious time alone with their husbands.

  ✔ Some women resent having to cook two meals. How nice of a husband to cook the second meal for his wife and himself. (Don't hold your breath.)

  ✔ Some couples know that for the good of the children, it's better to eat together as a family, no matter who's cooking what or how late the dinner is. This means the children's father and stepmother get high marks as parents.

+ Does he need new clothes? If he is in school, how much leeway does he have in picking his clothes, and how much do I have in exercising control over his purchases?

+ If he's a baby, do I introduce new stuffed animals as my welcome gift to him or will he feel more at home sleeping with his old favorites?

+ Will he accompany us to religious service? If he is very young, can he be depended upon or disciplined not to upset the other parishioners' attention to the services?

+ What are his needs at bedtime? Would I grow closer to him by supervising the bath or letting his biological father (or mother) do it? Should I read him a story at bedtime? Have a few minutes of play? Are prayers said—kneeling by the bed or in bed?

+ Is she afraid of the dark, and if so, what kind of night-light should we install?

+ Can we teach him not to come into our room at night when the door is closed?

+ Does he have a natural aptitude for sports or does he need to be encouraged? What are his favorite sports?

+ Does he have an artistic, musical, or other talent that should be developed with lessons?

+ Was he promised an allowance or raise in his allowance?

+ When he has to go to the doctor, should I take him instead of his biological parent? Will that cement our relationship or hurt it?

+ If he is very young, when should we start potty training and what should my role be?

+ Since he is in a new town or neighborhood, should I scout around immediately for playmates to bring over to our house to help him make friends?

+ Does he like to entertain classmates and friends at home?

+ How has he been disciplined in the past—and should we follow these guidelines?

When a Teenager Comes to Live with You

+ Will his sleeping quarters and desk afford him enough privacy?

+ Can I post rules about the use of the bathroom and make her obey them?

+ Will he accept the rule of no smoking in our house? Can I do something nice for him that would compensate for this strict rule?

+ Is her reading lamp good enough to help her study effectively? Does she have enough bookshelf space and storage area for her schoolwork as well as her tapes, videos, and CDs? How much help should I offer with her homework?

+ Can I talk him into eating healthier food than he is accustomed to? Can I correct his table manners?

+ Will she accept my offer to give her the house for occasional parties, provided there are no drugs or liquor on the premises and that an adult is upstairs (out of sight but definitely on the premises the entire time)? Will she agree to do a complete cleanup job after the party?

+ Is it better to forbid her smoking with her friends in our house and have them go elsewhere, or to permit her friends to smoke in our house but ask her not to?

+ Should I lend him my car on occasion, even if I think he drives too fast?

+ Can we afford to encourage her athletic activities, even if it entails the purchase or rental of special equipment, lessons, travel away for games, etc.?

+ Am I able to accept his constantly playing his music in the house, even if I hate it, provided he agrees to keep the sound down to a reasonable level?

+ Will she accept some gentle nudging on her manners, provided I carefully avoid making any comment on the absence of such training in her former life with her other parent?

+ Can I expect her to accompany us to church (temple, or mosque)?

- ✦ Should I motivate her to do volunteer work in the nonprofit sector of our community?

- ✦ Does my spouse handle the sex questions with my stepchild, or do I do it alone, or do we do it in tandem?

- ✦ Will I rein in my natural inclination to ask too much of this child? Will I be able to settle for lower expectations than I would like?

- ✦ Can we keep her on an allowance, as we do the other children, and encourage her to get a part-time job to give her more spending power?

- ✦ Will she accept our rules concerning telephone privileges and making excessive long-distance calls?

The more prepared you are for the visit or custody of your stepchild, the kinder stepparent you will be. You are making it much easier on the child, who probably arrives feeling disrupted by all that moving into someone else's home entails. By being kind to that child in establishing the rules of the house and the boundaries of discipline, you are teaching him or her to be kind back to you and to others.

I remember when one friend managed to emerge victorious and justified in a conflict with her new stepdaughter over excessive use of the stepmother's credit card. My friend was firm in dealing with what was really a serious infringement on her rights. "You're tough," I said admiringly. "You managed that conversation with great fortitude. Yet she obviously adores you."

"It would have hurt more to hold in what I felt was a reasonable concern," she said. "I would only have grown angrier and boiled over in an ugly way if I'd let it go. Now we both have had a civil talk and know where we stand. And if we continue to be open and respect one another's boundary lines, we'll get along just fine."

Some Quick Ways to Cool Conflicts in Stepfamilies

Too bad there is no lab where good chemical interactions in new marriages and steprelationships can be prescribed by wise heads and made up for the patients. The process usually takes careful planning, hard work, patience, compromise—and a healthy dose of self-control. One young single woman I knew who married a widower with five children astounded everyone with her mature, loving ways of unifying the family and motivating the children to start on the path to becoming very effective human beings. I suspected divine intervention, but when I asked her how she had performed this miracle, the answer came quickly. She had been asked this many times before.

"Whenever I wanted to say anything cross or critical to my husband or the children, whether justified or unjustified, I would abruptly leave the scene and go take a 'time-out.' I sought out a quiet spot, sat down alone, took some deep breaths, and swung my head back and forth from side to side a few times to relieve the tension in my neck. By the end of five minutes my time-out was over, and I was in charge of myself again. This was always a great source of amusement to the children, who wondered what crises had been averted by my sitting in silence and facing the wall, as I made them do when they were out of hand."

A new marriage actually provides the perfect opportunity to bury any negatives and turn all your energy toward carving out a fresh start with your new family. You can't remake the past, but you can certainly construct the future!

In a new marriage with stepchildren involved, it's hard to resist losing it when you're exhausted from dealing with someone else's child and coping with his or her unreasonable demands, just when you want to spend time alone with your new spouse. There's no justice in such a situation, because it seems as though one family member must give all the time, while other family members take all the time. Husband or wife may be saying silently, or openly, as the case may be, "Why do *I* always have to resolve the children's problems, particularly when they're not my children, they're yours?"

A working mother or father, returning home tired in the evening, may be totally unaware of how a rebellious child may have offended the baby-sitter or the parent who came home early from work. Husband and wife should discuss this openly and frankly. The couple should listen carefully to the report from the sitter or caregiver on the events of the day, because what's happening to their children in school, the way they play and interact with other children and the way they accept rules and regulations, should be a number-one concern to both parents.

Husband and wife need information, sympathy, and support from one another before they can give it effectively to the younger generation.

One creative, newly married stepfather put a stopwatch on the coffee table in the den and said to his wife, "Why don't we do it this way? You talk and complain for the first five minutes about your day at work and the antics of the children while I time you, then you time me while I complain for the next five minutes about my day and the children. Neither of us has to say, 'Are you listening? Do you hear what I'm saying?' We'll *really* listen to one another. Even if we don't have an immediate solution to the problem, sympathy soothes and heals."

The couple said this system worked. They are able to vent their gripes, calm their emotional storms, and earn proper sympathy from one another. If one of them is away on business, they have their session on the telephone. They have continued the custom now for several years, not every night, of course, but when either feels the need for it.

A child is a blessing, any child, but if you feel your new stepchild is anything but an affirmative part of your new life, remember that with your good heart, hard work, and intelligence, that child in time will probably become a great blessing. It's important to remember in any new marriage *not to feel sorry for yourself as a step-*

parent. Like having a bad cold, to be self-pitying is a lonely, unattractive condition. No one wants to be around you when you're hurting and showing it.

HARD WORK IS NEVER EASY, BUT A NEW FAMILY'S SUCCESS IS WORTH IT

A happy, successful new union of husband and wife with children and stepchildren is worth any effort that anyone contributes at any time.

The opportunities to show kindness to one's stepchildren are as important as feeding and clothing them. A stepparent's acceptance of this daunting challenge is a true test of character, because that stepparent may already have his hands full with his or her own children, plus trying to keep the new spouse happy and adjusting to that person's schedule, needs, and lifestyle. There may be added complications of trying to avert emotional and legal unpleasantness with the former spouse. Add to all of this stress the fact that the child may arrive in the stepparent's household badly spoiled, whiny, sullen, and undisciplined. Dealing with all of this and making a human being out of a petulant, sassy child is not fun and games for the stepparent, but the challenge is *to make the transformation fun and games* for the child.

What Kids Worry About in Stepfamilies

Children of divorced or widowed parents who remarry often say that the absolute rock-bottom worst part of the loss of one of their parents was the forced acceptance later of stepsiblings in the remarriage of one or both of their parents. Sibling rivalry in stepfamilies can become multiplied a hundred times over—even beyond measurement. ("Such evil tides that flow through such sweet breasts!") A child tends to think instinctively that his or her new stepsibling is:

- ✔ smarter than he or she is
- ✔ more popular

✔ better-looking

✔ greater in sports

✔ more of a winner in every detail

So, without detracting from your child's new stepsibling in any way, you've got a big job ahead of you in building up your child's confidence and making him aware of his own great self-worth. Don't make comparisons between your own child and his stepsibling, because that's what he's going to be doing all the time.

Tell your child or children that you have an enormous supply of love stored within you—enough for the newcomers to the household as well as for your own family. Convince them that your love for them grows stronger every day, and suggest that they can repay that love by treating their new stepbrothers or -sisters with kindness.

Children can never hear too often that they come first, whatever the situation—whether their other parent has died or left or been banished from the house, whether either or both parents remarry—when stepsiblings join the scene.

Jealousy in kids is usually pretty transparent. Take the case of fourteen-year-old Jenny, who accused her mother of showing favoritism toward her stepsister.

Her mother denied it. "I'm not giving Adrienne more attention than you, Jenny. How can you think that?"

"Yes you are. You didn't even come to ballet practice today with me. You stayed with her in her room."

"But she's sick."

"Not that sick, Mom."

"She was throwing up all afternoon. How would you have felt if you were sick and I left you to go watch someone practice her lesson?"

"What if we had both been sick? Would you stay with her or with me?"

Your children can and should be a great source of help to a child moving into a home where everything is new and strange, revolving around a new cast of characters. If there's a stepchild coming to your house who's the approximate age of your own child, make sure that right from the beginning he or she is invited to the same parties as your own child. This may require some lobbying of your child, who will probably initially resent having to share anything in the house—including you, his or her room, possessions, or a social life—with this "intruder." Be patient, make both feel important, but also be aware of how much you care about the success of this new marriage. Make them understand that you want this new family group to be supportive of one another, happy and functioning at full speed. Keep saying, "Do you know how important you are to all of us? To this new family? You have a key role. I'm *counting* on you."

Teach your own child to be creatively kind and helpful to a new stepbrother or -sister (in other words, to come up with some good ideas himself that would help the whole operation, instead of always having to be told to do this or that).

Answer each child's objections to the new arrangement, point by point. Remember to *listen*. Stay positive. "Listen, kids, it's going to work. It *will* work. We'll all see to it. No pouting, no sulking. Come out with your complaints and we'll solve the problems."

In order to solve the competitiveness problem, in addition to giving children and stepchildren equal attention, love, and support, they deserve equal space, wardrobes, amounts of toys, books, sports equipment, and the like. There should be no Cinderellas or ugly stepmothers and -sisters in today's society. Two stepsisters sharing a room have a better time of it if there is equal closet and bureau space. Room-sharing can be played like a game in which fair solutions to problems are decided by the children involved in conference with their parents.

It's an activity that teaches kindness.

How to Handle Common Gripes as Stepkids Get Together

Among the complaints most often heard are:

+ "I no longer have my own room. I can't even decorate it the way I want to. My 'roommate's' choices are given as much attention as mine."

+ "I don't have enough room for my things anymore. To begin with, I didn't have enough closet space and drawers; now, since he (or she) moved in, it is ten times worse."

+ "I don't have privacy in the bathroom anymore. It isn't even my bathroom now. I keep getting yelled at, 'Hurry up, hurry up.' If only my stepsister would get blamed as much as I do!"

+ "Someone else is sharing my telephone, and every time I really need to use it, she (or he) is on it."

+ "The food is different now—and there's never enough when my favorite foods are on the menu."

+ "It's harder work when I do my share of household chores, because there are more people in the house."

+ "I have to listen to my stepsister's (-brother's) TV programs as much as my own, because she says she's older and it's her right. That's not fair; it's not like it used to be."

+ "When I have a friend over, we have a hard time finding privacy."

+ "He (or she) smokes behind our parents' backs. I'd never do that, but I know better than to tell on him (or her)."

+ "He (or she) will get to go to summer camp (or go skiing) but there won't be enough money for me to go."

Some effective solutions might be:

+ "All right, if George got to pick the video this time, you'll be able to select it the next. We'll divvy up the right to choose."

+ "Yes, you can have your old bed, of course. We'll give your new stepbrother a bed just like it, so they'll be the same. Someday you'll really like the 'guy talk' you two can have after lights out in that shared room."

✦ "No, Naomi is *not* trying to push you out of your closet with her stuff. We'll measure the space so that all closet and shelf space is equal and we'll put up dividers."

✦ "I don't care if your stepbrother's muscles are bigger than yours. He's a year older. You can catch up. You're in just as good shape as he is. You don't measure muscle strength by centimeters!"

✦ "What if she did say she's prettier than you? She didn't realize that would hurt you. Give your stepsister some slack, will you? She's the one who came into this house, you didn't go into hers. She has it tougher, but you know something? You are going to be good friends one day. Just take it easy. It'll happen. And as far as who is prettier, you are both extremely pretty—in different but equal ways!"

✦ "You girls are competitive about shopping and malls and things. Why don't you two have a real conversation away from the subject of shopping, now that you're in the same family? Ask her about the sports she likes. Maybe you could arrange to play some games, and you can brief her about the good teams at school. Ask her about math, which I hear she does well in— maybe you could tell her about the language courses, which you do well in. Maybe you could end up helping one another in those subjects, who knows? The more you find out about one another, from one another, the better friends you'll be. We're going to make it work in this new family, please realize that."

Every time you hear a child voice one of these legitimate concerns, even if it's to someone else, stop and listen. Talk it over with him or her and write it down. If you have both agreed on a remedy, write that down, too. ("I'll tell Mary she can no longer borrow your sweater without your express permission, which will probably *not* be forthcoming, and you, in turn, will promise to cease making fun of her attempts to ice-skate, which she says humiliates her no end.")

In putting a child's complaints on the record, you have already soothed him by taking him seriously. Sometimes the only action you need take is to comfort him and promise that any injustices over which you have control will be corrected.

Recognize and sympathize with your children's and stepchildren's laments over the new living arrangements your new marriage has wrought. Hear them out, try to correct grievances, and show good faith to the new members of the household as well as to the old. *Listen* to your children. It's a kindness they desperately need when their whole world changes.

When the Visiting "Steps" Make It Tough Going for Mom

Sometimes a new mom has to contend with really rude stepchildren who come for weekends—children who have not been disciplined or taught their manners, and who constitute an enormous challenge for anyone to manage. She has often been portrayed by her new husband's ex as "a mean person." When her new stepchildren arrive for weekends, ungraced by any manners, unhelpful about doing any chores around the house, and with an attitude toward parental authority that can only be described as sassy, the household can become thoroughly disrupted. After all, the visiting children are doing all the things this woman's children are not allowed to do—and yet she is allowing her stepchildren to behave like this. Such visits might justly be called "weekends from hell."

It would be wonderful if the following developments could take place:

+ The father of the household—the biological father of the badly behaved kids—would communicate to his new wife how much he really appreciates what she's going through. He would tell her that he knows she has a real burden to bear, and that "your patience and forbearance are what make me adore you." (His wife, let's face it, really needs some buttering up to put up with this.)

+ *The father of the household might prepare his own children* for the fact that, now that there are two households involved in their lives, they are to obey their stepmother in *this* new household *as well as their mother at home.*

+ *The stepmom might make a special effort to be their pal,* to take them on special treat excursions. She might teach her stepdaughter how to fix her hair and do something special for her stepson. In other words, she should really try to gain their friendship, and usually, when a person goes to that much trouble, it is appreciated by those who benefit. Her own children will not appreciate this deferential treatment to their stepsiblings and they'll probably resent the time carved out of the weekend schedule for the other kids, but she can explain carefully that it won't last forever like this, that these visitors have suffered a lot of pain, haven't been taught the same things, and haven't been offered the same opportunities. "I need your help, kids," she might say to her children. "Your stepfather and I can't do this alone with them. I know that eventually they're going to come around to where they'll love and respect us and we'll *all* have a great time together. I *know* we can do it, but you'll be the most important factor in the success of it. You can *really* help me."

+ She can have some quiet talks with the stepsiblings. She can explain that if everyone has a better time, they'll be doing a huge favor for their mom, and the whole atmosphere of the house will change to a bright one.

A Stepmother Speaks About This Mutual Culture Shock

No one can predict how easy or tough it's going to be when a remarriage suddenly presents one of the partners with his or her first stepchild. As one friend put it, "When my stepdaughter walked into my life, I wanted to go right back to Nevada and undo everything I had just undone from my first marriage." Others know how to tough things out. The end result—a happy family—justifies the means of supernatural patience summoned by the parents.

A forty-year-old friend shuddered while describing to me her teenage stepson's arrival in her house the night she and her new husband returned from their wedding trip. She had no children of her own and barely knew the new stepson, who came from another coast and was to live with them permanently. The fact that they were almost strangers to one another was a grievous misstep, she later admitted. She should have taken the time and trouble to get to know him well before the wedding day.

"He entered the front hall for the first time, defiant, eyes glaring, nostrils flaring, like a bull entering the ring, pawing the dirt, sizing up his opponent—unfortunately, myself," she said, able to laugh about it now. "He was ready to circle and then attack me, so our first night of family life in our new house was not exactly a romantic occasion, I can promise you. My husband may have been upset at the lack of harmony between his son and me, but I . . . I was almost afraid for my life."

I protested, "But you and your stepson are great pals, so you certainly did something right."

"My husband wisely decided to stay out of it and let the two of us duke it out. It took about a year and a half of shadowboxing and confrontations—on everything from his sloppiness to his 'borrowing' my car without telling me. My behavior was not so perfect from his point of view either. He thought I was far too tough on him in the rules. 'Don't have such big expectations of me,' he kept protesting. 'But I do have big expectations of you,' I answered immediately, 'because you're your father's son, and I love and admire your father wholeheartedly, and somehow—somewhere—I'm going to find some of those same traits in you, or die in the attempt!'

"He will never know how hard I had to fight inside," my friend continued, "to accept this boy, to try to understand him, to be kind to him when I wanted to slam the door on him, his moods, and his insolence—and be rid of him."

"Was your husband any help?"

"None whatsoever," she laughed. "He simply couldn't see how nasty his son was to me, or how simmering with rage I was beneath the surface. My husband was having a rough time in his business those early days. I decided not to bother him with this problem at home, once I saw he really didn't 'get it' anyway.

"Then," Sandy continued, "I realized that all this time, I had been worrying about my husband and about me, but not bothering to get inside our son's heart, which must have been full of confusion and sadness. He was terribly let down by his mother, who lost custody of him to his father. He fantasized about what a really great mom she had been—when in fact she had been no mom at all. I realized that his father's and my worries were minuscule in comparison to his. That's when I began to do the right thing by that boy. He stopped fighting me and began to confide in me. I've never once criticized his mother. When he once said he appreciated that, I told him that as far as I was concerned *I* was also his mom, and immensely proud of it. He's been away at college since last August. I never thought I'd say this, but I miss his presence in this house—a lot. I can hardly wait for Christmas when he'll be home for vacation. The house will come to life again."

"You've done a great job with that boy, Sandy," I said, "because you took over an unhappy, anxious child and made a decent human being out of him."

"Thank you," she said, "you're kind to say that."

"No," I corrected her, "if anyone's been kind, it's you. I wish you could spread around some of that wisdom for inspiration to many women who aren't having that kind of success with their stepchildren."

"It takes time—quality time," she said. "The children feel so neglected, confused, and rejected during the time of separation, divorce, and all the changes they bring."

"How much time in a woman's day does it take, would you say?"

"Twenty-four hours a day ought to just about do it."

During an interview I conducted with a group of fourteen stepmothers and stepchildren, one of them announced that "twenty was the magic number," and the others unanimously agreed with her. When I asked for the meaning of the "magical twenty," it was explained that "after twenty years of simmering jealousies and misunderstandings, steprelationships in the family seem to work out just fine."

Patience must be a big player in this situation!

You Are a Great Stepparent If You . . .

+ *Attend all major sporting events,* class plays, and recitals in which
  your stepchild participates (unless the child's own mother or
  father will be present and would resent your being there).

+ *Respect the schedule made for the child's visits* to and from the
  other divorced parent, which means never casually canceling
  the visit or changing the time; having the child ready at the
  time he is to be picked up, with a properly packed suitcase;
  having his medicines with instructions carefully written out;
  and perhaps packing a little gift for his or her stepsibling
  whom he will be visiting for the weekend.

+ *Make a big fuss over the stepchild's birthday,* first communion, bar
  or bat mitzvah, school graduations, and all other ceremonies
  of life. If you, the stepparent, have your own children going
  through these same rituals, you should assure that celebrations, presents, and enthusiasm are dispensed in equal
  amounts to both sets of children. A diary should be kept with
  all these dates noted in advance, so that they are duly marked.
  To miss the birthday of a stepchild who's away at summer
  camp, for example, would be cruel. (Reschedule the celebration for when the child has returned.)

+ *Help with the child's homework whenever it is needed,* and show a sincere interest in his or her progress by keeping in touch with the
  child's teachers at school. The stepparents should know how the
  child is doing and in what subjects he might need some assistance. A stepparent can approach homework as interesting
  and hope that eventually the child will feel the same way.

  "If you study your French hard these next two weeks, let me
  help you, and do well on the big test, which I know you will, I'll
  take you to a French restaurant where you can order a superb
  meal for all of us *en français!*"

  "You know, I was pretty good at math in my college days,
  and I think I can assist with those tough problems you have
  from homework this week. Let me help and then someday you
  can help me with the new software programs for my company.

Who knows, if you get your math up to speed, we might be able to give you a paid job this summer."

+ *Give hearty congratulations for the good report cards,* as well as warm, constructive sympathy for the bad ones.

+ *Devote an equal amount of free time* to your own children and stepchildren in activities such as sports, shopping, going to movies, and enjoying the city's cultural events.

+ *Move fast with consolation* at a time of a great disappointment. For example, one child I know missed winning the national spelling championship by one word but was immeasurably cheered by the gift of a puppy from her stepmother. Another child missed going to a big city as a player on his high school baseball team for the final championship game because of a broken arm suffered at practice. His stepfather obtained a baseball for him signed by several Atlanta Braves, which made up for missing the team trip.

+ *Stand by when real trouble comes.* One young girl told me that when she was in the hospital in a coma, her mother and step-father, both of whom work, spelled one another twenty-four hours a day for four weeks to be there when she regained con-sciousness. ("It was then," she admitted, "that I knew I had a real dad in my stepfather, and that he loved me as much as my own father had.")

+ *Teach your stepchild the same values you have tried to instill in your own children*—particularly kindness toward others.

+ *Teach your own child how to help a stepbrother or -sister adjust to the new environment.* For example, if your stepdaughter's age approximates your daughter's, make sure that right at the beginning she is invited to the same parties to which your daughter is invited. Your daughter might call her picnic host-ess before the party:

"Grace, do you think there'd be a place at your Rollerblad-ing picnic for my stepsister Louise? She's new around here, she knows hardly anyone in the upper school, and it would be really neat if you'd let me bring her along." Don't expect your own daughter to continue to arrange for her stepsister to be included except for the first few times, but be sure to praise her for having been kind enough to do it at all.

Be specific in steps your child might take to help the newcomer, but don't suggest anything that would make him really uncomfortable:

"Show your new brother around school," you might request. "Teach him the ropes, sit with him at lunch at first and introduce him to everyone. Explain how he fits into the family. Act proud of him and build him up to the others. This is a hard time for him, so please don't tease him in front of the other guys."

"Did you ever think this was a hard time for me, too?" your son might retort. "I used to have a life. I used to have my own room, my own friends. Now you're telling me I have to do everything for Kevin. It's not fair, Mom."

"I know how you feel, but I wouldn't have asked you if I didn't think you were capable of being strong and good and kind. You are, you know. You're a terrific guy! I just couldn't handle all this without you!"

"Mom, you sure know how to get me to do what you want me to do."

"Do only what is kind and do what is comfortable for you. You're going to be a great role model for Kevin. He's lucky to have entered this family—in a large part because of you."

"I think you may have had something to do with that luck, Mom."

It's important to realize that a child wants—even needs—the stepparent to be proud of him. *Every small achievement in that boy's or girl's life should be dutifully marked.* Give your praise in private, if you have to, away from your own child who might be jealous, *but don't forget to do it.*

A

Final

Word

If you have stayed with me all through this book, you are a very kind person indeed, and I salute you!

Many of you have your own excellent ideas on how to make changes in our society so that our children can thrive more easily in it. Instead of our remaining in a state of paralysis because of the speed with which the moral structure around us is unraveling, perhaps we should pool all of those ideas and try out a variety of solutions. Perhaps it's time to put the old trial-and-error method of problem-solving into action.

Do me a favor. Take a walk for two blocks on a quiet street while you concentrate on everything that is bad and wrong with our society today. Then stop—and think about how you're feeling at that particular moment. Bad. Then walk on for another two blocks while your brain busily works on possible things you personally might do to help. Then stop—and think about how you're feeling at that particular moment. Good. I would imagine you have an entirely different attitude toward the world after the second walk, and that there's a spring in your step and that you find yourself going faster. You're probably saying to yourself, "I could do this; I could do that, too. I could say this, and I could say that."

Instead of being apathetic and depressed by the state of things, let's move ahead with ideas, answers, and hope for the third millennium. The opportunities for good changes are all there. We worry so much about societal ills, we forget about all the terrific societal *potential* around us. We should learn to feel the energy whizzing around in the air we breathe. Yes, there's pollution in that air, too, but concentrate on the mysterious energy. Maybe we can find some magical new technology to retrieve it from our atmosphere and convert it into constructive action.

If we listen to the streets around us, we might very well pick up the sounds and sighings of people—particularly the young—longing for things to be as they were in the days when a strong family prevailed, and when the promises of romance, idealism, and a "happily-ever-afterness" were the norm. The young have read about this time, and they've heard us talking about it and have seen the movies made in that era. They wonder what made it so. What was the fabric of those times, and how was it woven? The answer, of course, is the family.

If the traditional family isn't around all that much anymore, we can certainly make do with what we have. We can be "family" to one another's children. We can motivate children and help guide them to go where they'd like to go and to become what they aspire to be.

The fairy-tale "And they lived happily ever after" doesn't always play out as it should. People die, people divorce, and people remain single. People often move in and out of different families, weaving new patterns as they go. If there is one certainty, it's that everyone has the right to belong to a family. If at some point in life we have no family, we can make a new one ourselves. Friends become family. It's up to *us*.

As a child begins to develop into a human being, making that leap from a life of being bossed around in the home to a life of doing the bossing himself or herself in a home, the young person shows the results of an earlier exposure to certain virtues and values. It's readily apparent if those precepts were accepted or rejected. It shows up in the way young people approach their marriages and remarriages, in the way they handle or mishandle their children or their stepchildren, and in the way they step up to the plate to make a great life for themselves even if they never marry at all.

"Get a life!" is an often repeated phrase people say to one another. Everyone has a right to get, or at least to have *got,* a life at some point. Some have to work harder at it than others, but if any person can say that he has made a difference in a child's life, then that person does indeed have a life. There's a lot of happiness to be derived from being able to make that statement alone!

Index

About the Author

Letitia Baldrige's books on manners, business conduct, and human behavior have sold in the millions. In a cover story, *Time* magazine called her "America's leading arbiter of manners." Columnist Ann Landers describes her as ". . . the premiere authority on manners in America today, whose books are considered gospel."

She has had a distinguished career in government and business. In her diplomatic career, she served as Social Secretary at the American Embassy in Paris; she then became Special Assistant to Ambassador Clare Boothe Luce at the Embassy in Rome. During the John F. Kennedy Administration, she was Chief of Staff for Mrs. Kennedy and Social Secretary to the White House. Subsequently, she served as an advisor to four other First Ladies.

She has been a top executive in corporate life, and now is a marketing advisor to major companies and professional organizations, and runs a firm whose focus is management training in the field of human behavior. She also serves on many major corporate and nonprofit boards.

She is a legendary figure on national TV and radio shows, on the university lecture circuit, and in print media.

She and her husband, Robert Hollensteiner, live in Washington, D.C., have two married children, two grandchildren, and many godchildren, nieces, and nephews, all of whom have served as resources in her writing.